£30-00.

£15

psyco

↓

Psychoanalysis
in its Cultural Context

Edited by Edward Timms and Ritchie Robertson

AUSTRIAN STUDIES III

Psychoanalysis
in its Cultural Context

Edited by Edward Timms and Ritchie Robertson

AUSTRIAN STUDIES III

EDINBURGH UNIVERSITY PRESS

© Edinburgh University Press, 1992
22 George Square, Edinburgh

Set in Linotron Ehrhardt by
Koinonia, Bury, and
printed in Great Britain by
the Alden Press, Oxford

A CIP record for this book is available
from the British Library.

ISBN 0 7486 0359 X

Contents

Contents

List of illustrations

Stills from the film *Der Student von Prag* (1913), pp. 86–7:

1. The student (Paul Wegener) is visually terrorized by his *Doppelgänger* (also played by Paul Wegener).
2. The *Doppelgänger* interrupts the embrace of the student and the countess (Grete Berger) in the Jewish Cemetery.

Preface

In his keynote article on 'The Historiography of Psychoanalysis', Paul Roazen argues that 'it is only by putting Freud back into context that it will be possible to appreciate precisely what he achieved'. It is in this spirit that our volume *Psychoanalysis in its Cultural Context* is conceived. The history of psychoanalysis has been too exclusively centered on Freud. Indeed, Roazen suggests that Freud's own version of the history of the movement has triumphed by default. To achieve a more balanced view, it is necessary to take account of the ideas of his dissenting followers and forgotten adversaries. The people Freud attracted and repelled, as Roazen observes, make fascinating intellectual history.

The most controversial dimension of this cultural context is the late nineteenth-century debate about racial identity. Drawing on a wealth of recent research, Sander Gilman's article on 'Freud, Race and Gender' shows how biological conceptions of race became transformed into psychological categories. For Freud and his fellow analysts, being 'Jewish' meant participating in a shared set of intellectual and emotional attitudes. The problem for psychoanalysis, as for ethnopsychologists like Lazarus and Steinthal, was how to separate the psyche from the body. This problem was compounded by turn-of-the-century debates which associated Jewishness with femininity, indeed with the female body. Freud never entirely resolved the difficulties arising from this rhetoric of race, which had a distorting effect on his conceptions of gender.

Attitudes towards Jewishness and femininity are explored from another angle in Klaus Theweleit's article on Freud's 'Object-Choice', his engagement to Martha Bernays. Although only a small portion of Freud's letters to his fiancée are accessible, Theweleit's commentary reconstructs some of the patterns underlying Freud's choice of a wife: above all, his desire to transcend his humble Jewish origins by identifying with the more fully assimilated and intellectually distinguished Bernays family. Writing letters to Martha was for Freud a form of self-discovery, perhaps even the first phase in his process of self-analysis. But if Freud in a sense married his analyst, he was ultimately disappointed. Theweleit reminds us how Martha resisted all attempts to carry out psychological investigations within the family: 'Not in front of the children, Sigmund dear'.

A number of further articles deal with Freud's dissenting disciples. The 'Pathologization of Protest' is the theme of an article by Martin Stanton on Otto Gross, the anarchistic critic of patriarchy who was treated as a patient by Jung. By defining Gross as schizophrenic, Jung attempted to categorize Gross's cult of sexual promiscuity as pathological; and yet Jung himself invoked Gross's theory of polygamy to justify his own relationship with Sabina Spielrein. A second analysis with Wilhelm Stekel offered a more promising diagnosis by focusing on Gross's drug addiction. But Stanton shows that Stekel too attempted to marginalize Gross's political ideas, attributing them to repressed homosexuality.

Stekel also features in the unpublished memoirs of Fritz Wittels, written in New York around 1940. Introducing an excerpt in which Wittels describes how he came to write the first biography of Freud, Edward Timms suggests that the delayed publication of these memoirs raises disturbing questions about the suppression of sources. Although psychoanalysis deals with the ramifications of sexual drives, the history of the movement has been systematically desexualized, disguising the links between the Vienna Psychoanalytic Society and the erotic subculture. The chapter from the memoirs which is published in this volume gives a particularly vivid picture of Stekel, a figure whom orthodox histories of psychoanalysis have tended to marginalize. This suggests that a reassessment of the relationship between Freud and Stekel is long overdue.

Although feminist critics have made a valuable contribution to recent debates about psychoanalysis, little attention has been paid to the reactions of Viennese feminists during Freud's lifetime. This is the theme of an article by Harriet Anderson, which suggests that in the years 1900-1930 psychoanalysis and feminism formed an 'Ambivalent Alliance'. The aims of combating prejudices and raising consciousness made them natural allies, but the priorities of the feminists diverged from those of psychoanalysis. Their concern was with improved opportunities for women (Rosa Mayreder), sexual fulfilment in motherhood (Grete Meisel-Hess), the education of children (Emma Eckstein) and the understanding of social deviance (Therese Schlesinger-Eckstein). For feminists with this kind of social orientation, Adler proved to be a more valuable ally than Freud.

Another errant disciple whose work has tended to be forgotten is Otto Rank. In his article on 'Otto Rank and the *Doppelgänger*', Andrew Webber shows how creatively Rank combined his interests in dream, literature, art and myth. The early film *Der Student von Prag* provides Rank with a pictorial enactment of the pathological process of 'doubling', which he traces back to early nineteenth-century Romantic literature. These traumatic stories of double identity are attributed to narcissistic disorders in the personalities of their authors. Webber suggests that Rank, like Freud in his essay on 'The Uncanny', is too preoccupied with questions of psychological content to recognize the significance of 'doubling' for the structure of narrative (a question taken up with greater sophistication in post-Freudian theory).

Two further articles examine the divergent responses of literary authors to psychoanalysis. Robert Musil is a writer of such psychological sophistication that it is often assumed he must have been influenced by Freud. In 'Freud, Musil and Gestalt Psychology', Hannah Hickman reexamines this question, suggesting that the links with Freud are only secondary. Through his studies in Berlin, Musil immersed himself in an alternative psychological tradition which culminated in the Gestalt theories of Max Wertheimer, Wolfgang Köhler and Kurt Koffka. Their theory of perception in terms of 'unitary structures' is linked by Hickman with Musil's analysis of the idea of the soul 'playing billiards', creating patterns out of divergent stimuli. At a formal level, too, the concept of Gestalt is correlated with Musil's precepts about the structure of a page of prose.

The reactions of another Austrian author are analysed in Ritchie Robertson's article on Canetti's *Crowds and Power*. In his elucidation of this bewilderingly complex book, Robertson shows that Canetti attributes the behaviour of crowds to two primary urges: the desire to be separate and the longing for immersion in the mass. Despite his antagonistic stance towards Freud, Canetti does not altogether escape from the Freudian framework, since *Crowds and Power*, like *Beyond the Pleasure Principle*, presupposes a conflict between two fundamental instincts. This article also shows that *Crowds and Power* has a Nietzschean plot, involving the genealogy of the 'pack', in addition to the Freudian dialectic between group expansion and group control. A final section analyses divergent readings of Schreber's *Memoirs*, which Canetti interprets as an expression of political paranoia, where Freud draws attention to unconscious homosexual impulses.

The exploration of the cultural context of psychoanalysis is continued in two review articles. In the first, Sander Gilman sets out to explain why the study of Sigmund Freud has become 'big academic business', emphasizing how much still needs to be done even at the level of editions of primary source material. He suggests that books which emphasize Freud's 'Jewishness' tend to beg the question, if they fail to consider 'what kind of a Jew Freud was'. In a second review article, Simon Price reflects on Freud's passion for collecting antiquities. Recent publications have shown how Freud's tastes diverged from those of more conventional collectors. It was not the idealized human form created by the Greeks that fascinated him, but the part-animal figures of Egyptian art.

Each volume of *Austrian Studies* is designed to make the results of specialist research more accessible through a wide range of book reviews, as well as a close focus on one specific field. The discussion of psychoanalysis is rounded off by review articles which deal with other aspects of the human sciences: the fate of Austrian scientists in exile, discussed by J. M. Ritchie, and the poet-anthropologist Franz Baermann Steiner, whose aphorisms are analysed by Jeremy Adler. The volume concludes with a series of shorter reviews which monitor publications on a variety of historical, literary and musical topics, giving an indication of the diversity of recent research in Austrian studies.

Part One

The Historiography of Psychoanalysis

Paul Roazen

Although Freud had many notable precursors in the history of ideas, a broad consensus now exists that the distinctive set of doctrines known as psychoanalysis is nearing its one hundredth birthday. No doubt there will be some legitimate disagreement about exactly when in the mid-to-late 1890s this unique approach, created by Sigmund Freud, can be said to have begun. Some will perhaps decide to choose the time when Freud initially used the new term for his special way of proceeding. Others will think that it is more important to date its beginnings from the moment when Freud announced in a 1897 letter to his friend Wilhelm Fliess that he had abandoned the hypothesis that adult neurosis had its origins in childhood sexual seduction, and instead Freud began to believe in the powerful role that the fantasy life of patients can play in their irrational problems. Alternatively, one might propose that the most important turning point was when Freud substituted his version of free associations for the earlier therapeutic device of hypnosis. Finally, politically aware observers might want to argue that only in 1902, when Freud began formally to assemble a following around him, can psychoanalysis itself be said to be under way. As I see it, the fact that there can be legitimate disagreements on such an issue is itself a sign that the study of this field has finally, after so many years of amateur endeavours and sectarian squabbling, come of age as a legitimate academic discipline.

Chosen dates in history influence, as well as reflect, rival interpretative stances. Yet it would be agreed by most that in some sense psychoanalysis was decisively under way by the time of Freud's publication of *The Interpretation of Dreams* (1900). Certainly, it has often been pointed out that throughout the twentieth century, literature about all things psychoanalytic has been multiplying at an ever-increasing rate. There are now more psychoanalytic journals than ever before, and the number of practitioners is still on the increase. The situation in France today can serve as an instructive example; they have some sixteen Freudian organizations functioning, and one of them in Paris alone forms the largest single component unit of the International Psychoanalytic Association, which was founded by Freud in 1910.

Although the story of the history of Freud's school ought to include much more than just himself, embracing those he quarrelled with as well as those who

3

stayed with him through thick and thin, he continues to play a unique role in everything which has ever been written in connection with the system he created. Events since his death in 1939 have only seemed to heighten his stature. His continued dominance over the subject has to be traced to more than his own authoritarianism, which was a phenomenon of his culture and times as well as undoubtedly a special personal trait of his. I think it is telling how from his earliest writings he showed a sharp sense of history; he constantly introduced readers to the specific steps by which he had arrived at his ideas. Even with patients he could discuss his predecessors and his early struggles. Freud had a powerful sense of the future; he was early on convinced of his destined triumph, and therefore left no stone unturned to make sure of leaving behind something concrete that future historians could rely on. It is true that in 1885 Freud had written to his future wife about how he had undertaken to carry out 'an intention which a number of as yet unborn and unfortunate people will one day resent'. He went on to explain:

> Since you won't guess what kind of people I am referring to, I will tell you at once: they are my biographers. I have destroyed all my notes of the past fourteen years, as well as letters, scientific excerpts and the manuscripts of my papers. As for letters, only those from the family have been spared. Yours, my darling, were never in danger. In doing so all old friendships and relationships presented themselves once again and then silently received the *coup de grâce* (my imagination is still living in Russian history); all my thoughts and feelings about the world in general and about myself in particular have been found unworthy of further existence. They will now have to be thought all over again, and I certainly had accumulated some scribbling.
>
> But that stuff settles round me like sand-drifts round the Sphinx; soon nothing but my nostrils would have been visible above the paper; I couldn't have matured without worrying about who would get hold of those old papers. Everything, moreover, that lies beyond the great turning-point of my life, beyond our love and my choice of a profession, died long ago and must not be deprived of a worthy funeral. As for the biographers, let them worry, we have no desire to make it too easy for them. Each one of them will be right in his opinion of 'The Development of the Hero,' and I am already looking forward to seeing them go astray.[1]

It is telling about the passion of Freud's commitment to his work that even in the course of such an intimate letter, he described 'the great turning point' in his life as the love between himself and his fiancée, and, on an equal footing, his own 'choice of a profession'. He had prefaced his remarks to his future wife by telling her that he had been browsing in Russian history, and perhaps this attention to historiography helped lead him to think of the need to tidy up some of his own.

Freud was doubtless writing partly tongue-in-cheek about his future biographers and his pleasure in the anticipation of misleading them. Still, from Freud's earliest letters as a young man we know something of his youthful convictions about his immortality. And it would seem that his mother in particular shared his ambition to be a world conqueror.[2] He kept this unusual sense of himself until the end of his life; in 1938, on his way from Paris to London, on the boat-train at night he dreamt he was landing at the same town in England as William the Conqueror. Although Freud was at that stage physically feeble, having had cancer of the jaw for fifteen years, this highlights how he had retained his inner identity of being a warrior of the spirit.

It is clear that Freud could be a skilful political leader on behalf of the cause he founded. But one significant component of his immense historical success, in addition to his considerable capacities in building an organizational structure which would long outlast him, was his prescience in understanding the importance of keeping control of the story of the early development of psychoanalysis. We may know virtually nothing about what Freud admired in his early reading of H. T. Buckle or W. E. H. Lecky, or even what he picked up from Nietzsche,[3] but he knew in his bones that shaping the past is a key instrument to becoming dominant in the future.

Freud was so astute about historiography that at the opening of his Clark lectures in 1909 he declared: 'If it is a merit to have brought psychoanalysis into being, that merit is not mine. I had no share in its earlier beginnings. I was a student and working for my final examinations at the time when another Viennese physician, Dr Josef Breuer, first (in 1880–82) made use of this procedure on a girl who was suffering from hysteria.' Perhaps he was so extravagant about Breuer – with whom Freud had long since broken off all personal contact – because he wanted immediately to then give an account of Breuer's early treatment of the woman who has become famous as Anna O. But it is worth pointing out that not only has it been established that Breuer was not a success with Anna O., as Freud claimed at Clark, but that she ended up, after the cathartic treatment with Breuer, addicted to both morphine and chloral.[4] Equally striking is that by 1923 Freud added a footnote to his sentence declaring Breuer's priority in having 'brought psychoanalysis into being'; for Freud then wrote: 'See, however, in this connection my remarks in "On the History of the Psychoanalysis Movement", where I assumed the entire responsibility for psychoanalysis.'[5] Freud cut Breuer as an old man when he passed him in a Vienna street, but when Breuer died in 1925 Freud sent a condolence letter to the Breuer family, and published an obituary notice.

Freud's polemical 1914 pamphlet 'On the History of the Psychoanalytic Movement' was written after the series of difficulties he had had with Alfred Adler, Wilhelm Stekel, and Carl Jung. Freud remained furious with them all, as well as their various supporters, and in order to distinguish his own ideas from their dissenting views he let himself go in public in a way which was rare for him. James Strachey's splendid edition of Freud's works in English might have succeeded in highlighting just how upset Freud was, if Strachey had consulted more than the printed versions of Freud's published texts; for the original manuscript of 'On the History of the Psychoanalytic Movement' shows Freud to have been even freer with his partisanship than in the published version.[6] It seems to me extraordinary that Freud was so sure of himself as to have considered psychoanalysis, at such an early date, to be entitled to have a history. After all, there were then only a relatively small number of practising analysts, and Freud's influence was in those days far overshadowed by existing alternatives to psychoanalysis,

Equally surprising is that once Freud had launched his invective against his backsliding supporters, none of them shared Freud's own sense that something needed to be put into the history books. Freud's version of what had happened in those now epic pre-World War I struggles triumphed partly by default. Jung, for example, felt traumatized by what had happened between himself and Freud, and for years thereafter he bitterly complained in private how the Freudians had for a time succeeded in wrecking his clinical practice. Although he lived long enough to write an obituary of Freud, which was on the appreciative side, and discussed his difficulties with Freud in the autobiographical *Memories, Dreams, Reflections*,[7] by then the historical die had been cast. For those who had momentously differed with Freud it would always be an uphill battle to combat the account of things which Freud had put into the history books in a way which went unchallenged. Most subsequent controversies in psychoanalysis, long after Freud's death, have been too readily assimilated to the models of what happened before World War I. Not only was Freud stylistically the greatest writer among twentieth-century psychologists, but his decision to recount his own side of these now famous quarrels proved politically a key move on his part.

Part of today's wave of revisionist scholarship is able to thrive on showing how unbalanced was the account of what happened that flowed from Freud's own pen, an account too credulously swallowed by outsiders. For Freud's disciples shared his own keen sense of the significance of keeping the record straight from his own point of view. If independent observers have unwittingly been apt to adopt Freud's own viewpoint, rather than appreciate how pupils of his struggled to develop ideas of their own, even if it meant crossing swords with Freud, these dissenting ex-students of Freud's did little to help their own cause historiographically. Not only did those Freud stigmatized as heretics do little publicly to fight back, but their supporters did not have the same sense of history as Freud and his own loyal friends. Even now, after all these years, the Jung family for example has yet to authorize an official biography; and so there are important personal Jung archives still to be explored. We do not even have decent scholarly editions of Jung's works; tiny papers of Freud's appear with a considerable scholarly-seeming apparatus, while huge books of Jung's have been allowed to appear without even the semblance of decent editorial attention.

I am not suggesting that any of the so-called dissident figures in psychoanalysis can compare in stature with Freud as the first psychoanalyst. But as we know, there are many thousands of Freud's own letters still to appear in print, which can be counted upon to continue to alter our view of him.[8] As that striking passage from Freud's letter of 1885 about his future biographers going astray indicates, Freud's prose remains unmatched within all twentieth-century psychology. I believe Freud's unusual literary skills help account for the power his ideas still retain.

Through the creation of the psychoanalytic situation Freud was also able to exert an unparalleled degree of influence. When Erik H. Erikson once suggested that Freud's recommended therapeutic technique amounts to 'an exquisite sensory deprivation experiment',[9] he was identifying one means by which Freud could create converts to his cause. The relative absence of sights and sounds has specific psychological consequences, as does any use of the couch. By 1910, Freud's critics were complaining that he had indoctrinated his following. I suspect that Freud was not fully aware of the element of old-fashioned suggestion which was built into his own treatment procedure; he instead chose to think that psychoanalysts were capable of confirming what he ambitiously thought to be his findings. We still find naive people regularly talking about Freud's 'discoveries', instead of more modestly accepting the idea that in actuality what he was doing was forwarding a special way of looking at things.

It is one part of the story that the ideas of Freud's dissenting former students have been relatively neglected; fine recent biographies of Wilhelm Reich, Otto Rank, Karen Horney, and Melanie Klein, for instance, have helped remedy the situation.[10] But legitimate criticisms of psychoanalysis, written from completely outside Freud's fold, have scarcely ever been given enough of a hearing. A mythology has been allowed to thrive in which Freud is viewed as a wholly misunderstood genius unfairly maligned by an uncomprehending opposition. If, however, one examines reviews of Freud's works which appeared while he was still alive, the ones that are least worth reading today are those parrot-like accounts composed by loyal apostles.[11] The critiques offered by non-analysts, on the other hand, can be both insightful and respectful. Much that appears in the psychoanalytic literature today, which is supposedly an advance on previous professional thinking, turns out on examination to amount to reinventing the wheel.

I am not suggesting that what we confront in today's technical psychoanalytic literature can be considered unique. It has something to do with the ways in which classic authorities get cited in other fields as well. I am thinking, for example, of how the American founding fathers get quoted in Supreme Court decisions; it is sociologically important on behalf of national unity for people to believe they are living now under the same Constitution (with the acknowledged official amendments) which was written in the late eighteenth century. And so early American thinkers are often cited out of proper historical context to answer contemporary needs of today. Two commentators on the way historians have made use of Alexis de Tocqueville's great study, *Democracy in America*, make a similar point:

> If one may be permitted to speculate generally on the uses of classic authorities, one notes that historians often use words from the classic authorities as aids in achieving intellectual legitimacy. They are means of making an author's ideas more palatable by conveying them through familiar and universally acceptable symbols. Tocqueville's words have now become such symbols and are capable of evoking a mood of acquiescence toward the introduction of ideas quite remote from the

context in which their creator originally used them. They reassure the reader that the new formulation is linked to the mainstream of intellectual endeavor.[12]

Whatever desirable social purposes such mythologizing may accomplish, the creation of such false continuities is a central obstacle against which intellectual historians are obliged to struggle.

The situation is unusual within psychoanalysis in that we have so many publications by practising clinicians who have neither the leisure nor the training to perform academic research. Nor is it in their interest to promote impartial scholarship. So we have many journals which exist essentially for trade-union purposes. Independent research which in any way rocks the boat can not only become a threat to the way clinicians and their patients have ideologically organized their thinking, but also be perceived as a menace to their essential mode of being. I would not want to underestimate the way economic livelihoods could also be endangered. And so there are piles of psychoanalytic publications, each of which regularly cites Freud, but which instead of adding anything to the genuine history of the discipline is essentially using his words as 'classic authorities', making its own contemporary ideas 'more palatable' by linking them to isolated sentences that Freud once wrote. The body of Freud's work is so extensive that it is easy to place tortured constructions, useful for today, on what he originally wrote. Freud's broad influence has been such that a Marxist like Herbert Marcuse could adapt psychoanalysis to serve his own ideological purposes, and even trained historians have so credulously accepted conventional psychoanalytic teachings as to allow themselves to become partisan propagandists.[13]

It is a commonplace in the history of ideas that a great writer has to be understood in the context of those against whom he was writing. As Hugh Trevor-Roper once put it, 'St Augustine, St Thomas Aquinas, Descartes, Locke, Marx, all built up their systems against now forgotten adversaries.' It is my conviction that Freud does rank as a giant in intellectual history. Although I am myself citing that sentence from Trevor-Roper as a classic authority for my own argument, I do not want to be guilty of what has come to be known as Jesuitical reasoning by omitting his very next sentence: 'Vulgar disputants die with the disputes which have nourished them.'[14]

The problem for me with Trevor-Roper's second sentence is that it is apt to sound too much like Whig history, or history written on the side of the big battalions. The fact that Freud succeeded against his rivals, or that his early critics are now forgotten, says nothing about the merits of any of the arguments in which they were then engaged. Mikhail Bakunin scored a number of telling points against Karl Marx, for example, and yet even graduate students specializing in the history of socialism are in my experience unlikely to be familiar with Bakunin's thought. I am not suggesting that he was in any way Marx's equal as a theorist, but there is something obviously wrong in history-writing which is obsessed by success. Marx won out within the first Socialist International, and the history of our century has been uniquely influenced by him. We necessarily have to rely on the crude standard of survival in order to evaluate why any thinker deserves to be studied. But entirely aside from the advantage of understanding a writer in terms of the opponents he felt obliged to combat, it is notorious how some writers – such as Giambattista Vico – were unduly neglected in their own time.

If psychoanalysis were merely an aspect of the history of science, then it would make more sense to ignore those other figures who have fallen by the wayside. We are apt to think of science in connection with progress, and it follows that we should pay special attention to theories that win out as opposed to those that are discarded. Yet as intellectual historians we should be obliged to understand the Ptolemaic conception of the universe as well as the Copernican, and the phlogiston theory makes an interesting tale in the development of modern chemistry.

If one were to weigh Freud's concepts only in the cold light of science, however, I think his standing would seriously suffer. Whatever may be the case in France today (which has only belatedly caught up with the psychoanalytic revolution), in America, Freud's doctrines, popular even before World War I, are now under a medical cloud. While three decades ago psychoanalysts were regularly heads of American psychiatric departments all across the country, today it would be rare to have any hospital departments making such an appointment. Old-fashioned psychiatrists all along vigorously objected to the sectarianism among the psychoanalysts. And while these non-Freudian holdouts may have seemed anti-humanitarian, and sometimes been too tolerant of techniques like electroshock or even psychosurgery, they were fundamentally convinced that more was at issue, at least in the case of the great mental illnesses, than the purely psychological angle that most of the Freudians wanted to pursue. The gains made over the last generation in developing new and efficient drugs have given what is now known as biological psychiatry a standing which has, at least in America, eclipsed the analysts medically. Unfortunately, often in the history of ideas the baby gets tossed out with the bath-water, and the dangers of over-medication as well as slighting the interaction between patient and therapist are still with us.

Freud himself believed that there were what he called constitutional bases to the psychoses, although he was belated in even distinguishing between neurosis and psychosis. He warned his followers in the 1920s that they had better hurry in their psychological research lest the development of new treatment made it impossible to study problems which might soon be too easily curable. But again it has not been fashionable to see the extent to which Freud's commitment as a scientist could be at odds with his efforts as a therapist. And to the extent that he made his stand on purely scientific grounds, modern developments over the last generation have left some of his work high and dry. He may in the long run have contributed something unique to the attention that ought to be paid to the relationship between therapist and patient, but surely that would have struck Freud as paltry compared to the grandiosity of his aims.

It is only by putting Freud back in context that it will be possible to appreciate precisely what he achieved. It is not simply that in his own time the great mental diseases were even more mysterious than by and large they remain today. In addition, he was trying to introduce an element of humane attentiveness to human troubles that will always rank, I think, as a significant accomplishment. It may be that some of his disciples were so aloof from the need to bring about therapeutic improvement that in effect they imitated the therapeutic nihilism of the most benighted of Freud's contemporary rivals. In the face of pressing human dilemmas psychoanalysts, including Freud himself, could miss the wood for the trees, concentrating on abstract problems deriving supposedly from early childhood while overlooking distressing day-to-day difficulties, including the special setting of psychoanalytic treatment.

The truth of the matter is complicated in that Freud did not behave as a clinician at all in accord with his recommended techniques for his future disciples. Here an element of hypocrisy has crept into the history of psychoanalysis. Those who were intimate with Freud's own clinical practices knew perfectly well that he did not himself act as a so-called orthodox analyst is supposed to do. He talked, at least when he still had his health, a great deal; he recommended specific marriage choices; he treated addicts, and even those whom he acknowledged to be schizophrenics; and he gave his views on political and moral matters. Quite apart from his conscious intentions, the unique treatment situation he had arranged had an immense impact all of its own. Looking at photographs of Freud's consulting room it is hard to believe that any patient could have been in it without feeling the impact of Freud's own idiosyncrasies.

In part, Freud made his rules about how analysts were supposed to behave for the sake of beginners. Those technical papers were devised for the purpose of letting others know where he himself had originally gone wrong in his own practice. But even if allowances are made for the contrast between what Freud said and how he behaved, it is hard not to think that there was something phony about the way some of his followers disguised the liberties he took. Surely the fact that he personally analysed his own daughter Anna,[15] which was once a closely guarded secret, was as 'wild' a bit of analysis as anything Freud could have condemned in those former pupils of his whom he refused to recognize as legitimate psychoanalysts. If it was a matter of heresy to treat a patient sitting up, instead of lying on a couch, what did it mean to analyse one's own child? Perhaps one sentence of Freud's about Paul Schilder, whom despite Schilder's brilliance among Viennese analysts Freud came to disapprove of, can illustrate how arbitrary Freud could be. Freud wrote of Schilder in 1936: 'I must declare him unsuited to teaching psychoanalysis, quite regardless of whether others are more or less suited than he.'[16]

The Freud-Schilder difficulties remain to be explored. But even the most celebrated controversies in the history of psychoanalysis ought not to be looked upon only as scientific disputes, or even intellectual disagreements; they did of course contain differences of ideological approach, and the confrontation between Freud and Jung, for example, represents for me one of those enduring clashes between alternative temperaments and points of view. Just as Diderot and Rousseau were at odds about something more than a personality clash, Freud and Jung represent lastingly different outlooks in the history of ideas. For example, while Freud saw religion as in principle neurotic, though in practice sometimes acknowledging the legitimate and valuable functions religious beliefs could provide, Jung thought neurosis arose from a fundamental absence of meaning, and he sought in religion exactly that form of belief which he thought could rescue patients from the distress of an unduly secularized era.

The history of psychoanalysis has to be seen not just as a series of personal squabbles, although human differences could readily get blown up into theoretical proportions. What has been at stake, and kept the fires of conflict burning for so long, are rival world-views. If one wants to appreciate the quality of the differences between contending factions in the history of psychoanalysis, then the quickest way would be to pick up a book about the wars of religion in the sixteenth century.

Psychoanalysts in training in different organizational contexts rarely appreciate the terminology or techniques of alternative approaches. The movement known as self-psychology, for instance, initiated by Heinz Kohut in Chicago, has in many quarters of North America become the most fashionable example of psychoanalytic revisionism. Yet Kohut (who was subsequently denounced in private as 'anti-psychoanalytic' by Anna Freud) would not have dreamt of acknowledging Franz Alexander as a legitimate precursor, since Alexander had once been a leader among Chicago analysts and subsequently denounced as a deviationist. Jung is probably the single most seemingly sinister figure in the list of psychoanalytic iconoclasts, and although his notions about individuation ought to be more acceptable within the context of self-psychological thinking, he is still regarded as too much of a renegade to appear in orthodox psychoanalytic bibliographies.

Karen Horney, thanks to the successful impact of the feminist movement over the last generation, has reappeared within the so-called mainstream. And Melanie Klein, even though Freud loathed most of what she stood for, has also won a surprising degree of acceptance. The changes that do take place are likely to be accomplished slowly; the life of any effective organization means that the discipline provided by doctrine has to be changed only gradually and with deliberation. Psychoanalysis became a church whose unity had to be guarded against the threat of schism. And although claims have often, especially recently, been made for the existence of pluralism within psychoanalysis,[17] I think that ideological broad-mindedness remains more the exception than the rule.

Psychoanalysis has had its Ayatollahs, and even though I have never been a practising analyst, my own research has at times been deemed subversive enough to have called forth thundering anathemas.[18] Heresy-hunting is not something that only happened in the distant past of psychoanalysis, but has also taken place within my own lifetime. The power of mythology ought never to be underrated; independent historical research necessarily has to be threatening, since social unity rests on the power of unquestioned consensus. Psychoanalysis has no official Index of Prohibited Books, but the informal means of social control are every bit as powerful. If one were to ask any candidate in 'orthodox' psychoanalytic training who first invented the idea of a training analysis, these young professionals would almost certainly be unaware that it was in fact Jung who first proposed that all future analysts be themselves psychoanalysed. It is not a minor point of antiquarian curiosity, for the pros and cons of training analyses are scarcely ever debated.

The problem of myth-making is hardly peculiar to psychoanalysis. Mikhail Gorbachev may have successfully introduced many changes into Russian life, but as yet Leon Trotsky has not been fully rehabilitated. Some might say that whether or not Trotsky's ideas are now debated is a relatively trivial issue; but I think that one should never underestimate the power of ideology. After all, psychoanalysis itself rests on the basic conviction that how we think profoundly affects how we behave.

Trevor-Roper, who has written so tellingly about the Renaissance and Reformation, has conjectured about how formal ideologies come to lose their power. Such weakening of conviction takes place almost imperceptibly. 'To give precise dates to major intellectual changes is impossible. Intellectual systems are not destroyed intellectually by mere disproof; they are tied to social structures which, if themselves healthy, are prompt to repair local damage and to re-fortify weakened positions.' Trevor-Roper is worth listening to, I believe, since he is writing without any explicit interest in a doctrine like psychoanalysis, although I suspect that his studies of sixteenth and seventeenth-century Europe owe more than a little to his knowledge of the fate of Marxism in our own century. He argues that even when grand philosophic systems of thought 'have been discovered to be socially irrelevant, they do not dissolve at once; they live on in the minds of those habituated to them and only perish when that generation has disappeared and a new generation, in different circumstances, proves immune to their appeal. Even then, their decomposing relics may linger on in corners and perhaps, in time, generate new heresies.'[19]

It is beyond my competence to explain all the social sources of support for psychoanalytic thinking during the past hundred years. An examination of what has kept Freud's work so alive would require a comparative cultural analysis. For the Freud that succeeded in America is unlike the Freud that is currently flourishing, at long last, in France; and the English strand of psychoanalysis is unique, not to mention how other cultures have picked and chosen from within the broad doctrine that Freud first laid down.[20] Any generalizations about the sources of social support for psychoanalytic thinking would have to be linked to the specific circumstances of different national traditions.

Freud himself lived long enough to preside over the cross-cultural dissemination of his ideas. He selected disciples to carry on his calling in a variety of places, and even when he made misjudgements of character he persisted in his belief that, ultimately, he would triumph throughout the world. Even though he himself confessed to having little understanding of eastern religions, for example, he wrote letters to followers in both India and Japan. One of his favourites, Marie Bonaparte, undertook to finance anthropological field research by Géza Róheim in Australia. Freud himself stayed wedded to nineteenth-century convictions about how modern societies had evolved from so-called primitive cultures, and he never appreciated the requirements of modern field-work. Like Marx, he put forth his ideas with the conviction that they were universals.

Despite his conviction about his ultimate triumph, he was not willing to leave things to chance. And so when the first biography of him was published in 1924, written by an early member of his Vienna circle, Fritz Wittels, Freud did not let the occasion simply slide by. Freud wrote the author a detailed letter based on an advance copy of the book; and in Freud's library in London there is still a copy of his annotated edition of Wittels's study. Wittels later reprinted, with Freud's permission, extracts from Freud's letter to him. Later, Wittels was not only readmitted to the Vienna Psychoanalytic Society, but also published an article recanting his earlier candour.[21] A second book of Wittels's about Freud proved far less interesting; Wittels subsequently became a defender of psychoanalytic orthodoxy, and was one of those analysts who helped drive Karen Horney out of her teaching position at the New York Psychoanalytic Institute.[22] A close examination of Freud's detailed markings of his copy of Wittels's first biography would amount to an essay in its own right; but then one would have to take into account not only what Freud objected to, or approved of, but some striking passages which he chose not to comment on or challenge.

Wittels was sympathetic to Stekel; but Freud never forgave Stekel for what Freud deemed an unpardonable act of betrayal. And his unremitting capacity to bear grudges extended to a host of people he regarded as his enemies. Freud once approvingly quoted a passage from Heine that bears on his intransigence, which extended to the outlook he adopted toward his position in history. 'A great imaginative writer', Freud wrote in 1929, 'may permit himself to give expression – jokingly, at all events – to psychological truths that are severely proscribed.' Thus Heine (as quoted by Freud) confesses:

> 'Mine is a most peaceable disposition. My wishes are: a humble cottage with a thatched roof, but a good bed, good food, the freshest milk and butter, flowers before my window, and a few fine trees before my door; and if God wants to make my happiness complete, he will grant me the joy of seeing some six or seven of my enemies hanging from those trees. Before their death I shall, moved in my heart, forgive them all the wrong they did me in their lifetime. One must, it is true, forgive one's enemies – but not before they have been hanged.'[23]

While on holiday in the summer of 1931, Freud had 'composed what he called a "hate list" of seven or eight people.'[24]

This story about the construction of a hate list was told by Ernest Jones, who became Freud's authorized biographer. Jones commented that 'one would dearly like to know what names were on it', and regretted that only one of the identities could be reconstructed. It is typical that Jones was so closely identified with Freud's side of things that he did not seem to realize how lacking in charity he had made Freud seem. All of us who have studied the history of psychoanalysis are deeply indebted to Jones's research; he was permitted to see documentation that remains even now restricted. Jones was himself not lacking in the capacity to hate, and one does wonder sometimes whether his own personal version of Freud left out too much of Freud's unique generosity and outgoingness.

It is unfortunately characteristic of almost everything that has ever been written about Freud that it has been partisan. Freud himself had not wanted an official biography, but the Freud family came to feel that so many critical studies were coming out that it would be a wise act of statecraft to put them all in their place by depositing in Jones's hands the mass of documentary material they had at their disposal. While some of Freud's children had their reservations, in the end it was Anna Freud, the only one to have followed in his footsteps as an analyst, who overrode the natural objections that any family is entitled to have about a biographer invading their privacy.

One of the oddities of the choice of Jones as authorized biographer was that although he had been angling for the job for years, he made it sound in print as if he had been reluctant to undertake the task. Furthermore, he and Anna Freud were hardly on the best of terms. Jones had since the mid-1920s been sponsoring the work of Melanie Klein, Anna's bitter rival within child analysis; both Anna and her father thought that Klein was attacking Anna as a vehicle for getting back at Freud himself. Jones, then, was no personal favourite of either Anna or her father, although they both felt indebted to him for helping them escape to England after the Nazis occupied Austria in 1938. Only after Anna had read drafts of the first volume of Jones's biography did she decide to turn over in an unrestricted way the papers she had in her possession. Although Jones graciously dedicated his three-volume study to her, she remained privately lukewarm about what he had accomplished, although she and her allies knew that his version of things was good for the 'cause' they all championed.

Jones's books were successful not just in propping up a picture of Freud which was desirable from the orthodox psychoanalytic position, but in swamping almost all other writers by virtue of the authentic detail to which he alone had access. A few notable but isolated dissenting voices rose in protest. Erich Fromm, for example, wrote his short *Sigmund Freud's Mission* in an effort to show how Jones's own material could be used for different, 'revisionist' purposes.[25] And Bruno Bettelheim was courageous enough not only to review Fromm's essay favourably, but to publish his own separate critiques of Jones.[26] Among professional psychoanalysts, however, Jones carried the day; the orthodox Robert Waelder, for instance, made sure that he contributed an extended critique of Fromm's position,[27] while the liberals within the movement by and large did not seem to appreciate the power which creating a historical record could give. A notable exception to this generalization was Clara Thompson's book *Psychoanalysis: Evolution and Development.*[28]

Within the literary community as a whole Jones was to go unchallenged for an extraordinary period of time. Insiders within psychoanalysis knew, for example, that Jones's account of Sandor Ferenczi's last days was heavily biased; essentially Jones had accused Ferenczi of having had a mental illness which explained his difficulties with Freud, even though Freud's own obituary of Ferenczi had mentioned the physical disease of pernicious anaemia. But outsiders could be rougher on the 'dissidents' in psychoanalysis than even Jones. Perhaps the most telling example of non-analysts being even more partisan than the most fierce of the Freudians was how the eminent literary critic Lionel

Trilling could allow himself, with no basis in evidence, to exaggerate what he found in Jones. Trilling wrote in a review in the *Sunday New York Times Book Review* of Ferenczi and Otto Rank: 'Both men fell prey to extreme mental illness and they died insane.'[29] Even Jones was surprised at the length to which Trilling had taken Jones's own various diagnostic libels.

The stage was then set for the next generation of historians who, almost inevitably, have been branded as debunkers. Once Jones had finished rounding out Freud's version of his life, identifying completely with Freud's own side of a career filled with controversy, then any attempt to correct the idealizations that Jones had publicized was bound to appear like the work of detractors. Jones aspired to be definitive; and he quoted extensively from Freud's letters in the hope that it would deter any attempt to publish the correspondences in their entirety. Anna Freud too wanted nothing further after Jones. Her desire for control was such that, at the British Psychoanalytic Society, she rose to take exception to the forthcoming John Huston movie about Freud, even though the original screen-play had been written by Jean-Paul Sartre.

The results of Jones's orthodox historiography were not what he had anticipated. The excellence of his narrative served to attract even more researchers, but increasingly their allegiances would be to impartial scholarship as opposed to doctrinal loyalty. It is true that orthodox analysts continued to cite Jones as the last word; and other members of Anna Freud's party, such as Max Schur, could be counted upon to present a picture that she would find attractive.[30] Jones himself died shortly after the appearance of the final volume of his biography, but where power is concerned there are always those willing to pick up the mantle of the defence of the orthodox faith. In my opinion Peter Gay's recent work, including his *Freud: A Life For Our Time*, has been designed to launch what amounts to a Counter-Reformation in Freud studies.[31]

Anna Freud, right up until her death in 1982, watched over everything that appeared about her father. It is a safe generalization that she liked nothing that came out, not even Schur's book, apart from one notable exception: she thought that an article by Kurt R. Eissler about her father was splendid.[32] Starting with an attack on Franz Alexander, a particular battle that Anna Freud was still carrying on in one of her last publications,[33] Eissler became the official watchdog on behalf of psychoanalytic orthodoxy. He and Anna Freud worked together harmoniously. Even while Freud was still alive, Anna had been capable of exaggerating his dislikes; but after his death she was able to pursue her own agenda unchecked. She admitted to Jones once in a letter, while he was writing his biography, that she could be jealous of other women in Freud's circle. Basically she resented anyone whose link with Freud did not go through her. As the years passed she built up her own following, almost all of whom she personally analysed at least briefly; 'Miss Freud', as she came reverentially to be known, became so powerful as to intimidate almost anyone who tried to write about her father. One recent brouhaha in the history of psychoanalysis was the direct responsibility of both Eissler and Anna Freud. They took it into their heads that a youngish Sanskritist, Jeffrey M. Masson, who had graduated from the Toronto Psychoanalytic Institute, should succeed Eissler in charge of the

Freud Archives in New York City. Eissler had set up the Archives, with Anna Freud's half-hearted support, shortly after World War II. As time passed, and no doubt the advantages of tax deductions began to sink in, she gave the Archives her full support. The idea was that people would donate material to the Archives, and then the Archives would in turn give items to the Library of Congress in Washington, D.C. That way the Freud Archives was the official donor, and could place whatever restrictions it chose on the material it deposited at the Library of Congress. The dates embargoing items were wholly arbitrary; patient confidentiality was not a central consideration, and just as Anna O.'s real name, despite her family's objections, had been revealed by Jones, so Eissler felt free, after the death of Freud's former patient 'The Wolf-Man', to indicate his real identity as well.[34] Because of the arrangement under which the Library of Congress first agreed to accept the donation of Freud's papers, it remains helpless in the face of the partisanship that continues to this day to govern the operations of the Freud Archives.

The oddness of the choice of Masson in 1980 to be placed in charge of the Freud Archives was that he had had for years a bee in his bonnet about the sexual seduction of children. Neither Eissler nor Anna Freud could detect Masson's obsession with this theme; all they could see was that he was apparently bent on maintaining the glorification of Freud. He succeeded in charming them both. The fat was in the fire by 1981, within a year of his appointment, when he announced at a psychoanalytic meeting, and worse still to a *New York Times* reporter, that Freud had lacked the courage of his early convictions when he gave up the hypothesis that neurosis arose from childhood sexual abuse. Masson alleged that Freud had invented his theory of the Oedipus complex, and the significant role of fantasy, to curry favour with the Viennese medical establishment. Eissler then got the Board of the Freud Archives to fire Masson; Masson filed a legal suit, and an out-of-court settlement was finally agreed upon.

Eissler was subsequently eased out of his position at the Freud Archives; Anna Freud herself died in 1982, and one might have thought that the situation of psychoanalytic historiography would be radically transformed. It is true that no one now has to fear the force of Anna Freud's wrath, which could be considerable. For example, in my own case I did not realize how much at the time she had done behind the scenes against me because of her intense dislike of my second book, *Brother Animal: The Story of Freud and Tausk*, which first came out in 1969.[35] Only when I went through her papers at the Library of Congress in the summer of 1989 did I learn the full extent of her manipulations exerting pressure on publishers, reviewers, and other psychoanalysts. She participated in a shared fanaticism whose power extended to some of the most famous philanthropic foundations.

Although it would be unwise to be prematurely confident about the waning of cultism, it does seem to me that in the last few years the history of psychoanalysis has finally shown signs of becoming a subject which can be studied in universities with something like the objectivity which one can expect of similar topics. It is still true that too many people remain fiercely attached to fixed ideological positions. The power of therapeutic transferences is such that those who have been analysed by members of one school of analysis or another are apt to be irrationally attached to positions which cannot be defended on normal academic grounds. Still, I see real indications that the history of psychoanalysis is today being critically weighed by university scholars in a way which it has never been before.

The past ideological wars mean that, as compared to almost any other academic endeavour in the history of ideas, it is strikingly easy to be original in this area. All one has to do is to maintain a modicum of impartiality and thereby cut through literature which has been written by clinicians with no real idea of normal standards of scholarship. In addition, with the continued withholding of primary data, such as Freud's numerous correspondences, there is plenty of time to assimilate new material. It will be years before all Freud's letters finally appear. We are obliged to cross our fingers and hope that when these correspondences are finally accessible, people will be able competently to weigh the meaning of the feelings and events that are described there.

One danger in the current literature is that the pendulum may swing excessively in a scientistic direction. Practising clinicians have gone unchallenged for so many years that serious students of the history and philosophy of scientific methodology are able to make mince-meat out of most of the existing psychoanalytic literature. Freud can be seen, when judged by the severest standards of modern science, to appear naively ignorant of the need to verify his propositions.

Although Freud could undoubtedly deceive himself about how much of his work had been independently confirmed, at the same time I think there is a problem with importing into this field standards which are needlessly positivistic. Of course Freud's dream theory needs revision now; advances in biochemistry alone make many of his convictions seem elementary and misguided. Jung's theory of dreams, an alternative to Freud's, should have alerted people earlier to different possibilities that were available; it is impossible to make sense of what happened in the early days of psychoanalysis without taking seriously the various criticisms which were advanced against Freud by a wide variety of contemporary thinkers.

It should go almost without saying that by now we know much more about the nature of good psychotherapy. There is nothing sacred about the fifty-minute hour, and the use of the couch may, as some of Freud's earliest critics contended long ago, be inadvisable. Sophisticated therapists today are far more wary of artificially inducing regressions in patients than has been the case with orthodox psychoanalysis.

Nevertheless, all Freud's theories have to be seen in the context of his times. It would be anachronistic to look at him only from the perspective of what we now think to be true. We can better understand what Freud was doing with his patients thanks to the hindsight which the past century has given us; but we have to beware of the distortions which an exclusively present-minded orientation would impose on us. We should neither be appealing to Freud for ways of supporting the practices of orthodox analysis today, nor searching for ways of

17

making Freud seem foolish and misguided by standards which were not accessible to him.

The aim of studying the history of psychoanalysis ought to be to take us out of ourselves, and to provide a fresh perspective on some of our own least examined ways of thinking. Freud was laying down some fundamental challenges to traditional Western ethics. This is not a subject on which one can be either right or wrong in a way which is strictly verifiable. He created through his works a world which was different; he attracted articulate and sophisticated people who tried their best to make sense of some of the most fundamental issues in human experience. Freud was trying to say something lasting about the nature of both love and hate, and even though the subject is in principle an inexhaustible one, the ideas he proposed were memorable and telling.

I am not making a plea for apologetics about Freud, which are in any case unnecessary. Both as a thinker and writer he is capable of withstanding the closest scrutiny. The people Freud attracted and repelled make for fascinating intellectual history. The fact that many of his supporters were on an unacknowledged religious quest helps make them appealing since their search for salvation meant that they were soul-seekers. This religiosity also led to an unfortunate degree of intolerance, which has been an obstacle in the path of scholarship. But the length of time it has taken to breach the defences of credulous believers and unreflective sceptics means that now the study of the history of psychoanalysis has come of age.

Notes

1. *Letters of Sigmund Freud 1873–1939*, ed. Ernst L. Freud, tr. Tania and James Stern (London, 1961), pp. 152–3.
2. Paul Roazen, *Freud and His Followers* (New York, 1975; reprinted 1992), pp. 39–46.
3. Paul Roazen, 'Nietzsche and Freud: Two Voices from the Underground', *Psychohistory Review*, Spring 1991, 327–49.
4. Henri Ellenberger, 'The Story of "Anna O.": A Critical Review with New Data', *Journal of the History of the Behavioral Sciences*, 8 (1972), 267–79; cf. also Paul Roazen, Review of Hirschmüller's *The Life and Work of Josef Breuer*, *Psychohistory Review*, Winter 1991, 283–7.
5. Sigmund Freud, 'Five Lectures on Psychoanalysis,' *SE* 11: 9.
6. Sigmund Freud, *Selbstdarstellung*, ed. Ilse Grubich-Simitis (Frankfurt, 1971), pp. 141ff.
7. Carl G. Jung, *Memories, Dreams, Reflections*, recorded and edited by Aniela Jaffé, translated by Richard and Clara Winston (New York, 1965).
8. Paul Roazen, 'Tampering with the Mails': Review of *The Letters of Sigmund Freud to Eduard Silberstein 1871–1881*, *The American Scholar*, Autumn 1991.
9. Cf. Paul Roazen, *Erik H. Erikson: The Power and Limits of a Vision* (New York, 1976), pp. 70–2, 182, 191.
10. Myron Sharaf, *Fury on Earth: A Biography of Wilhelm Reich* (New York, 1983); E. James Lieberman, *Acts of Will: The Life and Work of Otto Rank* (New York, 1985); Susan Quinn, *A Mind of Her Own: The Life of Karen Horney* (New York, 1987); Phyllis Grosskurth, *Melanie Klein: Her World and Her Work* (New York, 1986).
11. Paul Roazen, Review of Kiell's *Freud Without Hindsight, Reviews of his Work (1893–1939)*, *Journal of the History of the Behavioral Sciences*, 26 (1990), 197–202.

12. Lynn L. Marshall and Seymour Drescher, 'American Historians and Tocqueville's *Democracy*', *The Journal of American History*, 55, 3 (Dec.1968), 516.
13. Paul Roazen, *Encountering Freud: The Politics and Histories of Psychoanalysis* (New Brunswick, 1990), pp. 121–4, 13–16, 263–4.
14. Hugh Trevor-Roper, *Renaissance Essays* (London, 1986), p. 104.
15. Roazen, *Freud and His Followers*, pp. 436–46.
16. John C. Burnham, *Jelliffe: American Psychoanalyst and Physician* (Chicago, 1983), p. 269.
17. Victor Tausk, *Sexuality, War, and Schizophrenia: Collected Psychoanalytic Papers*, ed. Paul Roazen (New Brunswick, 1991), pp. 1–28.
18. Roazen, *Encountering Freud*, Ch. 6.
19. Trevor-Roper, *Renaissance Essays*, p 192.
20. Roazen, *Encountering Freud*, Ch. 2.
21. Fritz Wittels, 'Revision of a Biography', *Psychoanalytic Review*, 20 (1933), 361–74.
22. Quinn, *A Mind of Her Own*, pp. 337–40.
23. Sigmund Freud, 'Civilization and Its Discontents,' *SE* 21: 110.
24. Ernest Jones, *The Life and Work of Sigmund Freud*, 3 vols (New York, 1953–7), III, 159.
25. Erich Fromm, *Sigmund Freud's Mission: An Analysis of His Personality and Influence* (New York, 1959).
26. Bruno Bettelheim, *Freud's Vienna and Other Essays* (New York, 1991), pp. 39–56.
27. Robert Waelder, 'Historical Fiction', *Journal of the American Psychoanalytic Association*, 11 (1963), 628–51.
28. Clara Thompson, with the collaboration of Patrick Mullahy, *Psychoanalysis: Evolution and Development* (New York, 1950).
29. Cf. Lieberman, *Acts of Will*, p. 400.
30. Roazen, *Encountering Freud*, pp. 215–18.
31. Paul Roazen, Review of Gay's *Freud: A Life For Our Time*, *Psychoanalytic Books*, 1 (January 1990), 10–17.
32. Kurt R. Eissler, 'Mankind at Its Best', *Journal of the American Psychoanalytic Association*, 12 (1964), 187–222.
33. Paul Roazen, Review of Sandler, Kennedy, and Tyson, *The Technique of Child Analysis: Discussions with Anna Freud*, *Journal of the History of the Behavioral Sciences*, 27 (1991), 281–3.
34. Paul Roazen, 'Psychoanalytic Ethics: Freud, Mussolini, and Edoardo Weiss', *Journal of the History of the Behavioral Sciences*, 27 (1991), 366–74.
35. Paul Roazen, *Brother Animal: The Story of Freud and Tausk* (New York, 1969; reprinted with new Introduction, New Brunswick, 1990).

Freud, Race and Gender

Sander L. Gilman

Freud's 'Jewish' identity has been long the topic for scholarly exegesis.[1] Recently Harold Bloom asked:

> What is most Jewish about Freud's work? I am not much impressed by the answers to this question that follow the pattern: from Oedipus to Moses, and thus center themselves upon Freud's own Oedipal relation to his father Jakob. Such answers only tell me that Freud had a Jewish father, and doubtless books and essays yet will be written hypothesizing Freud's relation to his indubitably Jewish mother. Nor am I persuaded by any attempts to relate Freud to esoteric Jewish traditions. As a speculator, Freud may be said to have founded a kind of Gnosis, but there are no Gnostic elements in the Freudian dualism. Nor am I convinced by any of the attempts to connect Freud's Dream Book to supposed Talmudic antecedents. And yet the center of Freud's work, his concept of repression as I've remarked, does seem to me profoundly Jewish, and in its patterns even normatively Jewish. Freudian memory and Freudian forgetting are a very Jewish memory and a very Jewish forgetting. It is their reliance upon a version of Jewish memory, a parody-version if you will, that makes Freud's writings profoundly and yet all too originally Jewish.[2]

My answer to Bloom's problem is only a very partial one. For Sigmund Freud, an acculturated Jewish medical scientist of late nineteenth-century Vienna, one of the definitions of the Jew which he would have internalized was a racial one and it is a definition which, whether he consciously sought it or not, shaped the argument of psychoanalysis. Given Freud's own analysis of many of his dreams, the latent or manifest content of which reflection the question of being 'Jewish' in a violently anti-Semitic world, this question seems to have been first raised by Freud himself.[3] Thus we can cite Peter Homans, who defines 'Jewishness' 'after the fashion of a key to its wax impression or a statue to a plaster cast of the statue – psychoanalysis emerged as the negative image, so to speak, of its Jewish surroundings.'[4] Homans sees the de-idealization of Jewish men to whom [Freud] had attached himself as the key to this movement; I see this de-idealization, in part, as the result of Freud's struggle with the very definition

20

of science which becomes central to his primary group orientation. Freud's seeming fixation on the biological explanation for psychological phenomena, a fixation which has greatly stirred the interest of historians over the past two decades, must be tied to his contemporary understanding of science as a domain in which debates about his own self are carried out.

For Freud in the 1870s, the idea of race is a confining, limiting factor, as it implies a biological, immutable pattern of development. After the turn of the century, it comes to acquire a more positive valence as a sign of the special status of the Jewish way of seeing the world. It moves from a purely biological category to a purely psychological one. In 1886, about the time Freud was studying with Jean-Martin Charcot in Paris, Gustav Le Bon, the French anti-Semitic sociologist, published his overt discussion of the inheritance of the psychological attributes of race, which he attributed as much to biology as to social environment.[5] Le Bon's views are central for Freud's later work on the psychology of mass movements, which are his unstated analyses of anti-Semitism. Freud found Paris to be as intensely anti-Semitic as his home in Vienna had been. He wished to reject Le Bon's biological view of race as 'the innumerable common characteristics handed down from generation to genera-tion, which constitute the genius of a race.'[6] For Le Bon, race stands in the 'first rank' of those factors which help shape the underlying attitudes of the crowd. Racial character 'possesses, as the result of the laws of heredity, such power that its beliefs, institutions, and arts – in a word, all the elements of its civilization – are merely outward expressions of its genius.'[7] And yet for the later Freud it is within the psyche, not the body, that the difference between Jew and Aryan exists. Freud does sense that there is a difference, unnameable perhaps, but a difference nevertheless. It is the unknowable essence of the Jew which anthropologists such as Richard Andree evoked. Unlike Andree, Freud provided this essence with a special, positive valence.

In 1926 Freud stated in an address to the B'nai B'rith, on the occasion of his seventieth birthday, that being Jewish is sharing 'many obscure emotional forces (*viele dunkle Gefühlsmächte*), which were the more powerful the less they could be expressed in words, as well as a clear consciousness of inner identity, the safe privacy of a common mental construction (*die Heimlichkeit der gleichen seelischen Identitat*).'[8] His contemporaries, such as Theodor Reik (along with Freud and Eduard Hitschmann, the only psychoanalysts to be members of the B'nai Brith), 'were especially struck' by these very words as the appropriate central definition of the Jew.[9]

Freud's version of the ethnopsychology of the Jew gave a new twist to Le Bon's claims concerning the biology of race. It evokes the Lamarckianism of William James's view of the transmission of 'the same emotional propensities, the same habits, the same instincts, perpetuated without variation from one generation to another.'[10] It is the uncanny nature of the known but repressed aspects of the mental life of an individual – about which Freud wrote in his essay on the uncanny – which haunts Freud's image of the internal mental life peculiar to the Jew. As he writes to his Viennese Jewish 'alter ego' Arthur Schnitzler: 'Judaism continues to mean much to me on an emotional level.'[11]

The debate about the meaning of what Philip Rieff sees as the Victorian and
Edwardian generalities about the 'persistent character of the Jews' must be
understood as part of the quest of the scientific psychology of the late nineteenth
century.[12] For Freud this sense of the psyche of the Jew had not only to do with
the structure of the Jewish mind but also with the Jew's emotional disposition.
Here he would have found substantial support in the work of William
McDougall, whose study of *The Group Mind* (1920) played a central role in
shaping Freud's own argument about the psychology of the masses.[13] McDougall
sees the fusing of the Hebrew tribes into a nation as having 'played a vital part
in its consolidation, implanted and fostered as it was by a succession of great
teachers, the prophets... The national self-consciousness thus formed has
continued to be not only one factor, but almost the only factor or condition, of
the continued existence of the Jewish people as a people, or at any rate the one
fundamental condition on which all the others are founded – their exclusive
religion, their objection to intermarriage with outsiders, their hope of a future
restoration of the fortunes of the nation, and so forth.'[14] Jewish self-
consciousness leads to the establishment of institutions which preserve this
'common mental construction'. It is this sense of common purpose, for
McDougall, but not necessarily for Freud, within the sphere of the political,
which defines the Jew. Central, however, is that all aspects of the Jewish mind,
including all the affective components, have their root in this 'common mental
construction'.

When Freud comments to his 'brothers' in the B'nai B'rith about their
common mental construction, he is also in a very specific way evoking the
presence of the Jewish body. Freud's major association with Jews in the 1870s
and 1880s was when he joined (and helped form) a new lodge of the B'nai B'rith
in Vienna.[15] 'B'nai B'rith' means 'sons of the Covenant'. While the name was
selected as a replacement for the title 'Bundes-Brüder' – a German-Jewish lodge
founded in New York in 1843 – the name evoked, for *fin-de-siècle* Viennese Jews,
a direct association with the image of circumcision. As Theodor Reik commented
in 1915:

> the bond which the primordial fathers of the Jews concluded with their
> god is represented ... as a glorified and emended account of an initiation
> ceremony. The connection of the *B'rith* with circumcision is just as little
> an accident as the covenant meal in which the worshippers of Yahweh
> identified themselves with him; and the giving of the law – *B'rith* can also
> signify law – which stands in such an intimate relationship to the
> concluding of the covenant (Sinai) should be set side by side with the
> procedures of the puberty rites.[16]

The sense of 'common mental construction' is associated closely with the special
form of the Jew's body and the ritual bonding which it signifies. Central to this
is the act of circumcision. And this is the salient marker of the male Jewish body
in *fin-de-siècle* medicine.

It was generally assumed in Europe at the time that there was a 'Jewish mind'
which transcended conversion or adaptation.[17] And this was usually understood

as being a fault. Ludwig Wittgenstein could comment about Jews such as Freud that 'even the greatest of Jewish thinkers is no more than talented. (Myself, for instance). I think there is some truth to my idea that I really only think reproductively ... Can one take the case of Freud and Breuer as an example of Jewish reproductiveness?'[18] The Jewish mind has no true originality. The Jewish mind is prosaic, as Freud wrote to Emil Fluss in the 1870s:

> How well I can imagine your feelings. To leave the native soil, dearly-beloved relatives, – the most beautiful surroundings – ruins close by – I must stop or I'll be as sad as you – and you yourself know best what you are leaving behind ... Oh Emil why are you a prosaic Jew? Journeymen imbued with Christian-Germanic fervour have composed beautiful lyrical poetry in similar circumstances.[19]

This view echoes the negative interpretation of the 'common mental construction' of the Jew as expressed in much of the anthropological and cultural debates of the late nineteenth century.

Such views of the Jews are statements about their pathology. And Freud concurs on a very basic level with the notion that the Jewish mind-set is pathological. In his lecture on 'Anxiety' (1917) he evoked the Lamarckian model of the inheritance of acquired characteristics in order to argue that the 'core' of anxiety is 'the repetition of some particular significant experience. This experience could only be a very early impression of a very general nature, placed in the prehistory not of the individual but of the species.'[20] Or, one might add, in the prehistory of the race. Freud goes on to say that this 'affective state would be constructed in the same way as a hysterical attack and, like it, would be the precipitate of a reminiscence.'[21] The anxiety of the Jew is analogous but not identical to the suffering of the hysteric. The male Eastern Jew is the quintessential hysteric for the medical science of the *fin de siècle*. It is the psychopathology of the Jew which is impressed on the individual through the experience of the collective.

The roots of this view lie deep in theories of ethnopsychology as formulated by two Jews, the psychologist Moritz Lazarus and his brother-in-law, the philologist Heymann Steinthal, in the 1860s. In the opening issue of their journal for ethnopsychology and linguistics, *Zeitschrift für Völkerpsychologie und Sprachwissenschaft* (note the linking of mind and language), they outlined the assumptions about the knowability of the mind.[22] Their object of study was the 'psychology of human beings in groups (*Gemeinschaft*)'. Unlike other fields of psychology of the time, where laboratory and clinical work was required in order to define the arena of study, ethnopsychology depended on historical and cultural/ethnological data. Their work was highly medicalized: Lazarus had studied physiology with the materialist Johannes Müller and co-founded the Medical-Psychological Society with the Berlin neurologist Wilhelm Griesinger in 1867. While they wished to separate their psychology from materialistic physiology, they were bound by the scientific rhetoric of the materialistic arguments about inheritance. They subscribed to a Lamarckian theory of mnemonic inheritance in the construction of the mind. The great laboratory

23

psychologist Wilhelm Wundt remained a leading proponent of their views of 'universal mental creations'[23] well into the twentieth century. And Freud makes extensive use of Wundt's explication of these views in his *Psychopathology of Everyday Life* (1901) and *Totem and Taboo* (1913).[24] The psychology of the individual, as one of Freud's other sources, the Princeton psychologist James Mark Baldwin commented, recapitulates the history of the 'race experience'. One can expect 'general analogies to hold between nervous development and mental development, one of which is the deduction of race history epochs from individual history epochs through the repetition of phylogenesis in ontogenesis, called in biology "Recapitulation"'.[25] The history of the human race was to be found in the development of the individual. But 'racial memory' has a very different connotation for a Jewish reader of Wundt and Baldwin.

Freud, like the ethnopsychologists, needed to separate the idea of the psyche from the body, needed to eliminate the image of the fixed, immutable racial composition which determines all thoughts and all actions. For all of these thinkers, the psyche was separate from, and yet still part of, the body. They wished to avoid the pitfalls of race, but found it impossible to separate the mind from the body.

Freud dismisses the Germanic 'Weltanschauung' as a 'specifically German concept, the translation of which into foreign languages might well raise difficulties.'[26] It is not the rigid paradigm of knowing which appeals to Freud, but rather the acceptance of the 'scientific' model, which, while it assumes the '*uniformity* of explanation of the universe', only does so 'as a programme, the fulfilment of which is relegated to the future'. Since the scientific outlook is not specifically Germanic, it is available to the Jew.[27] By the mid-1930s Freud can shrug his shoulders at the Nazi burning of his books, sensing that this action represents the German response to his own 'common mental construction': '"They told me," he said, "that psychoanalysis is alien to their *Weltanschauung*, and I suppose it is." He said this with no emotion and little interest, as though talking about the affairs of some complete stranger.'[28] It is Freud the positivist that dominates in his comprehension of the mind-set of the Jews.

Lazarus and Steinthal call these groups 'peoples' (*Völker*), but stress that they are constituted by the individuals which comprise them and are not fixed biological 'races.'[29] 'Human beings,' as Lazarus observes, 'are the creation of history; everything in us, about us, is the result of history; we do not speak a word, we do not think an idea, there is neither feeling nor emotion, which is not in a complicated manner dependent on historical determinants.'[30] The standards for defining a people are fluid and change from group to group. Thus the standards for being French are different from those for being German.[31] Even though a 'people is a purely subjective construction', it reflects itself in 'a common consciousness of many with the consciousness of the group.'[32] This 'common consciousness' exists initially because of the 'same origin' and the 'proximity of the dwellings' of the members of the group.[33] And 'with the relationship through birth, the similarity of physiognomy, especially the form of the body, is present.'[34] For them this 'objective' fact of biological similarity lays the groundwork for the 'subjective' nature of the mental construction of a people.[35] But the biological underpinnings of this argument are clear: for the

Irish eat potatoes as a reflex of being in Ireland, which makes them Irish, and they are Irish because they eat potatoes.[36] Could one not argue that Jews are Jews because they circumcise their male infants and they circumcise their male infants because they are Jews? The place where these acquired characteristics is localized is not the body, but within the language of the *Volk*. Lazarus and Steinthal are constituting a definition of group identification which is rooted in a biological (and, therefore, for them observable and demonstrable) relationship but which self-consciously builds upon this basic identity a sense of group cohesion. This is an answer to the argument about 'race' constructing the mentality of the group. Here it is the group which is constituted by the biological accidents of birth and dwelling, not by the inborn identity of blood. And yet it is the observable, biological which structures their argument.

Freud sees the construction of the mentality of a group as a reflex of biology tempered by the social context in which the individual finds himself. In *Civilization and its Discontents* (1930) he comments on the subjectivity of happiness:

> no matter how much we may shrink with horror from certain situations – of a galley-slave in antiquity, of a peasant during the Thirty Years' War, of a victim of the Holy Inquisition, of a Jew awaiting a pogrom – it is nevertheless impossible for us to feel our way into such people – to divine the changes which original obtuseness of mind, a gradual stupefying process, the cessation of expectations, and cruder or more refined methods of narcotization have produced upon their receptivity to sensations of pleasure and unpleasure.[37]

Freud places himself and the reader (the 'us') at some distance from the victim.[38] This works in terms of the historical images he evokes from antiquity, the seventeenth century, the sixteenth century, but the image of the pogrom, while obliquely 'historical' in that it reflects Russia at the *fin de siècle*, is also quite immediate to Freud. His attribution of this mind-set to allegedly distant times of stress separates himself out from what was occurring during his own experience, even while he wrote *Civilization and its Discontents*.

But Freud, as in his earlier review of Forel, in print rejected traditional definitions of 'race' as a category within the discourse of science. During his analysis of Smiley Blanton he commented: 'My background as a Jew helped me to stand being criticized, being isolated, working alone ... All this was of help to me in discovering analysis. But that psychoanalysis itself is a Jewish product seems to me nonsense. As a scientific work, it is neither Jewish nor Catholic nor Gentile.'[39] He wrote in a birthday greeting to Ernest Jones in 1929:

> The first piece of work that it fell to psychoanalysis to perform was the discovery of the instincts that are common to all men living today – and not only to those living today but to those of ancient and of prehistoric times. It called for no great effort, therefore, for psychoanalysis to ignore the differences that arise among the inhabitants of the earth owing to the multiplicity of races, languages, and countries.[40]

And this to an individual with whom he felt a 'racial strangeness' (*Rassenfremdheit*) at first meeting in 1908.[41] Jones himself records that Freud told him that 'from the shape of my head I could not be English and must be Welsh. It astonished me, first because it is uncommon for anyone on the Continent to know of the existence of my native country, and then because I had suspected my dolichocephalic skull might as well be Teutonic as Celtic.'[42] Jones's response to Freud's remark is couched in the language of racial biology. The use of these categories was simply taken for granted.

These contradictory remarks show that Freud resisted the idea of a group mentality and tried to restructure it. His conviction of the compatibility of both neutral science and ethnocentric perception is found in a letter written on 8 June 1913 to one of his most trusted Jewish followers, the Hungarian psychoanalyst Sándor Ferenczi:

> Certainly there are great differences between the Jewish and the Aryan spirit. We can observe that every day. Hence, there would assuredly be here and there differences in outlook on art and life. But there should not be such a thing as Aryan or Jewish science. Results in science must be identical, though the presentation of them may vary.[43]

This difference in 'spirit' is present and yet undefined. Many opponents of political anti-Semitism acknowledged that there were indeed 'many scientific Jews, but nowhere a Jewish science', to quote Anatole Leroy-Beaulieu.[44] Yet it was clear that Freud understood that his own identification as a Jew both provided the 'ground' for the new science of psychoanalysis and at the same time limited the claim of this new field of inquiry to be a 'neutral science'. In 1910 he had confronted his Viennese colleagues at the second Psychoanalytic Congress bluntly: 'Most of you are Jews, and therefore you are incompetent to win friends for the new teaching. Jews must be content with the modest role of preparing the ground. It is absolutely essential that I should form ties in the world of general science ... The Swiss will save us ....'[45] But the Swiss, at least C. G. Jung if not Eugen Bleuler, also tended to see psychoanalysis as a 'Jewish' science. Freud recognized this when he commented to Smiley Blanton in 1930 that he had tried to place Jung at the head of the psychoanalytic movement because 'there was a danger that people would consider psychoanalysis as primarily Jewish.'[46] Or to Abram Kardiner that he hated the idea that 'psychoanalysis would founder because it would go down in history as a "Jewish" science.'[47] Psychoanalysis had to be freed, but could not be freed from the Jewish mind which, at least in Freud's view, constructed it.

In a 1936 letter (written in English) on the death of his friend and early British supporter Montague David Eder, Freud evoked that 'common mental construction' which sets the Jew apart: 'We were both Jews and knew of each other that we carried that miraculous thing in common, which – inaccessible to any analysis so far – makes the Jew.'[48] He uses this rhetoric often in his exchanges with Jews. He can write to Karl Abraham on 3 May 1908 of their common 'racial identification' (*Rassenverwandtschaft*) as opposed to the 'Aryan' views of Jung.[49] Freud's letter reflects his anxiety about the labelling of psychoanalysis as a

'Jewish national affair.'[50] As he later wrote to Jones, science should be beyond such designations, but evidently is not. Both Freud and Abraham saw a grain of truth in this charge, rooted in the way Jews were assumed to see the world. Thus Abraham writes in a letter:

> I find it easier to go along with you rather than with Jung. I, too, have always felt this intellectual kinship. After all, our Talmudic way of thinking cannot disappear just like that. Some days ago a small paragraph in *Jokes* strangely attracted me. When I looked at it more closely, I found that, in the technique of apposition and in its whole structure, it was completely Talmudic.[51]

Freud's response does not deny this but rather rephrases this 'shared mental construction' in the following terms: 'May I say that it is consanguineous Jewish traits (*verwandte, jüdische Züge*) that attract me to you? We understand each other.'[52] Abraham's claim is that the Jews in psychoanalysis share a common discourse and he evokes, in a positive manner, the traditional negative label of 'Talmudic' for this approach. Both Abraham and Freud agree (and give a positive value) to the charge that the Jews possess a secret or hidden language, which is manifested in the way Jews use (or rather, abuse) language. This is the charge, which we have already seen widely stated, that Jews speak *Mauscheldeutsch*, that they speak differently from all others.

In 1912, when the break with Jung was clear, Freud in a letter to Ferenczi despairs of yoking 'Jews and *goyim*' in the service of psychoanalysis', for 'they separate themselves like oil and water.'[53] How Freud experienced the '*goyim*' can be seen in a letter to Otto Rank a month later when the 'Jews and *goyim*" become 'Jews and anti-Semites.'[54] Writing to Jung's former mistress Sabina Spielrein in August 1913, Freud says: 'We are and remain Jews. The others will only exploit us and will never understand or appreciate us.'[55] Or in writing to Theodor Reik in 1914 about his critique of the Lutheran pastor-psychoanalyst Oskar Pfister's theological understanding of psychoanalysis, Freud observes that Reik's comment is 'too good for those *goyim.*'[56] Not only are Jews different in terms of their mentality from Aryans, but this is an unbridgeable difference. Jews are unknowable to Aryans.

In Freud's comments on the 'Resistances to Psychoanalysis', he writes in 1926 that

> the question may be raised whether the personality of the present writer as a Jew who has never sought to disguise the fact that he is a Jew may not have had a share in provoking the antipathy of his environment to psychoanalysis ... Nor is it perhaps entirely a matter of chance that the first advocate of psychoanalysis was a Jew. To profess belief in this new theory called for a certain degree of readiness to accept a situation of solitary opposition – a situation with which no one is more familiar than a Jew.[57]

Even though Freud expresses both pride and fear that psychoanalysis will become identified as a Jewish undertaking, he also writes to the Italian psychiatrist Enrico Morselli[58] in 1926 that while he does not know whether Morselli's conception of psychoanalysis as 'a direct product of the Jewish mind' is correct, he would not be ashamed if it were. 'Although long alienated from the religion of my ancestors', Freud continues, 'I have a feeling of solidarity with my people (*Volk*) and realize with satisfaction that you are a student of a man of my race (*Stammesgenossen*), the great Lombroso.'[59]

It is not Judaism as a religion (which is 'of great significance to me as a subject of scientific interest') with which Freud identifies in a public letter in 1925, but rather the 'strong feeling of solidarity with my fellow-people (*mit meinem Volk*)'.[60] In his response to the greetings of the Chief Rabbi of Vienna on the occasion of his seventy-fifth birthday, Freud stresses the communal, psychological identity of the Jew:

> Your words aroused a special echo in me, which I do not need to explain to you. In some place in my soul, in a very hidden corner, I am a fanatical Jew. I am very much astonished to discover myself as such in spite of all efforts to be unprejudiced and impartial. What can I do against my age?[61]

Indeed the 1934 preface to the Hebrew edition of *Totem and Taboo* stated the case for a secular, racial (or at least ethnopsychological) definition of the Jew quite clearly:

> No reader of [the Hebrew version] of this book will find it easy to put himself in the emotional position of an author who is ignorant of the language of holy writ, who is completely estranged from the religion of his fathers – as well as from every other religion – and who cannot take a share in nationalist ideals, but who has yet never repudiated his people, who feels that he is in his essential nature (*Eigenart*) a Jew and who has no desire to alter that nature. If the question were put to him: 'Since you have abandoned all these common characteristics (*Gemeinsamkeiten*) of your countrymen (*Volksgenossen*), what is left to you that is Jewish?' he would reply: 'A very great deal, and probably its very essence.' He could not express that essence in words; but some day, no doubt, it will become accessible to the scientific mind.[62]

It is not only the Jew who is unknowable within the pantheon of Freud's scientific world. Freud's comments on the unknowability of the Jew are parallel to his claims about the unknowability of the feminine. For, just as the scientist does not know what the essence of the Jew is, neither does he know about the essence of female sexuality, even to its developmental structure: 'Unfortunately we can describe this state of things only as it affects the male child; the corresponding processes in the little girl are not known to us.'[63] This Freud wrote in 1923. It was part of a generally accepted view, echoed by *fin-de-siècle* sexologists such as Paul Näcke, that 'a man can never penetrate (*eindringen*) into the psychology of the female and vice-versa'.[64] Freud's comment echoes his earlier view in the *Three Essays on the Theory of Sexuality* (1905) that 'the significance of the factor of sexual overvaluation can best be studied in men, for their erotic life alone has become accessible to research. That of women – partly owing to the stunting effect of civilized conditions (*Kulturverkümmerung*) and partly owing to their conventional secretiveness and insincerity is still veiled in an impenetrable obscurity (*undurchdringliches Dunkel*).'[65] The pejorative tone of this description parallels the anti-Semitic rhetoric about the hidden nature of the Jew and the Jews' mentality widely circulated at the *fin de siècle*, not least in the medical literature of the age.

The language which Freud uses about the scientific unknowability of what makes a Jew a Jew is parallel to that which he uses concerning the essence of the feminine.[66] The rhetoric which Freud employs in all of these categories is taken from the biology of race, with its evocation of hidden essences and unknown forces shaping the actions of an individual. What can be known is only the essence of the male self: 'In consequence of unfavourable circumstances, both of an external and an internal nature, the following observations apply chiefly to the sexual development of one sex only – that is, of males.'[67] But is the Jewish male truly a male, or has Freud constructed a definition of gender, here the male, which would include himself within a category from which Jewish males are excluded? The assumption of the knowability of the self, as one can glean from Freud's own remarks, is not extended to the essence of the Jew, only to the essence of the male. The unknowability of the Jew, the hidden nature of the Jewish mind, replicates the discourse about the Jewish body and its diseased and different nature.

The problem of the knowability of the Other and the self provides the rhetoric at the heart of one of the most complex and debated aspects of Freudian theory, Freud's reading of the meanings of male and female anatomy.[68] In 1926 Freud (in his essay on lay analysis) referred (in English) to female sexuality as the 'dark continent' of the human psyche:

> But we need not feel ashamed of this distinction; after all, the sexual life of adult women is a 'dark continent' for psychology. But we have learnt that girls feel deeply their lack of a sexual organ that is equal in value to the male one; they regard themselves on that account as inferior, and this 'envy for the penis' is the origin of a whole number of characteristic feminine reactions.[69]

Elsewhere I have sketched the implications of this phrase in terms of the medicalization of the black female body during the nineteenth century.[70] But note Freud's vocabulary concerning the sense of inferiority attributed to the woman because of her 'envy for the penis'. The question of the woman's attribution of meaning to the female genitalia, specifically the clitoris, is raised by Freud in this context: 'Women possess as part of their genitals a small organ similar to the male one; and this small organ, the clitoris, actually plays the same part in childhood and during the years before sexual intercourse as the large organ in men.'[71] The view that the clitoris is a 'truncated penis' is generally rejected in contemporary psychoanalytic theory. To date, the only explanation for this view has been found in the arguments about homologous structures of the genitalia.[72] But little attention has been given to what Freud could have understood within this generally accepted model.

The image of the clitoris as a 'truncated penis', as a less than intact penis, reflects the popular *fin-de-siècle* Viennese view of the relationship between the body of the male Jew and the body of the woman. This clitoris was known in Viennese slang of the *fin de siècle* simply as the 'Jew' (*Jud*).[73] The phrase 'for a woman to masturbate' is to 'play with the Jew.' The 'small organ' of the woman becomes the *pars pro toto* for the Jew with his circumcised, shortened organ. This pejorative synthesis of both bodies because of their 'defective' sexual organs reflects the *fin-de-siècle* Viennese definition of the male as neither female nor Jewish.

But the clitoris, the 'Jew', becomes a sign of masculinity for Freud. As late as his essay on female sexuality (1931), Freud stressed the need for female sexuality to develop from the early masturbatory emphasis on the masculine genital zone, the clitoris, to the adult sexuality of vaginal intercourse. The clitoris, the 'Jew', is the sign of the masculine which must be abandoned if and when the female is to mature into an adult woman.[74] The 'Jew' is the male hidden within the body of the female for Freud. But it is the definition of the masculine aspect of the woman which must be transcended if she is to define herself antithetically to the male.

The analogy of the body and mind of the Jew to the body and mind of the woman was a natural one for the *fin de siècle*. Within German high and medical culture this image of the nature of the woman was already present. The entire medical vocabulary applied to the body of the female stressed her physical and mental inferiority to the male. And the terms used were precisely parallel to the discourse about the Jews. Thus the female, as Elaine Showalter has so brilliantly shown, is understood as being at great risk for mental illness.[75] But the female, like the Jew, also is marked by her smell. The female, like the Jew, is atavistic in her body and her mind. Cesare Lombroso, the founder of modern forensic anthropology and himself an Italian Jew, provided a reading of the origin of the sense of shame in the 'primitive'. He remarked that in the Romance languages the term for shame is taken from the root *putere*, which he interpreted as indicating that the origin of the sense of shame lies in the disgust for body smells. This he 'proves' by observing that prostitutes show a 'primitive pseudo-shame', a fear of being repulsive to the male, since they dislike having their genitalia inspected when they are menstruating. But the association between odour and difference also points quite directly to the image of the source of pollution. The smell of the menses is equated with the stench of ordure, both human and animal, in the public health model of disease which still clung to the popular understanding of illness during the late nineteenth century. Edwin Chadwick, the greatest of the early Victorian crusaders for public sanitation (who built upon the theoretical work of German writers such as E. B. C. Heberstreit) perceived disease as the result of putrefaction of effluvia. For Chadwick 'all smell is disease'.[76] The link between public sanitation and the image of the corrupting female (and her excreta) is through the agency of smell. Although so much is said about the nature of the female body, it is also claimed that science can never truly capture her essence, which is beyond the understanding of the male. In the later philosophical works of Arthur Schopenhauer, as well as in the medicalization of female differences in the work of Freud's contemporary, Paul Julius Möbius, the rhetoric of women's inferiority was coupled with the charge of unknowability.[77] The ultimate distance between the 'neutral' scientific observer and the object observed was the claim that the object could not share in the perceptual strategies of the observer. Whether Jew or woman was not germane; the central category was the difference in the object's ability to comprehend the world.

Freud redefined sexuality so as to diminish the stress on sexual anatomy, on the association with the sexuality of the 'normal adult'. When sexuality came to be defined against the idea of the degenerate, it was no longer possible to recognize the 'male' or the 'female' on first glance. Sexuality was now part of the mental structure of all human beings. And the bisexual nature of all human beings destroyed any specificity in the meaning of sexual anatomy. Each human being reflected the qualities of mind which were on the spectrum from the purely 'masculine' to the purely 'feminine':

> In the first place sexuality is divorced from its too close connection with the genitals and is regarded as a more comprehensive bodily function, having pleasure as its goal and only secondarily coming to serve the ends of reproduction. In the second place the sexual impulses are regarded as including all of those merely affectionate and friendly impulses to which usage applies the exceedingly ambiguous word 'love'. I do not, however, consider that these extensions are innovations but rather restorations; they signify the removal of inexpedient limitations of the concept into which we had allowed ourselves to be led. The detaching of sexuality from the genitals has the advantage of allowing us to bring the sexual activities of children and of perverts into the same scope as those of normal adults. The sexual activities of children have hitherto been entirely neglected, and though those of perverts have been recognized, it has been with moral indignation and without understanding.[78]

By eliminating reproduction as the goal of the sexual, Freud destroyed the argument that Jewish sexual practices (circumcision or endogenous marriage) were at the root of the pathology of the Jews. But if we were to substitute the word 'Jew' for the word 'pervert' in this passage, we would find a restating of the need to incorporate the liminal into the universe of the sexual. 'Jews' and 'perverts' are virtually interchangeable categories at the *fin de siècle*.

This phantasm of knowing on the part of the 'neutral' observer is also associated with the unknowability of the Jew. At about the same time as Freud commented on the unknowability of the Jew, he also complained to his friend and analysand Marie Bonaparte, Princess of Greece, that he did not know what women wanted.[79] All of these comments point toward the unknowability of the female body as that 'object' (in a Freudian sense) which is different from the self. But it also places the 'Jew' – in its slang sense of the clitoris – in the body of the female. But, of course, the essence of the Jewish body is both too well known to be hidden and too well hidden to be known. It is both 'canny' and 'uncanny' simultaneously.

31

Freud's contradictory statements about the meaning and function of race and racial identity and his assumption that race is a category vitiated by the new science of psychoanalysis form a central theme of recent research.[80] The very idea of the Jew, within the science which formed Freud and other Jewish physicians of the *fin de siècle* and which defined the high medical science of his day, is present in images, metaphors and deep structures of his own theory. It was the case that the image of the male Jew was 'feminized' during the course of Western (read: Christian) history. Indeed, in 1904, accepting the view that the Jews are a single race, the Elberfeld physician Heinrich Singer comments that 'in general it is clear in examining the body of the Jew, that the Jew most approaches the body type of the female.'[81] Singer's view echoes older anthropological views, such as that of the Jewish ethnologist Adolf Jellinek, who stated quite directly:

> In the examination of the various races it is clear that some are more masculine, others more feminine. Among the latter the Jews belong, as one of those tribes which are both more feminine and have come to represent (*repräsentieren*) the feminine among other peoples. A juxtaposition of the Jew and the woman will persuade the reader of the truth of the ethnographic thesis.

Jellinek's physiological proof is the Jew's voice: 'Even though I disavow any physiological comparison, let me note that bass voices are much rarer than baritone voice among the Jews.'[82] The association of the image of the Jew (here read: male Jew) with that of the woman (including the Jewish woman) is one of the most powerful images to be embedded in the arguments about race. And it can be found quite directly in the attacks on Freud and psychoanalysis. In responding to Felix von Luschan's attack on the new science of psychoanalysis in 1916, coming from one of the greatest 'experts' on the nature of the Jew, Freud can only express himself in a letter to Sándor Ferenczi in racial terms that 'an old Jew is tougher than a noble Prussian Teuton.'[83] Luschan's attack on Freud, Wilhelm Fliess and Hermann Swoboda sees them as a pseudo-religious collectivity parallel to Christian Science. He employs a phrase coined by Konrad Rieger for all of these 'pseudoscientific' undertakings: 'Old Wives Psychology' (*Altweiber-Psychologie*).[84]

When we turn to Freud's internalization of the image of his own difference, it is the relationship between ideas of race and ideas of gender in the *fin de siècle* which frames his answer. It is through the analysis of the theory in terms of its own critical presuppositions that the repression and projection of the the image of the Jew can be found in psychoanalytic theory – not within a theory of race (as is later to be found in the work of Jung) but within Freud's representation of the image of gender.

Drawing on earlier work published in 1925 and 1931, Freud wrote about the role of the scientist in resolving the question of gender in his comprehensive *New Introductory Lectures on Psychoanalysis* (1933 [1932]):

> To-day's lecture, too, should have no place in an introduction; but it may serve to give you an example of a detailed piece of analytic work, and I

can say two things to recommend it. It brings forward nothing but observed facts, almost without any speculative additions, and it deals with a subject which has a claim on your interest second almost to no other. Throughout history people have knocked their heads against the riddle of the nature of femininity–

> Häupter in Hieroglyphenmützen,
> Häupter in Turban und schwarzem Barett,
> Perückenhäupter und tausend andre
> Arme, schwitzende Menschenhäupter...

[Heads in hieroglyphic bonnets, / Heads in turbans and black birettas, / Heads in wigs and a thousand other / Wretched, sweating heads of humans...] (Heine, *Nordsee* [Second Cycle, VII, 'Fragen']). Nor will you have escaped worrying over this problem – those of you who are men; to those of you who are women this will not apply – you are yourselves the problem. When you meet a human being, the first distinction you make is 'male or female?' and you are accustomed to make the distinction with unhesitating certainty. Anatomical science shares your certainty at one point and not much further.[85]

This argument can be read as part of a rhetoric of race. First, let me translate this problem, which Freud articulates within the rhetoric of gender science, into the rhetoric of racial science: 'There is an inherent biological difference between Jews and Aryans and this has a central role in defining you (my listener) and your culture.' The 'you' which the 'I' is addressing is clearly the Aryan reader, for the Jewish reader is understood as but part of the problem. The Aryan is the observer, the Jew the observed. Upon seeing someone on the street the first distinction 'we' (the speaker and his listener as Aryans) make is to ask: 'Jew or Aryan?' and that distinction can be made with certainty based on inherent assumptions about differences in anatomy. Indeed, according to a contemporary guidebook, in Vienna the first question one asks about anyone one sees on the street is: 'Is he a Jew?'[86] This biological distinction can be clearly and easily 'seen' even through the mask of clothing or the veneer of civilization. The young American Jewish psychoanalyst Abram Kardiner recounts how he was rejected by a young woman he met at a masked ball in Vienna, once they unmasked and it was clear that he was a Jew.[87] But it was not merely social rejection that could follow. The threat of what it meant to be seen as a Jew was also articulated on the streets of Vienna. Martin Freud, Sigmund Freud's eldest son, notes:

> walking with [his aunt Dolfi, his father's youngest sister, who died in Theresienstadt] one day in Vienna we passed an ordinary kind of man, probably a Gentile, who, as far as I knew, had taken no notice of us. I put it down to a pathological phobia, to Dolfi's stupidity, when she gripped my arm in terror and whispered: 'Did you hear what that man said? He called me a dirty stinking Jewess and said it was time we were all killed.'[88]

The false assumption in Freud's text is that the uniformity of the identity of all 'males', as opposed to all 'females', can be made in terms of the form of their genitalia. Freud continues his argument to show that this physiological determinant is central in any discussion of the nature of sexual difference. He identifies himself as a male in this text, quoting a male author, Heine, who represented the Jew as the diseased feminine in *fin-de-siècle* culture, in the context of the impossibility of 'knowing' the truth about the 'dark continent' of the feminine.[89] For the anti-Semitic 'Aryan' reader, Heine's references would evoke quite a different set of associations than they have in the original text. Heine was (and remains) the primary Jewish writer in the German cultural sphere. Such readers might tendentiously have associated Heine's images not only with oriental turbans and Egyptian hieroglyphs but also with the sweat of ghetto poverty and the wigs of the shaved heads of orthodox Jewish brides, as hidden signs of racial, not merely sexual difference. Here is a Jew (Freud) citing a Jew (Heine) about an essentially Jewish focus, human sexuality. Freud can short-circuit this association only by constructing an image of the 'male' to which he, Heine, and his male, Aryan listeners can all belong.

The voice in Freud's text is that of a male and a participant in the central discourse of the scientific thought-collective about gender. In my racial rereading, the voice would become that of the Aryan and part of the Aryan thought-collective. The fantasy of Freud's identification with the aggressor in my retelling of this passage as a passage about race seems to be vitiated when Freud transforms the problem of the relationship between the subject and the object into a question of sexual identity. The 'male' is the 'worrier' (read: subject) and the 'female' is the 'problem' (read: object). But this assumes that Freud's definition of the male body as uniform and constant is the norm within his *fin-de-siècle* scientific thought-collective. The Jewish male body is different, is marked, in the act of ritual circumcision and in many other ways. It is not that the anatomy of the genitalia creates two independent (and antagonistic) categories of gender, but that there were three such categories – the male Jew's genitalia were understood as a marker of difference. In order to meet the challenges to the special nature of the Jew's body, Freud through his creation of a universal 'male' body transmutes categories of race into categories of gender. The power of these constructs is such that the fact that they are a reaction formation is obscured and they are accepted as the basis for the discussion of ideas of masculine and feminine gender as primary categories of Freud's system.

Notes

1. For a judicious summary of the debate about 'The Jewish Identity of Sigmund Freud', see Robert S. Wistrich, *The Jews of Vienna in the Age of Franz Joseph* (Oxford, 1989), pp. 537–82.
2. Harold Bloom, *The Strong Light of the Canonical: Kafka, Freud, and Scholem as Revisionists of Jewish Culture and Thought*, City College Papers, no. 20 (New York, 1987), p. 43.
3. See for example Immanuel Velikovsky, 'The Dreams Freud Dreamed', *Psychoanalytic Review*, 30 (1941), 487–511.
4. Peter Homans, *The Ability to Mourn: Disillusionment and the Social Origins of Psychoanalysis* (Chicago, 1989), p. 71.
5. Gustave Le Bon, 'Applications de la psychologie à la classification des races', *Revue*

Philosophique, 22 (1886), 593–619; also his *Rôle des juifs dans la civilisation* (Paris, 1985). Cf. the discussion of Le Bon's attitudes to the Jews in Robert Nye, *The Origins of Crowd Psychology: Gustave Le Bon and the Crisis of Mass Democracy in the Third Republic* (London and Beverley Hills, 1975), p. 56, and Elisabeth Roudinesco, *La bataille de cent ans*, 2 vols (Paris, 1982), especially I, 181–221 and 395–411.

6. *SE* 18: 74. All quotations from Freud, unless otherwise noted, are taken from *the Standard Edition of the Complete Psychological Works of Sigmund Freud*, ed. James Strachey, 24 vols (London, 1953–74), referred to as *SE*. Where the original German phrasing is particularly significant, a reference is also given to Sigmund Freud, *Gesammelte Werke, chronologisch geordnet* (Frankfurt, 1952–87), referred to as *GW*.

7. Le Bon, *The Crowd: A Study of the Popular Mind* (New York, 1960), p. 83.

8. *SE* 20: 274; *GW* 17: 49–53.

9. Theodor Reik, *Jewish Wit* (New York, 1962), p. 12.

10. William James, *The Principles of Psychology*, 2 vols (New York, 1890), II, 678.

11. Freud, 'Briefe an Arthur Schnitzler', *Neue Rundschau*, 66 (1955), p. 100.

12. Philip Rieff, *Freud: The Mind of the Moralist* (New York, 1959), p. 261.

13. *SE* 18: 83–5, 96–7

14. William McDougall, *The Group Mind* (Cambridge, 1920), pp. 159–60.

15. *B'nai B'rith: Zwi Perez Chajes Loge* (Vienna, 1976); H. Knoepfmacher, 'Sigmund Freud and the B'nai B'rith', *Journal of the American Psychoanalytic Association*, 27 (1979), 441–9.

16. Reik, 'Die Pubertätsriten der Wilden: Über einige Übereinstimmungen im Seelenleben der Wilden und der Neurotiker', *Imago*, 6 (1915–16), 125–44, 189–222; translation from Reik, *Ritual: Psycho-Analytic Studies*, tr. Douglas Bryan (London, 1931), pp. 91–166 (pp. 156–7).

17. See the discussion of this concept, without any reference to the psychological or medical literature, in Steven Beller, *Vienna and the Jews, 1867–1938: A Cultural History* (Cambridge, 1989), pp. 73–83.

18. Ludwig Wittgenstein, *Culture and Value*, ed. G. H. von Wright and Heikki Nyman (Oxford, 1980), pp. 18–19.

19. Freud, 'Some Early Unpublished Letters', tr. Ilse Scheier, *International Journal of Psychoanalysis*, p. 426.

20. *SE* 16: 396.

21. Ibid.

22. Moritz Lazarus and Heymann Steinthal, 'Einleitende Gedanken über Völkerpsychologie', *Zeitschrift für Völkerpsychologie und Sprachwissenschaft*, 1 (1860), 1–73. See in this context their letters: *Moritz Lazarus und Heymann Steinthal: Die Begründer der Völkerpsychologie in ihren Briefen*, ed. Ingrid Belke, 2 vols (Tübingen, 1971–86). On their relationship to late nineteenth–century medicine, see Heinz–Peter Schmiedebach, 'Die Völkerpsychologie von Moritz Lazarus (1824–1903) und ihre Beziehung zur naturwissenschaftlichen Psychiatrie', *XXX Congrès International d'Histoire de la Médecine, 1986* (Dusseldorf, 1988), pp. 311–21.

23. Wilhelm Wundt, *Elements of Folk Psychology: Outlines of a Psychological History of the Development of Mankind*, tr. Edward Leroy Schaub (London, 1916), p. 2.

24. On Freud and Wundt see Christfried Tögel, 'Freud und Wundt: Von der Hypnose bis zur Völkerpsychologie', in Bernd Nitzsche (ed.), *Freud und die akademische Psychologie: Beiträge zu einer historischen Kontroverse* (Munich, 1989), pp. 97–106. For the reciprocal influence, see Tilman J. Elliger, *S. Freud und die akademische Psychologie: Ein Beitrag zur Rezeptionsgeschichte der Psychoanalyse in der deutschen Psychologie (1895–1945)* (Weinheim, 1986); Carl Eduard Scheidt, *Die Rezeption der Psychoanalyse in der deutschsprachigen Philosophie vor 1940* (Frankfurt, 1986).

25. James Mark Baldwin, *Mental Development in the Child and the Race* (New York, 1898), pp. 14–15. See *SE* 7: 173.

26. *SE* 22: 158.
27. Jacques Le Rider, 'Freud zwischen Aufklärung und Gegenaufklärung', in Jochen Schmidt (ed.), *Aufklärung und Gegenaufklärung in der europäischen Literatur, Philosophie und Politik von der Antike bis zur Gegenwart* (Darmstadt, 1989), pp. 475–96.
28. Quoted in Reik, *From Thirty Years with Freud*, tr. Richard Winston (New York, 1940), p. 30.
29. Lazarus and Steinthal, 'Einleitende Gedanken', p. 5.
30. Lazarus, 'Über das Verhältnis des Einzelnen zur Gesammtheit', *Zeitschrift für Völkerpsychologie und Sprachwissenschaft*, 2 (1862), p. 437.
31. Lazarus and Steinthal, 'Einleitende Gedanken', p. 35.
32. Ibid., pp. 35–6.
33. Ibid., p. 37.
34. Ibid.
35. Ibid., p. 38.
36. Ibid., p 39.
37. *SE* 21: 89.
38. In this context see Dagmar Barnouw, 'Modernism in Vienna: Freud and a Normative Poetics of the Self', *Modern Austrian Literature*, 22 (1989), 327–44, on Freud's construction of fictions of the self.
39. Smiley Blanton, *Diary of my Analysis with Sigmund Freud* (New York, 1971), p. 43.
40. *SE* 21: 249.
41. Sigmund Freud, C. G. Jung, *Briefwechsel*, ed. William McGuire and Wolfgang Sauerländer (Frankfurt, 1974), p. 71; *The Freud/Jung Letters: The Correspondence between Sigmund Freud and C. G. Jung*, ed. William McGuire, tr. Ralph Manheim and R. F. C. Hull (Princeton, 1974), p. 145.
42. Ernest Jones, *The Life and Work of Sigmund Freud*, 3 vols (New York, 1953–7), II, 42–3. Cf. the description of this meeting in his autobiography: Jones, *Free Associations: Memories of a Psycho-Analyst* (London, 1959), p. 166.
43. Jones, *Life and Work of Freud*, II, 168.
44. Anatole Leroy-Beaulieu, *Israel among the Nations: A Study of the Jews and Antisemitism*, tr. Frances Hellman (New York, 1895), p. 51.
45. Fritz Wittels, *Sigmund Freud: His Personality, his Teaching, and his School*, tr. Eden and Cedar Paul (London, 1924), p. 140. This translation corrected many errors (listed by Freud) in the original German.
46. Blanton, *Diary*, p. 43.
47. A. Kardiner, *My Analysis with Freud: Reminiscences* (New York, 1977), p. 70.
48. Freud, *Briefe 1873–1939*, ed. Ernst and Lucie Freud (Frankfurt, 1960), p. 443.
49. Sigmund Freud, Karl Abraham, *Briefe 1907–1926*, ed. Hilda C. Abraham and Ernst L. Freud (Frankfurt, 1980), p. 47.
50. On the context of this exchange see Homans, *The Ability to Mourn*, pp. 35–41.
51. Abraham to Freud, 11 May 1908, in Freud and Abraham, *Briefe*, pp. 48–9.
52. Freud and Abraham, *Briefe*, p. 57.
53. Freud to Ferenczi, 28 July 1912, in Freud collection, Library of Congress; quoted in Peter Gay, *Freud: A Life for Our Time* (New York, 1988), p. 231.
54. Freud to Rank, 18 August 1912, in Rank collection, Columbia University Library; quoted in Gay, *Freud*, p. 231.
55. Aldo Carotenuto, *A Secret Symmetry: Sabina Spielrein between Jung and Freud*, tr. Arnold Pomerans, John Shepley, and Krishna Winston (New York, 1982), pp. 120–1.
56. Reik, *Jewish Wit* p. 33.
57. *SE* 19: 222.
58. Morselli was the author of *La psicanalisi: studi ed appunti critici* (Turin, 1926), which

argued that psychoanalysis was a Jewish discovery because of the Jews' predisposition to theoretical solutions for material problems. See also his essay 'La psicologia etnica e la scienza eugenistica', *International Eugenics Congress 1912*, 2 vols (London, 1912), 58–62.

59. Freud, *Briefe*, p. 380.
60. *SE* 19: 291; *GW* 14: 556.
61. Josef Philip Hes, ' A note on an as yet unpublished letter by Sigmund Freud', *Jewish Social Studies*, 48 (1986), 322.
62. *SF* 13: xv; *GW* 14: 569.
63. *SE* 19: 142.
64. Paul Näcke, 'Über Kontrast–Träume und speziell sexuelle Kontrast-Träume', *Archiv für Kriminal-Anthropologie und Kriminalistik*, 28 (1907), 1–19 (p. 13). See *SE* 5: 396.
65. *SE* 7: 151; *GW* 5: 50.
66. Sigmund Diamond, 'Sigmund Freud, his Jewishness, and Scientific Method: The Seen and the Unseen as Evidence', *Journal of the History of Ideas*, 43 (1982), 613–34.
67. *SE* 9: 211.
68. See the detailed overview of the psychoanalytic debates about 'penis envy' in Shahla Chehrazi, 'Female Psychology: A Review', *Journal of the American Psychoanalytic Association*, 34 (1986), 141–62.
69. SE 20: 212.
70. Sander L. Gilman, *Difference and Pathology: Stereotypes of Sexuality, Race and Madness* (Ithaca, 1985), pp. 76–108.
71. *SE* 15: 155.
72. See, for example, F. D. F. Souchay, *De l'homologie sexuelle chez l'homme* (Paris, 1855). This topic is central to the argument in Thomas Laqueur, *Making Sex: Body and Gender from the Greeks to Freud* (Cambridge, MA, 1990).
73. Karl Reiskel, 'Idioticon viennense eroticon', *Anthropophyteia*, 2 (1905), 1–13 (p. 9). Freud refers to this work in *SE* 10: 215, n. 1.
74. *SE* 21: 232–3.
75. Elaine Showalter, *The Female Malady: Women, Madness, and English Culture, 1830–1980* (New York, 1985).
76. John M. Eyler, *Victorian Social Medicine: The Ideas and Methods of William Farr* (Baltimore, 1979), p. 100.
77. On the image of the woman in *fin-de-siècle* medicine see Lilian Berna–Simons, *Weibliche Identität und Sexualität: Das Bild der Weiblichkeit im 19. Jahrhundert und in Sigmund Freud* (Frankfurt, 1984); on Möbius, see Francis Schiller, *A Möbius Strip: Fin-de-siècle Neuropsychiatry and Paul Möbius* (Berkeley, 1982). Freud distances himself from Möbius' s biological work on femininity, seeing the limitations present within the feminine rather as a reflex of the suppression of female sexuality in Western culture. See *SE* 9: 198–9 for Freud's rebuttal of Möbius.
78. *SE* 20: 38.
79. Quoted in Jones, *Life and Work of Freud*, II, 468. See William G. Niederland, 'The Source of Freud's Question about What Women Want', *American Journal of Psychiatry*, 146 (1989), 409–10.
80. See Le Rider, *Modernité viennoise et crises de l'identité* (Paris, 1990), pp. 197–222.
81. Heinrich Singer, *Allgemeine und spezielle Krankheitslehre der Juden* (Leipzig, 1904), p. 9.
82. Adolf Jellinek, *Der jüdische Stamm: Ethnographische Studien* (Vienna, 1869), pp. 89–90.
83. Jones, *Life and Work of Freud*, II, 119; see also II, 398–9.
84. Felix von Luschan, 'Altweiber–Psychologie', *Deutsche medizinische Wochenschrift*, 42

(6 January 1916), 20.

85. *SE* 22: 113.

86. Ludwig Hirschfeld, *Was nicht in Baedeker steht: Wien und Budapest* (Munich, 1927), p. 56.

87. Kardiner, *My Analysis with Freud*, p. 92.

88. Martin Freud, *Glory Reflected: Sigmund Freud – Man and Father* (London, 1957), p. 16.

89. See 'The Jewish Reader: Freud reads Heine reads Freud', in Sander L. Gilman, *The Jew's Body* (New York, 1991), pp. 150–68.

Object–Choice

Fragment of a Freud Biography

Klaus Theweleit
(translated by Edward Timms)

Marrying for love is a kind of madness, according to Freud. But it is a madness which follows rules. The basic rules are easily identified: in place of the normal recognition of reality according to specific demands of the reality principle we have here a fundamentally false perception of the love-object (an 'impairment of the ego', as Freud puts it). The primary characteristic of this false perception is the extravagant overvaluation of the loved object, in particular a sexual overvaluation and idealization of the object. This leads to an identification of the deluded subject with the overvalued and falsely perceived object, more specifically with the *female* object, for this psychological process is essentially male. Women, according to Freud, are only to a limited extent capable of this fundamental false perception called 'love'. 'Complete object-love', we read in his paper 'On Narcissism', is not to be found among women.[1]

Not necessarily an anti-feminist proposition, if construed in the way hinted at by Freud: for women are less *crazy* ('verrückt') than men, they are indeed more useful (what they are useful for, we shall soon see).

In his experience, Freud says, people fall in love in two principal ways: according to the attachment (or 'anaclitic') pattern and according to the narcissistic pattern. According to the *anaclitic* pattern one attaches one's love to the person from whom the first experiences of satisfaction derive: that is usually the mother, who held and nourished the child.

Those adults who in choosing their love-object take as their model not their mother but their own selves conform to the *narcissistic* pattern. They are plainly seeking themselves as a love-object, says Freud. He calls this a *disturbance* in the development of libido.

In his text on 'Narcissism' Freud identifies four forms of choice of female objects which, if one considers them more closely, all tend to be useful for the man who is involved with them; I say 'the man', because among other things I would like to show that Freud himself is that man. He designs a model for the choice of female love-objects which accords with the type of women he was connected with through processes of personal and institutional development: first, his patients; secondly, the women who became psychoanalysts under his guidance; thirdly, his wife and her sister; and finally his daughters, for whose

39

psychosexual development Freud here, in 1914, designs a model (his daughter Anna was to be the one who later showed herself to be capable of living up to this design). For each category of women there is a special kind of satisfaction deriving from the type of object-choice which applies to them; and each kind of choice has something advantageous for the creation of Freud's lifework, for the foundation and preservation of the kingdom of psychoanalysis.

Freud's Choice

In the beginning was – ? The sweet girl: 'Martha is mine, the sweet girl of whom everyone speaks with admiration, who despite all my resistance captivated my heart at our first meeting.'[2]

That 'first meeting' had occurred two months earlier. It is June 1882, Martha Bernays and Sigmund Freud are freshly engaged, but separated: the post travels between Vienna and Wandsbek near Hamburg. This is the first letter of the engaged man, one-and-a-half thousand further letters are to follow before the process of 'object-choice' is completed in 1886.

In the beginning was – resistance? Resistance, passion, conquest.

A 'chance acquaintance' with Freud's five sisters brought the bride into the bridegroom's house, 'where Sigmund and Martha met for the first time', as Ernst Freud puts it in his preface to the German edition of Freud's *Brautbriefe* (selected letters to his fiancée).[3] Ernst was born ten years after this event as the couple's fourth child and youngest son.

The pattern 'girl who is a friend of my sister' seems to be involved in this 'finding' of a love-object, then 'passion' which has evolved within two months into a 'possession': 'Martha is mine, the sweet girl –'

There is more to it than that. The sentence from Freud's first letter to his fiancée (relating to 'the sweet girl') continues: 'the girl whom I feared to court and who came towards me with high-minded confidence, who strengthened the faith in my own value and who gave me new hope and energy to work when I needed it most'.[4]

The phrase 'whom I feared to court' and the strengthening of faith in his own value suggest that a young women of (socially) higher status is being courted. The first gift that she brings into the relationship is the intensification of her lover's energy for work (what he 'needed most', as he puts it).

Marriage for social advancement ... object-choice as symptom ('passion') ... choice according to the usefulness of the bride for the man's energy for work: these forms are already familiar. There is consequently one word in Ernst Freud's account of how his parents first became acquainted which seems questionable, that little word which suggests that it was a *chance* acquaintance.

Chance is most probably not the mother of attachment in such a case.

A young scientist in Vienna, a neurologist, Assistant at the Physiological Institute, twenty-six years old, very gifted, descended from a poor (and rather disreputable) eastern Jewish businessman's family, poised between Jewish orthodoxy and assimilation into the western scientific (that is, atheistic) university profession, is thinking around 1880 about getting married: - what would his model woman look like? She would have to be from a westernized and assimilated Jewish family, daughter of a professor from the medical or some other faculty, and the family would have to be more affluent than Freud's own family. Isn't that right?

Freud's choice comes close to this pattern. Martha Bernays, writes Ernst Freud, 'came from a rather distinguished family from Wandsbek near Hamburg. Her grandfather Isaac (Chacham) Bernays was an outstanding rabbi in the city of Hamburg. Her father's two brothers are significant figures in German cultural history'.[5]

Indeed, they were both professors. One of them was Michael Bernays, a noted Goethe and Shakespeare scholar, the first ever Professor of Modern German Literary History (at the University of Munich), who for a time acted as reader for Ludwig II of Bavaria; the other was Jacob Bernays, Professor of Classical Philology at the University of Bonn, the first professor at any German university not to have been baptized. Martha's father is no longer alive at the time when she becomes acquainted with Freud; he was not a professor but a businessman like Freud's father; but a businessman in a better financial position, more assimilated to western ways and less marginal than Freud's father: Berman Bernays, who in his final years was Assistant to the Viennese economist Lorenz von Stein. The uncle, Professor Jacob Bernays, is also no longer alive. He died a year before their engagement. The other uncle, Michael Bernays (the only one of the three brothers to renounce the Jewish faith, becoming a partisan of Wagner), is still alive and acts as a surrogate father-in-law for the couple, together with Martha's brother Eli, who supports the family after their father's death. Thus Freud falls in love if not quite with the proverbial professor's daughter, then with a niece linked through the social code with two professorial uncles ... a daughter from the sphere to which he himself aspired, indeed a daughter from precisely the kind of socially superior family into which he would like to be accepted/converted, turning his back on his own Galician, orthodox Jewish, small-scale commercial family background.

All that could still accord with Ernst Freud's concept of 'chance' or with the workings of the probability principle. The significance of these constellations for Freud's experience of love would be utterly impossible to establish, but for the fact that we know the game which Freud himself played with this constellation; and this contains surprises of a special kind. The uncles were, after all, professors of a special kind. One a Goethe and Shakespeare specialist; the other a classical philologist and Aristotle specialist - not professors of medicine, but then Freud himself did not simply want to become a professor of medicine but: - something that was represented by these two uncles.

Uncle Jacob Bernays had concerned himself particularly with the Aristotelian concept of catharsis, his publications appearing between 1852 and 1880. Freud's biographer Sulloway observes on this subject:

> In Vienna, as elsewhere, this whole subject was much discussed among scholars and in the salons and even assumed for a time the proportions

of a craze. According to Hirschmüller, by 1880 Bernays's ideas had inspired some seventy German-language publications on catharsis, a number that more than doubled by 1890.[6]

For readers of early Freud that naturally rings a bell: *cathartic method* is the first name which Freud gave to what was later to be known as the psychoanalytic process. The concept derives from *Studies on Hysteria* (1895), it is developed in the description of the treatment of Anna O., who herself called the 'cathartic process' *chimney-sweeping* - a colloquial equivalent for what catharsis really means. Sulloway concludes: 'It seems very possible that an intelligent girl like Anna O. might have been acquainted with the subject and have unconsciously incorporated this knowledge into the dramatic plot of her illness.' The only thing to say against this would be that the tendency of psychoanalytic authors to attribute the knowledge and mode of experience of 'intelligent girls' to the 'unconscious' is probably ineradicable. If it is indeed the case, as Sulloway suggests, that for Anna O., i.e. Bertha Pappenheim, a friend of Martha's, *cathartic method* derives directly (even if unconsciously) from Martha's Uncle Jacob, then in the case of Freud, whose knowledge of Uncle Jacob's work was not merely unconscious, we can conclude that in collaboration with Breuer he took the decision to relate his book of 1895 to the publications of this particular uncle, among other sources; that is to say, he chose to make his literary debut as heir to the catharsis-specialist Jacob Bernays and as husband of Jacob's niece Martha.

After 1895 Freud's collaboration with Breuer comes to an end together with the hope of developing the *talking cure/catharsis* into *psychoanalysis*. (Instead, Freud discovers the sexual abuse of daughters as the foundation of hysteria: a truth, but an obstacle to the development of psychoanalysis.)

When in 1897 he sets about the task of elevating the interpretation of dreams into the 'royal road to the unconscious' and places it at the centre of the psychoanalytic process, he shows how closely connected he is with Martha's other uncle, the Goethe/Shakespeare-Bernays, for his description of the breakthrough to the process of *interpretation of dreams* is peppered with textual references to Goethe and Shakespeare. In October 1897 Hamlet and Oedipus are still competing in Freud's writing for the position of central figure in the psychoanalytic scenario. And Freud identifies the significance of dreams as repositories of experience by means of three lines from a poem by Goethe.[7]

The connection with the works of the Bernays professors, Jacob and Michael, is an unmistakable component of Freud's publications and Freud's writing up to 1899. Can this be chance? A game? A compliment to Martha? Or proof that he really belongs to his 'new family'? What could be a better way of emphasizing this than by linking his own work to that of those renowned uncles. Freud is concerned, like all heroic pioneers, to invent his own personal history; to create himself all over again, but differently from his procreation through his physical parents. The woman chosen for marriage is *always* of special significance for the process through which the husband himself redefines his origins and personal history: she shows the way to other historical worlds; this is indeed her function.

This particular woman appears very well suited for playing a special part in the process. Which part she personally should play was something that Freud conveyed to her in a letter just four weeks after their engagement; a *programme* for Martha.

Hamburg, July 1882. While searching for a printer for writing paper that should have a personal monogram, Freud stumbles on the traces of another Bernays, Martha's grandfather Isaac; a gift from providence (or product of ingenious research), which Freud, in a letter to Martha dated 23 July 1882, skilfully turns to his advantage. When is a letter not a letter? When the text expresses a literary pose, as so often later, when Freud begins to expound a case history reminiscent of a novella. It is not addressed to 'my dear girl' in the intimate second person singular, as the letters generally are, it has neither a proper beginning nor a signature, but refers to Martha in the third person, as a character in a story. Martha, turned into literature, reads what follows:

> My girl came from a family of scholars and wrote – for the time being only letters – with untiring hand, thus spending the little money she had on notepaper. So I decided to acquire some notepaper for the dear industrious child and chose some on which she could write to me only. An M and S intimately entwined, as the generosity of the engravers grants us, renders every page useless for intercourse save between Marty and me. The man from whom I ordered this despotic paper on Friday could supply it only on Sunday; 'for on Saturday', said he, 'we are not here. It is one of our ancient customs.' (Oh, I know that ancient custom!)[8]

Martha is one day, like her learned uncles, to graduate from notepaper to writing as a profession, and these sheets of M & S notepaper are to be regarded as practice for that purpose (just as Freud himself in this letter is trying his hand again as a writer); after this first part of the programme of hope, the focus of the text shifts to the old engraver, whom Freud stuffs full of Jewish wisdom, translated by Freud into wisdom of a more topical kind, interlaced with the turns-of-phrase of a love letter: 'Jerusalem is destroyed and Marty and I are alive and happy', which are then turned into philosophy of history: 'if Jerusalem had not been destroyed, we Jews would have perished like so many races before and after us. The invisible edifice of Judaism became possible only after the collapse of the visible Temple.' After these introductory flourishes comes the kernel of the story, its 'extraordinary incident' – the narrative of the old man:

> We owe our education to one single man. Years ago Hamburg and Altona formed one Jewish community, later they separated; until the Reform movement came to Germany, instruction was carried out by inferior teachers. Then it was realized that something had to be done, and a certain Bernays was called and chosen to be 'Chacham'. This man has educated us all. – The old Jew was about to embark on his achievements, but I was more interested in Bernays the man. Was he from Hamburg? No, he came from Würzburg, where he had studied at Napoleon's expense. (Oh, the myth-forming power of mankind!)

(Oh, the myth-forming power of Freud in the process of re-telling his tale!)

> Bernays came here as a very young man, thirty years ago he was still living here. Did you know his family? 'Me, I grew up with the sons.' I now remembered two names, Michael Bernays in Munich and Jacob Bernays in Bonn. That's them, he confirmed, and there was also a third son, who lived in Vienna, and died there. I also knew something about this third brother, whose name remained so much in the background.

(Berman Bernays, Martha's father, whose name Freud himself does not mention in his story.)

> The father's rich talents were divided among his sons. The father had been a linguist, an interpreter of the Scriptures, and had left behind him some distinguished children. Thus one son chose languages, the material of which became the scientific work of his life, the second one is still teaching the appreciation of the subtleties and the wisdom which our great poets and teachers have put into their writings. The third son, a serious, reserved man, dealt with life on a level even more profound than is possible for science and art: he was above all a human being and created new treasures instead of interpreting old ones. Glory to the memory of him who presented me with my Marty!
>   Imagine if my old Jew, who was now talking with such enthusiasm about the teachings of his master, could have guessed that his customer, allegedly a Dr Wahle from Prague, had this very morning kissed the grand-daughter of his idol! He went on to recall the memories of his youth, and traits of Nathan the Wise now began to appear in what he said.

What a fanciful impulse (impulse on a knife edge) to introduce himself to the old engraver (and to his fiancée reading the letter) as 'Dr Wahle': 'Former admirer of Martha and friend of Freud', says Ernst Freud in a footnote. A play with identities and with the figure of the victor in the wooing of Martha; and not only Napoleon has to be included in the genealogy, but Nathan the Wise and Lessing, whose monument on the Goose Market in Hamburg is alluded to at the beginning of the letter. This continues an earlier playful reference to Lessing: on their engagement day, 17 June 1882, Martha had given him her father's ring. Freud, who wore the ring on his little finger, had a smaller copy of the ring made for her and declared hers to be the authentic ring, since she was loved so much by everyone (a reference to the parable of the three rings in *Nathan the Wise*). Everything is ingeniously angled towards the writer of this *story*, the one and only suitable candidate for the hand of the grand-daughter of the old *interpreter* of the Scriptures, whose mantle Freud in July 1882 is ready to inherit (as he is that of all uncles). And now comes the message of the patriarch Isaac B.:

> The Jew, he said, is the finest flower of mankind, and is made for enjoyment. Jews despise anyone who lacks the ability to enjoy. (I couldn't help thinking of what Eli, to his credit, once disclosed about his philosophy when in his cups: *Homo sum.*)

(Eli is Martha's brother, whom the prudent Freud does not neglect to mention.)

> The law commands Jews to appreciate every pleasure, however small, to pronounce a blessing over every fruit which makes him aware of the beautiful world in which it is grown. The Jew is made for joy (*die Freude*) and joy for the Jew. The teacher illustrated this with the gradual importance of joy in the Holy Days.

That is not only the law for the Jewish *man*. Freud assures his fiancée that his own joyous self (Freud/*Freude*) is also good for the *Jewish woman* and that *this* Jewish woman is precisely for him.

> A customer arrived and Nathan became a merchant again. When I took my leave I was more moved than the old Jew could possibly guess. If he ever came to Prague, he said, he would give himself the pleasure of looking me up. He won't find me in Prague, but as substitute I will offer him –

Freud didn't invent him, that old man. The old man who helps him to invent the name-plate that is to hang over the entrance to the Bernays/Freud marriage. Final sentence of the letter:

> And as for us, this is what I believe: even if the form wherein the old Jews were happy no longer offers us any shelter, something of the core, the essence of this meaningful and life-affirming Judaism will never be absent from our home.

A beautiful name-plate for love, certainly. The element of joy (*Freude*) offered by orthodox religion is to be carried over into the secular happiness of the couple; this letter plays freely with the linguistic significance of the name of its author; there cannot be many texts in which Freud so joyously inscribes as his motto the 'e' which is missing from his name.

The motto is intended for M & S. The correspondence continues for four long years. The letters deal with everything that interests Freud, using Martha as addressee for a process of writing that is a form of self-discovery and that *succeeds* in discovering itself. Through the process of writing these letters to his fiancée Freud becomes an *author* just as Kafka does through writing his letters to Felice Bauer. They are the record of Freud's first approach to psychoanalysis.

Following a suggestion made in the commentary by Ernst Kris, first editor of the letters Freud later wrote to Fliess, it is often claimed that as recipient of these letters Fliess exercised the function of long-distance analyst for Freud. It is suggested that what subsequently became known in the analytic situation as 'transference' actually developed between Freud and Fliess. To me Fliess seems to play a different role: as the second man in the male partnership necessary for the evolution of psychoanalysis, that productive 'male couple' in which Freud after a period of collaboration gained the upper hand and then *consciously* accomplished his victory. But I think that the letters written to Martha Bernays during the time of their engagement had that kind of function for Freud; they strike me as I read them as the earliest (and at times astonishingly far-reaching) first phase in the development of the process known as 'psychoanalysis'.

In particular, I would like to draw attention to the long letter to Martha written on 2 February 1886 – too long to be quoted here. Addressing Martha, Freud analyses himself – the letter resembles what would later be known as the transcript of an analytic session.

Putting the matter provocatively, I would suggest it is not unimportant both for Freud as a person and for the development of psychoanalysis that its first discovery occurred in a love letter.

Among other things, Freud discloses to Martha in this letter that the 'mild neurasthenia', from which he tended to suffer, 'always left me as though touched by a magic wand, whenever I have been with you'.[9]

Martha, his love for Martha, writing about his love for Martha becomes for Freud a means for eliminating neurotic tendencies; writing to his fiancée letters about love for his fiancée cures neuroses, says Freud.

The letter also refers to sexual abstinence, which Freud appears to have practised in these years (the equivalent of his subsequent appeal to his patients to avoid 'acting out' their sexuality, since this interferes with the work of analysis).

Freud was working, especially in his letters from Paris, on a transformation of his engagement relationship into a psychoanalysis, a transformation of the stream of letters into the first form of self-analysis with the assistance of his fiancée as a transference figure.

Through this project Martha, without knowing it, becomes an analytic authority. Perhaps it would be an exaggeration, though it would not be entirely nonsensical, to say that for Freud the wish to marry his analyst was fulfilled (before women analysts existed together with the rules which make it difficult to marry them).

The programme for Martha and for himself which emerges from the letters organizes in the first instance a replacement of his own family history, an *improvement* on it through Martha's relatives: those uncles are superior brothers for a father to have, compared to the jailbird Uncle Josef with his counterfeit roubles (that coded figure who haunts the *Interpretation of Dreams*); and Eli is a different kind of brother, supporting the Bernays family far more conscientiously than Freud's own older brothers with their dubious business in Manchester, who admittedly also support 'the family', but probably with counterfeit money and forged notes of credit. A wish-fulfilment brother and uncles to gladden the heart: – useful both for Freud's writing strategies and for his personal development.

Secondly, Martha's father is a far more respectable businessman than his own father, Jacob Freud; a father who furthermore is no longer among the living: the position of father in the Bernays family is in part vacant (offering scope for one's own expansive drive), but more importantly it represents what could paradoxically be called the 'absent impediment'. It is one thing to receive a woman from her father's hand, another to win her by challenging the father's position of power. Freud repeatedly describes himself in the letters to Martha as a rebellious student, as an oppositional type confronting various authorities. Now such rebellious sons (-in-law) are always perceived (at least in the eyes of fathers who have daughters to give away) as irresponsible adventurers and subversives, whom one can grant anything in life with one exception: responsibility. Giving away one's daughter falls into this category.

Object-choice according to the condition that the bride has no father is a factor which not infrequently intensifies the feelings of the man in love.

Then thirdly there is the old Jew Isaac/Nathan Bernays, through whom Freud can connect himself with a kind of Jewish didactic tradition which had been abandoned or had never existed in his own family; in addition, the linkage between this tradition and westernized Hamburg rationalism in the style of Lessing. [...]

Freud the psychoanalyst was later to coin a term for complex causal chains intertwined and secured in this way: overdetermination. Overdetermination in the formation of symptoms, in the encoding of dream images ... in the construction of the beloved. Freud married Martha Bernays as an overdetermined symptom: symptom of the bridegroom's recovery of his 'capacity for work and love', guarantor of the transformation of his personal history, overdetermined ally in a process of growth.

Freud's capacity for projection, which construes the Martha of his desire according to his need for a specific kind of 'Martha', in no sense falls short of the *generosity of the engravers* in the intertwining of the signs M & S. The letters to his fiancée are addressed just as much to the imaginary locus of being *mutually intertwined* and to the woman whom he sees at the side of the person he will one day become as they are to the (more real) Martha to whom he is engaged and to Martha his analyst. [...]

Martha Freud later failed to fulfil, or only partly fulfilled, his wish to make out of her something different from what she probably was. Perhaps that is one of the reasons why Freud no longer remembers, or no longer wishes to remember his own kind of object-choice, when thirty years later he sets about the task of meditating on the mechanisms of falling in love. The choice of Martha Bernays involved disappointments.

She neither became the writer he wished her to become (scarcely possible considering the six children to whom she gives birth during the first nine years of marriage), nor does she appear to have taken a lasting interest in 'psychoanalysis', and that must have weighed more heavily on the development of their relationship and the evolution of Freudian theory.

This emerges from various comments of Freud's, most clearly from a letter to Fliess dated 8 February 1897. Freud would like to find out from Fliess whether the latter has observed 'when disgust first appears in small children and whether there exists a period in earliest infancy when these feelings are absent. Why do I not go into the nursery and experiment ... ? Because working twelve-and-a-half hours I have no time for it, and the womenfolk do not support my researches.'[10]

The *womenfolk*, that means Martha Freud and her sister Minna Bernays, who is four years younger and who together with Martha brings up the Freud children. After her engagement to Ignaz Schönberg, a friend of Freud's who was mortally ill with tuberculosis, had been ended by Schönberg himself, Minna joined the Freud household in the 1890s.

At some point in her life together with Sigmund, Martha must have withdrawn her interest from 'analysing': not in front of the children, Sigmund dear; a division of the spheres of influence between the Freud womenfolk and Freud the man.

So Freud with his six children (Anna, the youngest, is just one year and three months old) has to put his questions about children's behaviour to Wilhelm Fliess, father of two, whose wife Ida shares his enthusiasm for the observation of children. That is bitter for a theorist of the sexuality of young children, especially as there is no possibility of drawing on the clinical investigations of others.

Notes

This article is translated from Klaus Theweleit, *Objektwahl (All You Need Is Love)* (Basle and Frankfurt, 1990), pp. 14–15, 57–71 and 74–5. We are grateful to the author and to the publishers Stroemfeld/Roter Stern for permission to include it in our collection.

1. *SE* 14: 67-102 (p. 88).
2. *Letters of Sigmund Freud 1873-1939*, ed. Ernst L. Freud, tr. Tania and James Stern (London, 1961), p. 25. We are grateful to the publishers, Hogarth Press, for permission to quote extensively from this edition.
3. Sigmund Freud, *Brautbriefe*, ed. Ernst Freud (Frankfurt, 1988), p. 8.
4. Freud, *Letters*, p. 25.
5. Freud, *Brautbriefe*, p. 7.
6. Frank J. Sulloway, *Freud, Biologist of the Mind* (London, 1980), pp. 56-7.
7. *The Complete Letters of Sigmund Freud to Wilhelm Fliess*, tr. and ed. Jeffrey Moussaieff Masson (Cambridge, MA, 1985), p. 274.
8. For this and the following quotations, see Freud, *Letters*, pp. 35-40.
9. Freud, *Letters*, p. 213.
10. *Letters of Freud to Fliess*, p. 230.

The Case of Otto Gross

Jung, Stekel and the Pathologization of Protest

Martin Stanton

Until the late 1970s little was known about Otto Gross (1877-1920), except that he was a bright star in the psychoanalytic firmament before World War I, who seemingly rapidly faded into obscurity. The publication of the *Freud/Jung Letters* in 1974 considerably changed this perception, not least because it became evident that Gross was an important figure in a crucial period of Jung's development, notably in 1909, at the same time that the Sabina Spielrein affair loomed large. In 1979 Emanuel Hurwitz, a medical assistant at the Burghölzli mental hospital in Zurich, published a major study of Gross, which included extensive reference to Jung's case notes on Gross, which were housed in the hospital's archive.[1] Hurwitz pointed out that these notes gave a picture of the Gross case very different from *Freud/Jung Letters*. Jung's notes portray Gross as a passive participant in the 'treatment', whereas the correspondence with Freud reveals that Gross was actively engaged in a mutual analysis with Jung. The publication of some of Sabina Spielrein's notes and letters from this period added a further twist to this complex history, because she clearly believed that Jung's behaviour towards her was considerably inspired by Grossian ideas.[2]

In the light of these contradictions, it is obviously important to examine the broader context of the Otto Gross case, principally to assess Gross's impact on Jung's work and thought during this period. Two important difficulties hinder such an exercise. First of all, there is no English edition of Gross's work, and Hurwitz's essential biography also remains untranslated. Secondly, critics have tended to be convinced by Jung's pathologization of Gross and not bothered to look further at his ideas. To help overcome these difficulties, this article proposes both to provide a brief survey of research on Gross's life and work, with particular reference to his relationship to Jung, and to propose an added context for Jung's pathologization of Gross: namely, to contrast Jung's comments with those of Stekel, with whom Gross was in analysis in 1914. It is hoped that this contrast will provide some insight into the reasons for Jung's contradictory attitude to Gross, as well as some appreciation of the mutual dynamics involved.

Let us begin with a biographical sketch of Gross. He was repeatedly praised by Freud (in his letters to Jung) as 'such a fine man, with such a good mind', capable of 'outstanding work, full of bold syntheses, and overflowing with ideas'.

Indeed, in 1908, Freud went so far as to list Gross with Jung as the only hope for creative development within psychoanalysis.[3] Ernest Jones, who met Gross in Munich that same year, believed that he was suffering from 'an unmistakable form of insanity'. But Jones claimed to have gained his first practical experience of analysis through Gross, describing him as 'the nearest approach to the romantic ideal of a genius I have ever met ... such penetrative power of divining the inner thoughts of others I was never to see again.'[4]

As a habitué of the bohemian coffee houses in Munich, Gross used to practise analysis across the table, between pool games and the occasional assignment with his large number of casual lovers, with whom he used to share cocaine, opium, and frugal vegetarian meals. A strikingly handsome man, he was painted and sketched by many of his expressionist artist friends from the review groups *Der Blaue Reiter* and *Die Brücke*. His charismatic effect extended far beyond psychoanalytical circles. In 1907, he had a celebrated affair with Frieda von Richthofen, who later married D. H. Lawrence. She describes this in her memoirs, and allots Gross the intriguing pseudonym of 'Octavio'; some of her biographers and critics, like Martin Green, have even extended the influence to Lawrence himself, seeing *Sons and Lovers* as an exposition of Grossian ideas. 'He was a marvellous lover,' Frieda wrote. 'He never let one sleep. He talked and talked ... He took drugs ... He talked to you while he was loving you. He was so wonderful, and so awful.' In a similar vein, Lawrence himself wrote: 'Sex is the kind of magnetism that holds people together, and which is bigger than individuals, but you don't have sex with everybody ... not directly ... but indirectly ... sex is always being *PERVERTED* into something else ... all the time ... and something else is always being perverted into sex.'[5]

Grossian look-alikes certainly flourished in expressionist literature of the time: in Walter Hasenclever's play *Der Sohn* (1913), for example; in Franz Werfel's autobiographical novel, *Barbara oder die Frömmigkeit* (1929); and in Oskar Maria Graf's *Wir sind Gefangene*. Gross certainly provided the psychoanalytic theory to back the major literary breakthroughs proclaimed in 1915 at the Dadaist Cabaret Voltaire in Zurich, notably the 'Schrei' (scream), and its technical exploitation in 'Schreitaktik', which awakened primal libidinal protest in the somnolent audience by sounds just missing words, or voices too loud to articulate the phrase. This primal protest element was derived directly from Grossian ideas.

Other Grossian portraits of the period came from the anarchist circles in Munich. Gross declared himself an anarchist at the turn of the century, and involved himself in a number of anarchist community projects, notably one called Monte Verità in Ascona in Ticino, Switzerland, which he helped found in 1903, with the help of his newly-wed wife Frieda Schloffer, Hermann Hesse and the expressionist poet Erich Mühsam.[6] This community laid down the foundations of Gross's anarchist strategies, notably something he called the 'orgy' ('Orgie'), a word chosen for its shock effect at the time. In fact, this concept was based on a complex theory of how 'mother right could undo the authority structures of father right' which in short meant that 'free spirits' should advocate that women alone should choose their partners in any community that accepted promiscuity. Of course, the hippyesque venture did not last long. Locals complained bitterly about the nudism and revelries, and participants reverted quickly to the 'bourgeois' security of coupledom. Nonetheless, Gross did manage to integrate some of his psychoanalytic theories into a major anarchist programme of the day, notably that proposed by the briefly successful Bavarian Soviet Republic established in April 1919. This revolutionary movement involved his close friends Franz Jung, Gustav Landauer and Erich Mühsam. The main principles they derived from Gross were as follows: that psychoanalysis was potentially a revolutionary technique; that its aim was to remove social conditioning, notably the largely unconscious submission to the set lines of patriarchal authority, and to release the primal subversive energy of libido; finally, this in turn implied free love, which to Gross meant diversifying the relationships in which individuals engaged. This meant, in practice, active support of communal structures to reduce neurotic dependence on the bourgeois family, and promoting instead general sexual freedom. Curiously, though, he was against homosexuality, which he called 'next-room eroticism' ('Nebenzimmererotik') and denounced as regressive, conservative, and counter-revolutionary. Indeed, the whole issue of homoeroticism became central to his own personal analyses, as we will see presently.

Gross was most renowned in anarchist circles for his militant form of feminism, though some, notably his close friend Franz Jung, doubted his motives, suspecting him of being manipulative: 'For me', he said, 'Otto Gross signified the experience of a first and great deep friendship; I would have unhesitatingly sacrificed myself for him ... For Gross himself, I was perhaps no more than a figure on the chessboard of his intellectual combinations, which could be moved back and forth.'[7] Gross was most heavily criticized professionally for his 'analytical treatment' of women patients, notably Regina Ullmann (referred to in Jung's case notes as 'the Jewess'), Lotte Chattemer (whom Gross provided with drugs to commit suicide), and finally Sophie Benz.[8] Benz was a young cabaret singer whom Gross analysed in the Café Stephanie, then seduced and advised to leave her long-term lover, Leonhard Frank, and become promiscuous, lest she become enmeshed in the 'lethargy of father right'. Gross introduced her to cocaine, on which she overdosed in 1905. He claimed this was an accident, but the coroner returned the verdict of suicide, suggesting that she had been led astray. Not surprisingly, Leonhard Frank vowed publicly to take revenge.

Finally, one should mention yet another Otto Gross case: the celebrated struggle with his father, Hans, who was an eminent professor of law at the University of Graz. Hans Gross repeatedly attempted between 1909 and his death in December 1915 to have his son institutionalized for treatment of his drug addiction, which he claimed was responsible for his political views and anti-social behaviour. In November 1913 Otto Gross was indeed interned for six months for psychiatric treatment at his father's behest. Of course, Otto Gross, and indeed most of the German libertarian left, saw this as an obvious case of the abuse of patriarchal power. From December 1913 on, numerous publications, including *Die Aktion, Revolution,* and *Die Zukunft,* featured the affair. The politics of the press campaign, though, did not exactly correlate with the micro-politics of the Gross family: as Hurwitz and other critics have pointed out, the family did consistently bail Otto out from dire situations involving the police, and frequently saved him from starvation and destitution. Equally, the family's attempts to discredit Otto's views as drug-induced delusions can scarcely be justified, despite their undoubted generosity.

This raises the whole issue of the pathologization of Otto Gross, particularly in the psychoanalytic context in which he features both as a 'case', and as a radical innovator. To some extent, the confusion between Gross as patient and Gross as analyst is compounded in Jung's account, because Gross was a recognized specialist in Jung's chosen field, 'dementia praecox', several years before Gross became a patient of Jung's: a patient whom Jung ironically diagnosed as precisely a case of 'dementia praecox'. In *The Psychology of Dementia Praecox* (1907), Jung extensively elaborated on and criticized Gross's notion of 'independent but synchronous chains of association' in psychotic patients, and argued instead for an innate 'connectedness' in all associations, be they neurotic or psychotic.[9] Ironically, Jung later revised his views in favour of those of Gross, notably as 'synchronicity' developed into a major Jungian concept.[10]

Some insight into Jung's countertransferential dynamics towards Gross is provided by Wilhelm Stekel's account of his analysis of Gross in 1914 at Bad Ischl, a fashionable Austrian holiday resort. This appears in volume 8 of Stekel's *Störungen des Trieb- und Affektlebens,* which has been translated under the title *Sadism and Masochism.*[11] Both Jung and Stekel regarded the main aim of the analysis as treatment for drug addiction, and indeed Gross agreed with both of them that he would stop taking drugs and enter into no new sexual affairs whilst in analysis. It is extraordinary that, despite this common aim, they should give such different accounts of Gross's condition. Jung, for example, wrote:

> Dr Gross tells us that he puts a quick stop to the transference by turning people into sexual immoralists. He says the transference to the analyst and its persistent fixation are mere monogamy symbols and as such sympto-matic of repression. The truly healthy state for the neurotic is sexual immorality ... I feel Gross is going along too far with the vogue for the sexual short-circuit, which is neither intelligent, nor in good taste, but merely convenient, and therefore anything but a civilizing factor.[12]

It is interesting to note here Jung's use of the term 'immorality', because in contemporary letters to Sabina Spielrein he preferred to refer to Gross's 'libertinism'; the moral tone was clearly restricted to Jung's public performance, because in practice he was much more in line with Gross's arguments than he could afford to admit, notably during his relationship with Sabina Spielrein, who was both his lover and the first analysand he diagnosed as schizophrenic. At the time, Spielrein wrote to Freud: 'Now he [Jung] arrives, beaming with pleasure, and tells me with strong emotion about Gross, about the great insight he has just received (i.e. about polygamy); he no longer wants to suppress his feeling for me.'[13]

Even more interesting is that neither Gross nor Spielrein is mentioned in the published version of *Memories, Dreams, Reflections.* There is simply an account of Jung's fight against his own self-diagnosed psychotic episodes, elaborated conceptually through the struggle of personalities one and two. Now at this time, precisely, he was writing to Freud expressing his conviction that it was Gross who was psychotic, emphasizing that he, Jung, was spending hours with Gross in order to achieve the first psychoanalytic cure of a case of dementia praecox. 'I am afraid', Jung wrote to Freud on 19 June 1908, 'you will already have read from my words the diagnosis I long refused to believe and which I now see before me with terrifying clarity: Dem. praec.' He added:

> In spite of everything he is my friend, for at bottom he is a very good and fine man with an unusual mind. He is now living under the delusion that I have cured him and has already written me a letter overflowing with gratitude, like a bird escaped from its cage.[14]

The bird had in fact escaped its cage, and Gross did believe himself cured, though not of 'dementia praecox', but of drug addiction. He explained this in a letter: 'Dear Jung, I climbed over the asylum wall and am now in the Hotel x. This is a begging letter. Please send me money for the hotel expenses and also the train fare to Munich. Yours sincerely.'[15] Freud's response to Jung about Gross is interesting. He wrote on 21 June 1908 questioning Jung's diagnosis and suggesting 'toxin paranoia'. A year later, on 3 June 1909, Freud wrote to Jung praising Gross's book *On Psychopathic Inferiorities* as 'another outstanding work' and suggesting it reflected a brilliant mind, with hints of 'neurotic regression'. But Freud was prepared to admit that even this diagnosis could be the product of his own obtuseness.[16] Jung replied briefly that he had not read the book so he could not pass comment. At precisely this time, the Spielrein affair surfaced in the correspondence. Though, he did not totally suppress the reference to Gross, Jung wrote:

> She was, of course, systematically planning my seduction, which I considered inopportune. Now she is seeking revenge ... Like Gross, she is a case of fight-the-father, which in the name of all that is wonderful I was trying to cure *gratissime* (!) with untold tons of patience, even abusing our friendship [the friendship between Freud and Jung] for that purpose.[17]

It is quite clear that Jung was aware of both his own projections and concomitant blindness in this 'clinical' situation. Writing to Freud about Gross on 25 May 1908, he admitted: 'Whenever I got stuck, he analysed me'.[18] This is a simple admission, which is nonetheless extremely important, and often overlooked in the secondary literature on Jung.

In this context, it is useful to compare Jung's clinical account of Gross with Stekel's. Stekel quite clearly did not diagnose Gross as suffering from 'dementia praecox', but from extremely infrequent psychotic episodes; even this diagnosis he qualified by doubts about the prominent role of drugs in determining Gross's behaviour. Ironically, unlike Jung, Stekel had been a great admirer of Gross before the analysis, and even afterwards described Gross's *Three Essays on Inner*

Conflict [1920] as 'simply wonderful'; in his obituary of Gross in 1920, Stekel described him as 'a misunderstood genius'. [19]

Nonetheless, in this brief analysis, ended by the outbreak of war, Stekel attempted to present Oedipal reasons for Gross's political views, notably for his 'feminism' and his attacks on patriarchal authority, which he ascribed to homosexual 'priming' ('Zündung'). In fact, Stekel attributed Gross's rejection of homosexuality to unconscious repression. And he offered an interesting interpretation of Gross's advocacy of free love, based on an extrapolation from six dreams. Gross's orgies, according to Stekel, followed a ritualistic pattern: he liked to send the woman he desired at that moment into the next room where a chosen close friend would then make love to her, during which time Gross would masturbate and wait for her to return before achieving orgasm. This, of course, as Stekel noted, kept the male worlds apart, except for the woman's possible transmission of disease. In fact, Gross contracted gonorrhoea from Sophie Benz, and was still suffering from it at the time of his tragic death from a mixture of drugs and starvation in spring 1920.

Of course, Stekel's extrapolation of this ritual, and his diagnosis of latent homosexuality, must be treated with a certain amount of caution. First of all, Stekel was renowned for his journalistic talents, which led other members of the Vienna Psychoanalytic Society to dismiss his writings as inconsistent and unreliable.[20] Critics have also noticed that the Grossian ritual was neither private nor secret, at least as an imaginative motif, and indeed figured in the literary output of both Gross himself and of his friend Hermann Hesse, notably in the story *Klein und Wagner*.[21] It therefore remains questionable whether this imputed pathology related more to conscious literary activity than unconscious fantasy. Furthermore, like Jung, Stekel found in Gross a stimulating foil for his own clinical interests. In 1914 he began elaborating a controversial thesis that homosexuality was inverted heterosexuality, and that all analysts had to do was expose the unconscious defences that structured homosexual drives. In addition, Stekel maintained that analysis of these defences could actually promote free love, and that promiscuity was neither necessarily regressive nor undesirable as a social norm.[22] Indeed, rumours about Stekelian promiscuity with patients figure almost as prominently as the Grossian kind in the correspondence of the early analysts, although incontrovertible evidence is singularly lacking.

In conclusion, it is possible to observe various levels of identification in both Jung's and Stekel's treatment of Gross. It is especially interesting that Stekel disputed Jung's diagnosis of 'dementia praecox', and that Jung formally discounted Gross's 'sexual immoralism', though he used Grossian formulations to account for his own promiscuity at the time. Moreover, Jung failed to perceive latent homosexuality as the major unconscious structure prefiguring the aetiology of Gross's condition. Obviously, it is easy with hindsight to illustrate the ways in which medical diagnosis concealed countertransferential dynamics, especially in situations where psychoanalysts disagreed on diagnostic categories. It is much more difficult to represent how such countertransferential dynamics actually selectively censored or obscured material that did not fit into those categories; in short, to show how a given pathologization generated its own separate pathology. It is clear that both Jungian and Stekelian diagnoses reduced Gross's political radicalism to set clinical parameters: for Jung, Gross's attack on patriarchal authority simply displayed classic paranoid features, whereas for Stekel it exemplified latent homosexual drives. Both diagnoses ignored the politics of Gross's own account of his condition, namely his theorization of the psychoanalytical process in terms of liberating mother right and repressive father right. As we have seen, Gross argued that the transference itself was structured by the repressive dynamics of monogamy: either the analytical exchange followed authoritarian lines through the doctor's imposition of patriarchal authority, or it made concessions to 'libertinism' based on mother right, which in turn suggested promiscuity. Ironically, both Jung and Stekel, in different ways, opted in Grossian terms for the monogamous position, but articulated unconsciously in their own countertransference all the options offered by the promiscuous position. Grossian ideas in this sense haunt both their accounts of his condition, not to mention their own clinical preoccupations of that period. In this way, through identification with aspects of Grossian pathology, they both redefined their own particular pathologies in terms of the peculiar logic of their patient. The thrust of Gross's politics may therefore have been formally repressed in the set diagnosis, but it subsequently reemerged in the countertransferential dynamics of the clinical situation.

Notes

1. Emanuel Hurwitz, *Otto Gross: Paradies-Sucher zwischen Freud und Jung* (Frankfurt, 1979).
2. Aldo Carotenuto, *A Secret Symmetry: Sabina Spielrein between Jung and Freud* (London, 1984), p. 107.
3. *The Freud/Jung Letters*, ed. William McGuire, tr. Ralph Manheim and R. F. C. Hull (London, 1974), pp. 126, 154 and 227.
4. Ernest Jones, *Free Associations: Memories of a Psycho-Analyst* (New York, 1959), pp. 173–4.
5. Martin Green, *The von Richthofen Sisters* (New York, 1974), p. 153.
6. See Martin Green, *Mountain of Truth: The Counterculture Begins – Ascona, 1900-1920* (London, 1986).
7. Quoted in *Otto Gross: Von geschlechtlicher Not zur sozialen Katastrophe*, ed. K. Kreiler (Frankfurt, 1980), p. 93.
8. See Jacques Le Rider, 'De la psychanalyse à la révolution', in Otto Gross, *Révolution sur le divan* (Paris, 1988), p. 28.
9. C. G. Jung, 'The Psychology of Dementia Praecox', in *Collected Works*, 22 vols (London, 1954–83), III, 29-30.
10. Jung, 'Synchronicity', *Collected Works*, VIII, 8.
11. Wilhelm Stekel, *Störungen des Trieb- und Affektlebens*, vol. VIII (1927), section 12: 'Die Tragödie eines Analytikers'.
12. *Freud/Jung Letters*, p. 90.
13. Carotenuto, *Secret Symmetry*, p. 107.
14. *Freud/Jung Letters*, p. 156.
15. Jones, *Free Associations*, p. 174.
16. *Freud/Jung Letters*, p. 227.
17. Ibid., p. 229.

18. Ibid., p. 153.
19. Wilhelm Stekel, 'Otto Gross: in memoriam', *Psyche and Eros* (New York), No. 1 (July 1920).
20. Martin Stanton, 'Wilhelm Stekel: A Refugee Analyst and his English Reception', in *Freud in Exile: Psychoanalysis and its Vicissitudes*, ed. Edward Timms and Naomi Segal (New Haven and London, 1988), pp. 166–7.
21. Josef Dvorak, 'Opiumträume in Bad Ischl: Wilhelm Stekel analysierte Otto Gross', *Forum* (Vienna), September 1985, p. 45.
22. Wilhelm Stekel, 'Sexuelle Aufklärung', *Das Ziel* (Vienna), No. 2 (May 1913).

From the Memoirs of a Freudian

Fritz Wittels
(edited by Edward Timms)

Editor's Introduction

Fritz Wittels was born in Vienna in 1880 and died in New York in 1950. He was a prolific author of both psychoanalytic and literary works, but he is best known as Freud's first biographer. His book *Sigmund Freud: His Personality, His Teaching and His School* was published in English translation in London in 1924, having appeared in German the previous year. This is a first-hand account of Freud's early career, written by one of the early members of the Vienna Psychoanalytic Society. At the time of publication the book created controversy, since it criticized certain authoritarian tendencies in Freud's personality. However, its full significance only becomes apparent when it is compared with the alternative account which Wittels wrote in English in New York around 1940: his unpublished memoirs.

These memoirs, recently located in a New York archive, raise important questions for historians of psychoanalysis. The obvious question is why a document of such importance should have remained unpublished for almost fifty years. The answer is suggested by a handwritten note which the present editor discovered among Wittels's papers in New York, probably written by his widow Poldi Goetz Wittels. After her husband's death in 1950, she had evidently tried to find a publisher for the memoirs, only to be told that they could not be published for fear of upsetting 'Jehovah's children'. Since Wittels, taking issue with Freud's dictatorial tendencies, suggests in the memoirs that Freud suffered from a 'Jehovah complex', this is evidently a reference to loyal disciples who wished the great man's authority to remain unchallenged. They would have been outraged (perhaps they still will be) by the frankness with which Wittels writes about the early controversies in which Freud and his followers were involved.

The non-publication of Wittels's memoirs draws attention to one of the most disturbing features of the psychoanalytic record: the *suppression of sources*. Historians of the movement have from the very beginning been frustrated by problems of access: letters suppressed or destroyed, materials still kept under lock and key in the Library of Congress. Freud himself records that he set out to make life difficult for his biographers by destroying in 1885 'all my notes of the past 14 years, as well as letters, scientific excerpts and the manuscripts of my papers'.[1] And later in life, if Freud had had his way, his letters to Wilhelm

Fliess would also have been destroyed. Wittels's memoirs, left for decades to gather dust in a New York archive, provide further confirmation of this pattern. Indeed, Wittels reveals in the memoirs that even his Freud biography of 1923–4 was subjected to a form of censorship. For that biography originally contained an account of the scandal which led to Wittels's resignation from the Vienna Psychoanalytic Society.

Wittels first became a member of the Society in 1907, and for three years he was one of Freud's favourite disciples. But in 1910, abruptly and without explanation, he resigned. The memoirs make it clear that Wittels's resignation was due not to doctrinal disputes but to a quarrel about a woman, the enigmatic Irma Karczewska. The memoirs provide the explanation which the biography omitted: that Wittels became involved in a conflict over Irma with his former friend, the satirist Karl Kraus. As a result he was expelled from Kraus's circle, but he took his revenge by publishing a scurrilous novel, *Ezechiel der Zugereiste* (Ezechiel the Visitor from Abroad). This novel recorded the adventures of easily recognizable caricatures of Kraus, Irma and other members of the bohemian *demi-monde*. Kraus retaliated by suing Wittels for libel, and since the publication of the novel, together with the scandalous court case, threatened to bring the psychoanalytic movement into disrepute, Freud felt he had no option but to expel Wittels from the Society.[2]

The chapter suppressed from Wittels's biography of Freud showed how closely the supposedly scientific activities of the Psychoanalytic Society were entwined with the erotic pursuits of the Viennese *demi-monde*. Since Wittels, despite his reservations about Freud, was concerned to maintain the reputation of psychoanalysis as a science, it was only natural that he should have decided to suppress this chapter. Instead of publishing it, he sent that draft chapter privately to Freud in the hope of gaining his approval for this strategy of suppression. In a letter of 24 December 1923, quoted in the memoirs, Freud replied: 'You were right not to insert in your book the chapter which you sent me. It belongs to a different continuity.'

This concept of a 'different continuity' draws attention to a second principle of psychoanalytic historiography: *No sex please, we're scientists*. Freudian theory deals with the cultural and emotional ramifications of sexual drives. But the history of the movement has been systematically desexualized. Wittels's unpublished memoirs reveal that his relationship with Irma, far from being completely separate from his psychoanalytic investigations, was the inspiration of one of the papers he presented to the Vienna Society. This was the meeting of 29 May 1907, when Wittels read a paper entitled 'The Great Courtesan'. When we look up the *Minutes of the Vienna Psychoanalytic Society*, however, we read: 'There is no protocol preserved for the meeting on May 29 1907.' All that survives is a footnote giving the title of Wittels's paper and the list of those who attended. Recent investigations have shown that such erasures of erotic experience abound in the history of psychoanalysis. Jung's involvement with Sabina Spielrein provides an outstanding example.

This leads to the third fundamental problem raised by Wittels's memoirs, the problem of *emotional ambivalence* It is particularly difficult for people writing from within the psychoanalytic movement to give a balanced account of the development of their own profession. For anyone who accepts the basic tenets of psychoanalysis it is by definition impossible to write about Freud and his theories objectively. Freud is so emphatically the founding father of the movement that his followers inevitably find themselves entangled in an Oedipal ambivalence, caught between the impulses towards dependence and revolt. Wittels glosses over this problem in the preface to his Freud biography, claiming to be writing with 'detachment'. Psychoanalysis (he continues) 'is a scientific method independent of its discoverer's personality'.[3] When we recall that Freud and Wittels had quarrelled and separated over the Irma Karczewska affair about a dozen years earlier, we are bound to treat these claims with scepticism.

Here again the unpublished memoirs are enlightening. For with hindsight, looking back on those early disputes from the vantage point of a successful New York analyst around 1940, Wittels does achieve a higher degree of detachment. In the memoirs he frankly acknowledges the subjectivity of his earlier book, drawing attention to two key problems for the Freud biographer. The first is identification, a problem emphasized on the very first page: 'All of his disciples identify with Freud. They are not aware of this mechanism within themselves'. The second is ambivalence – indeed the title Wittels originally intended for his memoirs was 'Ambivalence as Fate'. For in his account of the writing of his Freud biography he now acknowledges that the book, far from being objective, had expressed 'a mixture of ambivalent feelings and aims. On the one hand I wished to punish the bad father; on the other hand, as I see it now, I hoped to be welcomed back as the prodigal son.'

The frankness with which Wittels acknowledges his punitive aim draws attention to a fourth methodological problem: *factional infighting*. The history of psychoanalysis has never been harmonious. Indeed, its most prominent feature has been the tendency towards rivalries and factions. Given that Freud was the father of the movement, it was inevitable that there should be a revolt of the sons (the revolt of the daughters came much later). In the early 1920s, when Wittels wrote the Freud biography, he had himself become a friend and follower of Wilhelm Stekel, the former colleague whom Freud detested. When Freud received a copy of the original German edition of the biography, he felt so provoked by the pro-Stekel perspective that he insisted on changes being made in the English version.

It is only in the memoirs that the full extent of Wittels's debt to Stekel is revealed. Indeed the memoirs, as the following excerpt will show, greatly enhance the received image of Stekel, whom more orthodox histories of psychoanalysis have tended to marginalize. Freud attributed his break with Stekel to a dispute over control of the *Zentralblatt für Psychoanalyse*, accusing Stekel of having done a secret deal with the publisher which amounted to 'treachery'.[4] Wittels's account shows that there were more fundamental divergences, stressing the contrast between Stekel's intuitive approach to psychoanalysis and Freud's insistence that it should be regarded as a 'science'.

This excerpt thus suggests that a reassessment of the links between Freud and Stekel is long overdue. After all, if Freud really believed that his erstwhile colleague was a charlatan, why did he draw so heavily on Stekel's theories in the dream symbolism section of the *Introductory Lectures* of 1917?[5] The excerpt from Wittels's memoirs also reveals that as late as 1927, in preparing his paper on 'Fetishism', Freud asked him for information about Stekel's approach to the subject. Such details serve as a reminder that Freud's achievement needs to be assessed in a context that takes proper account of the writings of his contemporaries.

Wittels's description of Stekel's 'peculiarly magic nature' raises one further question: the question of *institutional orthodoxy*. It is clear that serious historiographical problems arise from a desire to defend psychoanalysis as an institution. The history of the movement has tended to be written from inside, by practitioners with a vested interest in propping up Freud's prestige. Freud himself established the pattern in 1914 with his 'History of the Psychoanalytic Movement'. And the biography by Ernest Jones, regarded for many years as definitive, is also partisan in its defence of Freudian orthodoxy. More recently, the widely acclaimed biography by Peter Gay has continued this tradition. The aim is to present psychoanalysis as a success story, relegating to footnotes or appendices the mass of evidence that might undermine the claims of psychoanalysis to scientific status and therapeutic value.

Wittels was himself committed to psychoanalysis as an institution. Paradoxically, this erstwhile rebel ended his career as a successful analyst in New York, defending Freudian orthodoxy against the deviations of Karen Horney.[6] But there was another more irreverent dimension to his personality: that impulse which led him as a young man to become embroiled in so many escapades and which prompted him towards the end of his life to write a more truthful account of his involvement with Freud and his followers. Wittels's memoirs are written in a spirit that subverts institutional orthodoxies. Thus the publication of the complete text may stimulate a radical reinterpretation of the origins of psychoanalysis.

Reconciliation with Freud

(from the manuscript of Fritz Wittels's memoirs)[7]

After an interruption of about six years I returned to psychoanalysis. The man who helped me find my way back was Wilhelm Stekel, one of the oldest pupils of Freud, who, in 1912, two years after me, succumbed to the centrifugal forces around the master. Stekel died in England in the spring of 1940. Made wiser by my experience with Karl Kraus, taught to be silent about former friends, I will not talk here about Stekel's character, which is not always judged favourably. It is easier for me to say little about him because my relations with him were never as intimate as were those with Kraus. I had known Stekel since 1906, having met him first at Freud's round table but I had little close personal contact with him then. In 1920, I met him again in the streets of Vienna. He told me, in his narcissistic way, of his great successes, his books, his patients, and his pupils. He also told me how Freud had injured him and how, despite his successes, he still suffered under this injustice. That was grist to my mill. There was little I had to tell Stekel because he was well informed about my rupture with Freud. The tempter rose again in my life, this time, however, in the form of one to whom I came to owe gratitude, although Freud later did not think so. It is my opinion that I would not have found my way back to psychoanalysis without the help of Stekel.

Stekel's was a peculiarly magic nature. Without Freud's discovery Stekel would never have known that the dream spoke a language which could be understood. But once he was given the key he became a dream interpreter whose equal I have never seen. He could read the dreams of his patients as easily and readily as other people read books. Much of our knowledge of dream symbols came from him. He recognized the symbol of death in dreams ('Every dream is a picture puzzle with the question: Where is death?'). He knew that right and left meant right and wrong, described bisexual symbolism in dreams, found out that the figure five represented the hand, twelve the last hour and divined the meaning of many more symbols in the picture language of the dream which had not yet been recognized by Freud. As easily as he saw through dreams, Stekel was aware of hidden aims and unconscious fears in listening to his patient's communications. He startled his patients and although he helped them sometimes, he also often confused and bewildered them with the force of his interpretations. Stekel knew little of the so-called resistance analysis carefully elaborated by Freud's school, had not much use for systematic methods in general and was proud of it. Freud commented on Stekel's methods of practising analysis: 'We are told that savages put their ears to the ground and in this way are able to hear the tramping of horses for miles. Civilized man cannot do this, but he has the telephone and wire which send him messages from much greater distances; in other words, we have science and its methods.'

When analysing, Stekel was almost absent-minded and his strange ease in understanding reminded one of the accomplishments of mediums. He must have had some procedure but we could recognize none to study, and as a teacher he was rather incoherent. A man with such qualities had to become an offence to scientists. He was like the mental arithmeticians who call out the results without using any observable method. Science, however, demands not only results but methodical evidence leading to the results as well. It is distrustful of magicians and rightly so. Stekel was often wrong, too, and had a way of gliding over his mistakes with facility and without compunction. But here we would pass judgements on character and these I have promised to avoid.

To me he spoke of the old days, of how I had come to the psychoanalytic round table as a young fighter and how later, after my breach with Kraus, I had collapsed as though I were no longer the same conquering man. But I had to resume my destiny, he knew I would. He had his own school now, he said, and Freud's school was entangled in mysticism and philosophy while true analysis, the medical work, lay with Stekel. I knew little then about the latest events of the movement and some of what he said seemed justified. I told him that I did not think it possible for me to find my way back to psychoanalysis without Freud. He contradicted me on this; it was, he said, quite simple. My psychoanalytic knowledge and talents were repressed because of defiance. I should go through an analysis which he was willing to carry out and after this I would know more of the subject than any one of Freud's pupils. All my knowledge and understanding would again come to the fore. I followed his advice and I must confess that I had in this analysis most shaking experiences and I made discoveries which surprised me greatly although I had practised analysis myself since 1908. Intellectually I had known all the mechanisms many years, but almost nobody is actually convinced of them until he has himself felt through analysis their blind and irresistible power. Stekel's method was not to have any. Not always did I lie on a couch. He lived in a suburb where the city bordered on the woods and sometimes in the night we walked over snowfields scantily lit by the last city lights and he analysed me while we slowly walked together side by side. The idea must be horrifying to any classical analyst and I myself do not pretend that it was a method to be recommended. Whenever Stekel felt that he had something to say he stopped. I stopped, too, and in a completely dispassionate voice, as though it were a matter to which he was utterly indifferent, he stated terrible facts, dug out the big shocks of life of which one had either known nothing before or whose importance to one was by no means clear. Stekel's beautiful police dog ran ahead of us, his cane in mouth and returned again and again without the cane. 'It is a valuable stick! A souvenir!' Stekel would exclaim and my analysis was temporarily disrupted while the dog was made to seek for the cane in the snow drifts. It was regularly found and as regularly brought back, after which the mysteries of our story slowly continued.

I have kept the impression, although my memory may be wrong, that my analysis in the snow yielded better results than on the couch. The trouble with Stekel's analysis was that it almost invariably reached an impasse when the so called negative transference grew stronger. In this phase of the work patients become unruly and a special technique is to be used to enable the analyst to deal with this unpleasant but unavoidable and even helpful part of the work. Stekel was too narcissistic for that. He took criticism and reproaches from the patient as a personal offence and cut the analysis short when, in the Freudian sense, it was just about to begin, with the patient's frustrated feelings coming to the fore. For this reason his analyses lasted a relatively short time and this was the point on which he prided himself. He claimed that this was 'active therapy' as opposed to the long 'orthodox' analyses which he derided. Inasmuch as the negative transference, by the nature of psychoanalysis, comes sooner or later to the surface, his analyses could not last long. Here was one of his numerous inconsistencies. The fundamental rule of psychoanalysis is that the patient must say whatever comes to his mind. It is inconsistent first to pledge a man to spill it all out and then, when in strict accordance with the rule he does so and manifests aggression towards the analyst, to rebuke him. Once a patient said to him: 'How long will I have to come to you? I am sick and tired of it.' Stekel replied: 'You do not have to come any more; your treatment is at an end.' He was gravely offended that a patient could say such a thing to him who was the great expert, interpreter and benefactor. Instead of revealing the phenomenon of negative transference, he dismissed the ungrateful neurotic.

This, however, did not always happen. If he liked his 'analysand' and if he hoped to win a partisan for the future (as in my case), he took plenty and could treat negative transference, too. It was quite clear to him that I felt superior to him in many respects and had him analyze me only because I was too proud to go back to Freud. He was particularly cautious with me and – I gladly admit it – quite efficient. He said that Freud had treated me the wrong way throughout. To him, Stekel, it would have been easy to keep me from publishing *Ezechiel*; Freud could have succeeded, too, were it not for the fact that he had been blind in the matter since he had lost so many friends himself. We discussed the crucial point of my sweet letters to Kraus after Freud had recalled them to me;[8] and Stekel said this was nothing at all, hardly worth mentioning. In matters of ambivalence, however, he was not trustworthy and I did not accept his judgement wholeheartedly.

Shortly after my analysis with Stekel was finished or it may have been while it was still in progress, Mr E. P. Tal, a publisher, called to ask me whether I would be willing to write a survey of psychoanalysis understandable to the layman. He had in mind more the general scope of Freud's work than the medical aspect of psychoanalysis. He had first asked Stefan Zweig, but Zweig had declined because, as he said, he did not feel competent for the task. Tal asked him who, in his opinion, could write such a book and Zweig answered that he did not know of anybody. When Tal mentioned my name, Zweig replied: 'Yes, I think he would be the man to do it.' I do not know whether Zweig remembers this conversation but it was in this way that I was honoured with an order to which I probably owe my present position in America.

In my analysis with Stekel there was, as one may imagine, much talk about my book, *Ezechiel*. We discussed the entire episode with its roaring complexes, its shifting ambivalences and its nucleus in the father problem. To undertake, while in analysis, to write another book whose impetus lay in a personal relationship was certainly a dangerous enterprise of which my analyst should have warned me. A book written under these circumstances was liable again to become ambivalent and aggressive, to represent psychoanalysis and its creator subjectively rather than with the desired objectivity. Kraus had been a bad father and I had punished him. Now Freud was a father, too, and a bad one in that he had rejected me. Stekel buttressed my opinion that he was a bad father and an argument never settled, never quite forgotten was stirred up anew.

I did not know how to proceed at first. Stekel produced enormous volumes without interruption. They came out of his clattering typewriter with inconceivable ease. He could not understand what there was to think about. He said: 'Sit down and write!' I, however, realizing that I had reached another turning point in my life, spun myself deeply into psychoanalytic literature, Freud's publications in particular, for half a year. I knew all Freud's works well, anyhow; those of the first decade of the century I had discussed with Freud and our groups as they appeared one after the other. Those of the second decade I read as fast as they were published, as did all his pupils.

Drawing anew into Freud's *Interpretation of Dreams* and other works, his *Psychopathology of Everyday Life* and *History of the Psychoanalytic Movement* especially, I found that although he repeatedly said that the public had no right to pry into his private life, he had published so many details of his personal life that it was possible to construct a biography of the man and his work without further study and therefore without indiscretion. No authorization was necessary if I used but printed material with a few interpolations of my own. This was quite a discovery. Stekel had told me a few things about Alfred Adler and C. G. Jung which I had not known and as both of us judged the defections of these two psychologists in much the same way that Freud himself did, no specific consultation with the master was needed in this matter either. The only sore point was Stekel himself. Freud could not bear the sight of him and missed no opportunity to point this out verbally or in writing. The real aim of my book was to show Freud that I, from my more distant position, knew him and psychoanalysis better than did the pupils by whom he was daily surrounded. It was a kind of *El Cid* ambition, inspired, perhaps, by the comments of the king during the banishment of the knight from the Spanish Court: 'Why, banished though he is, he serves me better than any one of you!' This, I hasten to add, though I knew it not at the time, was a piece of self-analysis which I perceived later on. I overplayed my hand; I was not as wonderful as I thought.

The style of the book was not uniform. Expressions of admiration and reverence alternated with hard, occasionally ironic criticism. Freud's doctrines were presented in a readable form and not without inspiration. I later had to admit that the critical sections of the book were partly untenable; other parts (including my remarks on anxiety, on certain 'Freudian blunders', and on the concept of his book on dreams) I not only could support myself but saw accepted by Freud.

Again I had produced a mixture of ambivalent feelings and aims. On the one hand I wished to punish the bad father; on the other hand, as I see it now, I hoped to be welcomed back as the prodigal son. In addition, I was grateful to Stekel. He had been of help to me and I wished to help him in the public eye. It is strange to say that this book, with its manifold and seemingly incompatible aims, was a complete success. It is out of print today and I do not intend to prepare a new edition. It was published in German before the Christmas of 1923 and a year later in English and French. It made my name internationally known to those interested in Freud, regardless of whether they were for or against him. I was introduced, at uncounted lecture desks in Europe and America, as Freud's biographer; yet I was, as Freud later said an 'unsolicited biographer.'

I had just finished my book when I learned, to my utter consternation, that Freud was very ill and had to be operated upon because of cancer of the maxillary bone. Had he died, my book would have become meaningless to me. It contained my settlement with the man whom I loved and admired. Long ago I had been 'naughty' and he had punished me. My biography was naughty again with the not outspoken aim of being recalled to favour in spite of it or perhaps just because of it. I felt that I had been aggressive but brilliant. All depended on his reading my effusion. And then I learned that he was caught in the grip of a dangerous disease. My enemies assumed, on the contrary, that I had written my book with the purpose of being the first in the market after the man's death. He recovered, fortunately, and survived his first operation for sixteen years.

Around Christmas time in 1923 I sent my book to Freud who received it with undisguised surprise. His first impression of the book was not unfavourable. A few days after receiving my book he wrote me a letter which I published one year later, with his authorization, in the English edition. He also corrected a few matters of fact in my text and these corrections I included in the English edition. His letter contained several scathing comments on Stekel and I asked for permission to omit them in the publication which was then pending. He permitted the omission of one particularly offensive part; two others had to remain. My book is now out of print and I repeat the letter here as it was published (in translation) in 1924, still omitting the strongest condemnation of Stekel but adding, however, another passage which I had then suppressed for obvious reasons. Here it is: 'Perhaps you know that I was seriously ill and although I have recovered there is still reason to see in my experience a warning of a not too distant end. In this state of partial removal I may be permitted to ask you to acquit me of the intention to disturb your relation to Stekel. I am only sorry that it gained so decisive an influence on your book about me.' And the letter:

> You have given me a Christmas present which is very largely occupied with my own personality. The failure to send a word of thanks for such a gift would be an act of rudeness only to be accounted for by very peculiar motives. Fortunately no such motives exist in this case. Your book is by no means hostile; it is not unduly indiscreet; and it manifests the serious interest in the topic which was to be anticipated in so able a writer as yourself.
>
> I need hardly say that I neither expected nor desired the publication of such a book. It seems to me that the public has no concern with my personality, and can learn nothing from an account of it, so long as my case (for manifold reasons) cannot be expounded without any reserves whatever. But you have thought otherwise. Your own detachment from me, which you deem an advantage, entails serious drawbacks nonetheless. You know too little of the object of study, and you have not been able to avoid the danger of straining the facts in your analytical endeavours. Moreover, I am inclined to think that your adoption of Stekel's standpoint, and the fact that you contemplate the object of study from his outlook, cannot but have impaired the accuracy of your discernment.
>
> In some respects, I think there are positive distortions, and I believe these to be the outcome of a preconceived notion of yours. You think that a great man must have such and such merits and defects, and must display certain extreme characteristics; and you hold that I belong to the category of great men. That is why you ascribe to me all sorts of qualities many of which are mutually conflicting. Much of general interest might be said about this matter, but unfortunately your relationship to Stekel precludes further attempts on my part to clear up the misunderstanding.
>
> On the other hand, I am glad to acknowledge that your shrewdness has enabled you to detect many things which are well known to myself. For

instance, you are right in inferring that I have often been compelled to make detours when following my own path. You are right, too, in thinking that I have no further use for other people's ideas when they are presented at an inopportune moment. (Still, as regards the latter point, I think you might have defended me from the accusation that I am repudiating ideas when I am merely unable for the nonce to pass judgement on them or to elaborate them.) But I am delighted to find that you do me full justice in the matter of my relationship with Adler...

I realize that you may have occasion to revise your text in view of a second edition. With an eye to this possibility, I enclose a list of suggested emendations. These are based on trustworthy data, and are quite independent of my own prepossessions. Some of them relate to matters of trifling importance, but some of them will perhaps lead you to reverse or modify certain inferences. The fact that I send you these corrections is a token that I value your work though I cannot wholly approve it.[9]

It seems to me that no one who reads this letter can gain the impression that Freud felt deeply hurt by my book. On the contrary; Freud must have seen the glorification of his personality which I had in mind. The evident sincerity of the interspersed criticism, harsh though it sometimes was, enhanced the magnitude of the man and his work. Where the sunlight is strong, so to speak, the shadows lie deep. Of course one may say the very opposite: that criticism coming from a man who obviously valued him highly, condemned him. Readers adopted one or the other of these outlooks according to their attitude towards Freud. People who saw Freud regularly in those days have tried to convince me that Freud was bitterly against my book from the beginning. This, I repeat, was not to be deduced from his letter nor from his subsequent behaviour towards me. I rather think that his pupils and friends were much more antagonistic towards my book than was he himself in the beginning and that it was they who turned him against it, particularly when his opponents took my remarks out of context and quoted me as though I were one of their kind, an enemy of psychoanalysis.

The next thing I did was to attempt to reconcile Freud with Stekel, a foolish attempt because it was doomed from the start to fail. In one of Freud's publications he says of Stekel that his break with him was caused by 'matters which it is hardly possible to make public.' Even more spiteful is the passage in which Freud refers to 'Stekel, so serviceable in the beginning, and afterwards so utterly untrustworthy.' When I learned that this publication was just about to be reprinted for a new edition I asked Freud to change these hurtful allegations. Freud replied:

> I should like to do you a favour. Of course I could not suppress my criticism of Stekel; even less could I speak about him in a way adequate to his own self-appreciation. However, if the substitution of a milder term for a harsh word can diminish his offence and make himself adopt more polite forms, I do not wish to stand in the way.

Therefore, the very day your letter came I asked about the new printing of my essay, *History of the Psychoanalytic Movement*, and learned that it was too late to do anything. The printing was done and the sheets at the bookbinder's. So everything has to remain as it is.

Very truly yours,
Freud

Readers who knew Freud and his feelings towards Stekel will recognize the diabolic humour of this letter.

In the year 1925 my relations with Stekel came to an end. No sooner did Freud learn about this event which he had anticipated than he invited me to come to see him. The immediate motive for this invitation was scientific, as always with Freud. I had sent him a manuscript and he wished to discuss it with me – as in the old days. In this way I came back to the man whose teachings, in my younger years, has struck me with such force, whom I had had to leave and on whom, in defiance and bitterness, I had not called for more than twelve years. When I left him his hair and beard were dark and only slightly grizzled. There he sat, the same man and yet another one. His name had become an idea and legend was woven about his now snow-white head. I could certainly not argue with him any more. His big cause was mine, my small cause belonged to the past. He said: 'You have not altered much.' I could not say the same about him and kept quiet. I remembered a comparatively young man whom, in 1906, I had once asked to a consultation and who had returned downtown with me afterwards in a one-horse hansom cab. He held a small India rubber stethoscope in his hand and asked me whether I had been satisfied with him. Incredible that this man's name was Dr Sigmund Freud!

His first question was: 'In order to make things easier for me, tell me in what relation you are to Stekel?' It was always Stekel and clean-cut separation from him that mattered first. When I replied that I did not see him anymore, he said: 'I do not ask you why you separated. All I ask is how could you stand him so long!' There was something vindictive in his voice. I later learned that he blamed Stekel rather than myself for the part of my book which he disliked. I replied: 'You, Professor, could stand him much longer than I.' With this remark I alluded to the twelve to fourteen years during which Stekel had been one of his most prominent pupils, editor of his magazine, spokesman before the public and scientific collaborator. I do not wish to repeat what more he said about Stekel on the occasion of this first conversation with me after the long pause because it was too bitter. I mention here but one sharp pun: 'I have committed two crimes in my life; I called attention to cocaine and I introduced Stekel to psychoanalysis.'

Cocaine, though abused by drug addicts, is a drug of paramount importance. Stekel, too, has cured patients, made discoveries, but had, in Freud's eyes, come to be a nuisance. The comparison is, in a way, almost complimentary to Stekel, the assets of cocaine by far outbalancing its dangers.

He asked me why I had not come to him directly instead of having come through Stekel. I said: 'Because you did not invite me.'

He: 'You never asked for an invitation.'
I: 'I wrote you often.'

He: 'Yes, but your letters were always quarrelsome. Your book was scarcely the right way to bring you back to me, either.'

We then turned to scientific subjects and I do not remember how long I stayed with him but it was a long time and he dismissed me with the words: 'I'll be glad if I have won you back for psychoanalysis of the non-Stekel brand.'

We shook hands in grand style and nothing indicated that he resented my book except perhaps, as occurred to me much later, the fact that he did not look in my face when we separated that night.

After this conversation our relations became almost cordial as far as this was possible with one of Freud's 'Nordic' temperament. Between 1925 and 1928 I published four books on psychoanalysis.[10] He wrote to me: 'Dear Doctor, You probably know that I am biased and like well most of what you write...'

Or: 'Your little book for which I am very grateful is again very good and contains most excellent passages...'

I saw him often in these years. We discussed scientific questions and problems of organization. He sent me patients for treatment and once, in 1927, he even did me the honour of sending me to Munich when he was invited to lecture on psychoanalysis at the psychiatric institute there and did not feel well enough to accept himself. In the Viennese group of the psychoanalytic association which I frequented, following his wish and my own, I found less benevolence in the beginning. Younger members, particularly, were not sure whether they liked my return. I complained to Freud who advised me to hold on and show the members that I was a 'valuable acquisition.'

'Some', he said, 'cannot forgive you your book on me.'

I formally reentered Freud's organization in 1927. It was no longer what I had abandoned under dramatic circumstances, but had become part of a worldwide international organization. Dr Paul Federn, the vice-chairman, asked me what I intended to do in the matter of my book. I did not consider it urgent because I was under the impression that Freud himself did not take it very seriously. It seemed that way to me then. I promised that I would do something when an occasion presented itself, either in a possible second edition or in another publication in which I could revert to the subject. My book was then four years after publication and no longer in the foreground of public interest.

Freud continued to write me most amiable letters of which I take the liberty of publishing two more because they are of general interest. His paper on fetishism to which the letters refer was published in 1927, so that the discretion he asked of me is no longer needed.

Semmering (Villa Schueler)
July 31st 1927
Dear Doctor:
Perhaps you will be surprised that I ask you for a literary favour. Undoubtedly, however, you will soon understand. In these years I have had the opportunity of carrying several analyses of fetishism and in each case I found a surprisingly simple solution. I wish to make it the subject of a small communication. But there is somebody who has written a fat

volume about the subject. Following the rules of scientific usage, I should read the book and make sure that the shrewd somebody has not found my solution, little likely though this may be. However, I cannot bring myself to do so; I cannot overcome an inner resistance like an instinct for cleanliness. I know well enough that this should not be so, but with age one easily acquires whims and becomes inclined to stick to one's stubborness.

This time I find useful what I regret so much in your past. You certainly know Stekel's book on fetishism. Is it possible for you to tell me in a few sentences to what conclusions this author comes with regard to the nature and the aim of the fetish? My request is, of course, valid only in case he does express any such conclusion and if it is not too strenuous for you to extract it. In the negative case, notify me on a postal card; in any event be good enough to keep quiet about this confession of an idiosyncrasy which was hard enough for me to acquire.

With cordial greetings,

Yours,
Freud

I am not quite sure whether I succeed in conveying through this translation the sometimes dancing, sometimes grim humour that lies between the lines. At any rate, I was able to tell him that Stekel traced the fetish back to ten different determinants in the unconscious of the pervert. At which came the following letter nine days later:

Dear Doctor:
Many thanks. You have rendered me a good service which makes my publication possible. I will gladly reveal to you in compensation – but keep it still for yourself – that the fetish is not anything tenfold but something very simple, namely, the equivalent for the once imagined and so highly valued penis of the woman (mother's), and therefore a product of defiance against castration and defence against homosexuality.

With cordial greetings,

Yours,
Freud

This is not the place to discuss the value and importance of Freud's statement on fetishism. I would not even produce these letters here were it not for the documentation of Freud's cordial attitude; and even that might sound boastful and I would not speak about it were it not important to contrast this attitude with events which will be reported later.[11]

Notes

1. *Letters of Sigmund Freud 1873–1939*, ed. Ernst L. Freud, tr. Tania and James Stern (London, 1961), p. 152.
2. For a detailed account of this episode, see Edward Timms, 'The "Child-Woman": Kraus, Freud, Wittels, and Irma Karczewska', *Austrian Studies*, 1 (1990), 87–107.

3. Fritz Wittels, *Sigmund Freud: His Personality, His Teachings and His School,* tr. Eden and Cedar Paul (London, 1924), Preface.

4. *The Freud/Jung Letters,* ed. William McGuire, tr. Ralph Manheim and R. F. C. Hull (London, 1974), p. 541.

5. A note in the Standard Edition (*SE* 15: 149) emphasizes the debt to Stekel's theory of dream-symbolism, acknowledged by Freud in the fourth (1914) edition of *The Interpretation of Dreams,* but not in the *Introductory Lectures* themselves.

6. See Susan Quinn, *A Mind of Her Own: The Life of Karen Horney* (London, 1987), pp. 337–40.

7. 'Reconciliation with Freud' is taken from the typescript 'Wrestling with the Man: The Story of a Freudian' by Fritz Wittels, M.D. This excerpt is published with the kind consent of John R. Wittels, son of the author; the Abraham A. Brill Library, custodians of the Wittels papers; and Yale University Press, who are preparing a book edition of the memoirs (to be edited by Edward Timms). The text of this excerpt is reproduced with minor alterations to clarify meaning or correct orthography.

8. The episode of the 'sweet letters to Kraus' is explained in *Austrian Studies,* 1 (1990), 98–105.

9. When this letter was reproduced in the Standard Edition (*SE* 19: 286–8), a footnote drew attention to the 'short omitted passage [which] contains a further reference to Stekel and a remark about Freud's own illness'.

10. In a typewritten footnote Wittels indicates that the books in question were *Die Befreiung des Kindes* (Stuttgart, 1927; published in English in 1933 under the title *Set the Children Free!*); *Die Technik der Psychoanalyse* (Munich, 1926); *Die Psychoanalyse: Neue Wege der Seelenkunde* (Vienna, 1927); and *Die Welt ohne Zuchthaus* (Berne, 1928).

11. In a later section of the memoirs, Wittels discovers that Freud's 'cordial attitude' in 1927 was misleading, since 'he had not told me [...] how much he disliked my book and how hurt he felt by it'.

Psychoanalysis and Feminism:
An Ambivalent Alliance
Viennese Feminist Responses to Freud, 1900–30
Harriet Anderson

Psychoanalysis and modern feminism seem to be involuntarily joined in an alliance through their shared claim to make the unconscious conscious. The critical potential of psychoanalysis lies not only in questioning all that is regarded as normal and customary but also in uncovering the unconscious desires which normality and custom conceal. And there is no other movement of liberation which is so intensely concerned with the psychic structures of the oppressed as is the women's movement. Consciousness-raising, that is, making unconscious influences conscious with the aim of reducing their unquestioned effectiveness, is one of the principal vehicles of the feminist movement as of psychoanalysis. The alliance between the two might be a firmly forged one. And yet, many in the women's movement see Freud and psychoanalysis as epitomizing the oppression perpetrated by the enemy or at best as advocating the fateful law of the father. Freud's theories about the particularities of the female psyche and his tendency to trace gender-specific psychosexuality back to biological destiny, as well as the latent complicity of analysts with the patriarchal status quo and their widespread blindness to the structures of oppression, make many modern feminists wary of if not downright hostile to analysis. The alliance is ambivalent or even acrimonious.[1] Freud, however, did not fully develop his theories on femininity until after he had formulated the main ideas of therapeutic analysis. How then did those feminists react who were engaged in the first women's movement in Freud's Vienna? What kind of an alliance was forged between these women and psychoanalysis?

Women active in the organized women's movement in Vienna in the early decades of this century by no means passed psychoanalysis by in silence. 'An outstanding dialectician of psychology and in addition a monomaniac of his own system', commented Rosa Mayreder, the middle-class Viennese feminist, in 1916 on her compatriot and contemporary Sigmund Freud.[2] For the socialist Therese Schlesinger-Eckstein, on the other hand, Freud was the author of 'works of genius';[3] and the eugenicist Grete Meisel-Hess saw him as possessing 'greatness.'[4] Freud however did not return the compliment. He considered feminist claims to equality misguided and unrealizable and saw the strivings of 'the emancipated woman' as merely symptoms of the envy and hostile bitterness women harboured towards men.

Yet the paths of feminists and psychoanalysts in Vienna crossed in several places, both on the organizational and the personal levels. Freud was, for example, called upon to act as an expert at the investigation organized in 1905 by the left-liberal Cultural-Political Society which dealt with marriage law reform, a theme of burning concern to the women's movement. The feminists Grete Meisel-Hess, Henriette Herzfelder and Camilla Theimer also contributed to this inquiry.[5] Along with Rosa Mayreder and Grete Meisel-Hess, he also signed the declaration of the German League for Mothers' Protection in 1911, which called on men and women to contribute to the work to be done to protect motherhood and reform sexual life. The declared aim was to contribute to the striving 'for the organic and intellectual perfection of the human race and therefore the creation of the firm basis for a higher human culture, for more noble and at the same time happier conditions of living'.[6] This organizational connection extended to personal and therapeutic contact. Freud was a good friend of the Eckstein family of which the sisters Therese Schlesinger-Eckstein and Emma Eckstein were members. He treated Emma, probably the Irma of Freud's dream of Irma's injection, who then it seems went on to become an analyst herself.[7] And in addition, in 1915 he briefly treated Rosa Mayreder's husband, Karl, for depression, until (as we shall see) Rosa put her foot down. This contact was organized by Paul Federn, who probably came to know Rosa Mayreder through the activities of his sister Elsa. Elsa was active in the Vienna Settlement movement which was largely an off-shoot of Vienna's women's movement.[8]

It was not only Freud, but also Alfred Adler, who had a special significance for the feminists. Eight years after the consultations with Freud, Adler in his turn was called in by Rosa Mayreder to treat her husband, only to be sneeringly dismissed by Karl, with his wife's approval, with the words: 'And this fat gentleman with his smarmy bonhomie thinks he can help me with his worn-out phrases!'[9] Indeed, after Adler's visit, Rosa Mayreder noted in her diary that 'Dr Adler did not forbear to commit the usual neurologist's stupidities'. She even wondered whether the profession of neurologist 'does not lead to diminished intelligence'.[10] Others in the feminist network were however more receptive to Adler. A collection of essays entitled *Heilen und Bilden*, edited by Adler and others, was given a positive review in *Neues Frauenleben*, the journal of the more radical wing of the Austrian women's movement. There Adler was called 'a courageous and individualist researcher who had made it his goal to illuminate the dark domain of the neuroses'.[11] And indeed one of the early generation of female doctors, Margarete Hilferding (wife of the socialist political economist Rudolf), was active both in the women's movement and as an Adlerian analyst, becoming the first woman member of Freud's Wednesday Club in April 1910.[12] She left however in October 1911 along with Adler to become a member of his Society for Free Psychoanalytical Investigation. There was thus a network of organizational and personal connections which brought the psychoanalysts and the feminists together. How far was there, however, a similar network of ideological connections which might have led to a coherent alliance?

That there was a convergence on the ideological level is of course indicated by the fact that both Freud and the feminists supported the declaration of the

German League for Mothers' Protection. This advocated above all a more lenient attitude to the unmarried mother and her child and condemned the widespread marriage of convenience along with the morality which supported it. And indeed, it was this questioning of the moral status quo which brought, in the feminists' eyes, their own concerns and Freud's together. This point was emphasized by Meisel-Hess in 1916:

> The greatness of a doctor of our day, the greatness of Freud consists above all in the fact that he was one of the first to give his newly won clinical material firm foundations which resulted in completely new moral perspectives. ... He has drawn on material which lay completely hidden, has thrown quite new light on it and has had the courage to make moral demands ....[13]

For these feminists, then, psychoanalysis provided scientific backing for their own demands for a changed morality.

This meant that Freud was turned into a supporter of women's endeavours for sex reform. Meisel-Hess for example saw the repression of sexual needs in patriarchy to be one of the roots of the 'sexual crisis' which she identified in *Die Sexuelle Krise* (1909). This was the first volume of her three-part socio-psychological investigation of the essence of sexuality and its relations to the social question, war, morality, race, religion and in particular monogamy. Here Freud's ideas could be cited in support, as Meisel-Hess clearly recognized. 'Of course', she confidently asserts,

> we have here to take account of Professor Freud's fundamental insights into neuroses, psychoses and psychoneuroses and their connection with sexual misery ... Professor Freud explains that neuroses and psychoses necessarily occur as a result of inadequate sexual satisfaction ... The consistent prevention of reproduction and sexual life altogether makes people ill, both men and women; all social circles are ailing as a result of this abnormal way of living.[14]

After quoting from Freud's seminal essay on 'Sexuality in the Aetiology of the Neuroses', she goes on to assert the need for more relaxed sexual relations outside marriage (although marriage still remains the ideal) and above all to argue for the acceptance of unmarried motherhood.

However, eugenicist rather than ethical considerations predominate in this defence of motherhood, as Meisel-Hess herself proudly admits. It is this that distinguishes her from those other feminists, the 'women's righters' ('Frauenrechtlerinnen') as she calls them.

> I reject the many 'ethical' reasons, with which some women's righters tend to propose this demand ... It is time to let undistorted truth hold sway, I base my remarks here on natural science and natural right, on the will of nature and the social will which speaks through the species, on the clear demand of unsullied instincts.[15]

It is instincts and nature, then, which are for Meisel-Hess to be dominant, for they can lead humanity out of its present misery to a higher level of health and happiness. And it is the fulfilment of natural instincts which in her view Freud supports. She thus also pays tribute to Freud's investigation of 'the strange disturbances of the soul' which occur from the 'repression of certain facts and events' in childhood.[16] Yet she is, unlike Freud, less interested in reconstructing childhood traumas than in the consequences of repression and concealment for sexual relationships in adulthood. 'In the case of the polygamous man', she claims in her later study of monogamy, 'emotional repressions of the most monstrous kind take place.' She therefore comes to the conclusion that 'real sexual happiness can always only mean: me and you and you and me, and no theories, however ingenious, will ever manage to transform what is in truth the death of loving sensibility – sexual adultery – into anything else'.[17] Meisel-Hess thus uses her vision of Freud's ideas to support her own view of morality, a view which in fact discounts Freud's evaluation of the necessity of repression for the existence of culture. Although she, too, insists on the necessity of making the unconscious conscious, for her this means a re-evaluation of instinctual life. Meisel-Hess may have been one of Freud's most enthusiastic feminist supporters, but she was a highly selective one.

As the feminists themselves readily admitted, the new morality presupposed an awareness and understanding of human nature which the well-brought-up young lady's education certainly did not provide. They thus took it upon themselves to fill the gap and directed their attention, amongst other things, to the role of the 'good' mother as educator and moral guardian. Emma Eckstein addressed the issue in her pamphlet *Die Sexualfrage in der Erziehung des Kindes* ('The Sexual Question in the Education of Children', 1904), building on a crucial aspect of Freudian thought, namely the importance of infantile sexuality. Eckstein focuses on masturbation by children and how the mother should best react if she find it practised by her child. On the one hand she sees masturbation as an expression of a childhood sexuality which the thinking woman, who is equated with the good mother by almost all feminists, will learn to confront. 'As soon as she [the thinking woman] has learnt to regard the sexual functions as an important factor in the development of every person from childhood on, she will cease to conceal the damage and danger from her own eyes with the cloak of modesty', Eckstein confidently predicts.[18] However, this does not mean that masturbation is to be condoned. It is an enemy to be fought, an expression of those natural drives which must be tamed and subdued, she urgently warns.[19] Indeed Eckstein goes so far as willingly to admit that force might be necessary to fight this vice.

> It will barely be possible to prevent a child from executing this harmful habit without having to torment it with a bandage, light restraint or another means of force. Yet is would be very falsely applied sentimentality to refrain from using this temporary limitation and annoyance.[20]

However, Eckstein is not only a stern moralist, for she also sees masturbation as the child's reaction to the withdrawal of love by those persons closest to it.[21] She therefore in addition recommends love and affection as antidotes. Eckstein, like Freud, is above all concerned to bring the sexuality of children out of the dark, but unlike him she makes this a special concern for women as mothers. In order to be good mothers they need to be made aware of the realities of life and its darker sides, even if this means defying conventional moral norms. And those realities include for her, as for Freud, infantile sexuality.

Writing in the 1930s, Therese Schlesinger-Eckstein also found Freud's view of human beings, their instinctual economy and their need to repress, useful as support for her campaign for new moral norms. For her, as a committed socialist, this change was to be applied less to sexuality than to the morality surrounding social deviance, in particular criminality and its treatment. She argues, following Freud's model, that all people are forced to regulate their instincts in order to adapt to the demands of culture. Criminals are those unfortunates who for social reasons have not achieved this as successfully as others. For Schlesinger-Eckstein the so-called 'criminal' is 'a creature which is not socially adapted ... the instinctual drive which must be repressed is typical of all people, ... but in the case of the criminal character the censor fails to a high degree ...'.[22] In accordance with this view Schlesinger-Eckstein pleads not for retributive justice but for the re-education of offenders and for their humane treatment. The insights of psychoanalysis are invoked in support of a fundamental change in thinking about crime and punishment.

> Siegmund [sic] Freud has shown us in his works of genius what a tremendous even if unnoticed task every human being has to achieve in order to learn to master his natural drives to the extent that he can succeed in gradually growing into the world of culture ... Freud also teaches us, however, that every failure and every limitation of this development exposes the victim to all kinds of suffering and danger, from self-torment and fear of people and all other forms of nervous illness to hate of others, insanity and crime.[23]

The solution to the problem, Schlesinger-Eckstein continues, also lies with psychoanalysis, 'the first method of treatment which promises to be successful in the struggle against those antisocial acts'. For, 'every parents' evening which communicates modern pedagogic insights, every psychoanalytical or individual-psychological working party or advice centre is able to contribute much more to the future decrease of crime than any number of prisons and the establishment of a new penal law'. Psychoanalysis is here made into the legitimator of one of the feminists' main concerns, namely the establishment of a morality of compassion.

These feminists, then, used psychoanalysis to give backing to their demands for the moral improvement of society, which were central to the feminist vision. Even more central, however, was the organized women's movement itself and its open struggle against women's oppression by men. And here again psychoanalysis was used as an explanation and legitimation, even if not always in the most judicious way, as the work of Grete Meisel-Hess demonstrates. For her, women's enforced sexual abstinence outside marriage is the reason for their militancy. She notes that, according to Freud, women are denied opportunities for 'abreacting' their sexual drives. This is for her the reason why 'our time is so uncannily overstocked with weeping, fighting, deeply dissatisfied young women who are thoroughly tired of their lives'.[24] The spectre of the feminist as the sexually frustrated old maid raises its head again, but is given a psychoanalytical touch by being explained in terms of sexual wishes lying in the subconscious and barricading the freedom of the conscious.[25] Meisel-Hess was, however, careful to point out that the emotional impotence of the modern man also played its part, for it made him unable to love the sexually mature, independent woman. And in this claim Freud could be called upon as an authority, for as Meisel-Hess explains,

> The inability to love ... this highly specific phenomenon of our times is pathological in nature; it has its roots in an illness which Professor Freud in Vienna calls sexual neurosis ... Freud calls this condition 'the conflict between libido and sexual repression' ... That is exactly ... what we can so often encounter nowadays.[26]

Others explained women's organized attempts at emancipation in rather different psychological terms. Schlesinger-Eckstein, for example, approvingly referred to the connection identified by Adler between the drive to power of both the working class and women and the social conditions of powerlessness which these two groups were subjected to. She paid tribute to Adler's theory of 'masculine protest', which linked women's unconscious frustrations with their unremitting struggle against oppression. The label 'masculine protest', she observed, was 'perhaps not completely happily chosen'. But she acknowledged that this concept led Adler to become a 'theorist and promoter of women's emancipation'; for he, like other psychoanalysts, saw making unconscious wishes conscious the goal of psychoanalysis.[27] Adler was thus considered to have made a valuable contribution to the feminist programme of consciousness-raising as the basis of emancipation. Indeed, he was even seen as supporting the feminist assault on the excessively masculine character of culture with his own attack on the over-evaluation of masculine qualities and his call for women's equality.[28] Psychoanalysis and feminism seemed then to be joined in an amicable alliance.

Yet it was an alliance which was also ambivalent. Psychoanalysis was to support feminism, not to change it, and some feminists did not hesitate to raise a critical voice at points where analysis did not appear to promote their particular brand of feminism. This meant that different feminists reacted in differing ways to the same idea. Thus Meisel-Hess accepts aspects of psychoanalysis with regard to adults and the existence of their sex drives, but in contrast to Emma Eckstein balks at the investigation of infantile sexuality and in particular of Oedipal feelings. This she disparagingly calls the 'tendency, everywhere, in every disturbance of emotional balance ... to look for the effect of infantile erotic and in particular incest feelings, that is, for repressed sexual feelings towards the parents!'[29] This she condemns as a 'fateful wrong turn which threatens to degenerate into a mania and in fact cultivates an abnormal direction for the instincts'.[30] Oedipal theories challenged her eugenicist ideal of the healthy family and in addition detracted from the absolutely central significance which her feminism allotted to adult and in particular female sexuality and its cultural context.

The Oedipus complex was challenged from another angle by Rosa Mayreder. Central to Mayreder's feminism was less the catastrophic effect of the repression of sexuality than the way in which a woman's development of a sense of individuality was frustrated by complex social ramifications. One of these ramifications was the slow but sure collapse of the iron rule of the paterfamilias and the resulting rebellion of the sons against the fathers. It was in this connection that Mayreder questioned the Oedipus complex, suggesting that social jealousy on the part of the sons would make more sense than sexual jealousy as an explanation of the element of rivalry in this relationship.[31] It was an idea which earned her the ridicule of the psychoanalytic establishment,[32] but which has subsequently been developed by other commentators.[33]

Mayreder's criticism has, however, a further significance, for it points to the fundamental difference between early feminism and psychoanalysis. Feminists placed greater emphasis on the social than on the psychological dimension. This difference becomes quite clear when the attitudes of Freud and the feminists to the question of marriage and divorce expressed during the inquiry of 1905 are juxtaposed. For Freud it was a biological and emotional problem, not a question of natural equality or rights; he emphasized the necessity of women's sexual fulfilment for psychic health and pointed out the disadvantages women were under, giving as an example the need to marry at a very early age and in complete emotional immaturity. But he attributed this to nature, not to social constraint.[34] Biology, not cultural disability is Freud's focus. This contrasts with the position of the feminists, who emphasized social factors. For example, they drew attention to the pressures operating on divorced women and pleaded for such women's protection from social disadvantage, something Freud ignored.[35] This difference gives a political edge to some of the feminists' writings. Schlesinger-Eckstein in particular emphasized the importance of social milieu in modifying the instincts. She claims:

> The more favourable the material conditions are in which someone lives, the less repression of drives is demanded of him, the more loving and understanding his educators are, the more easily will he succeed in repressing and sublimating the antisocial part of his instincts.[36]

This leads her, like Adler and Wilhelm Reich, to express the wish that the working class be made acquainted with the basic ideas of Freud's psychology and its healing application and that the workers' health insurance firms be given the means to support analysis.[37]

Criticism did not, however, remain confined to sober argument. For Mayreder, at any rate, analysis left the realm of the intellectual to touch the personal, intimate level and to release more hostile feelings. This is hardly surprising, for the contradictions between intellectual feminism and the realities of life as a woman were thereby made emotionally more apparent. Psychology was for Mayreder both an intellectual and a personal concern. She is on the one hand a highly psychologizing thinker, who eagerly explains cultural phenomena in psychological rather than material terms. For example, much of what she says about masculinity and its relationship to culture is reminiscent of Freud's essay of 1908, '"Civilized" Sexual Morality and Modern Nervousness'.[38] Yet, unlike Freud, Mayreder makes this modern nervousness gender-specific and sees it as the main obstacle which men must overcome in order to make a new form of partnership between the sexes a real possibility. Despite her resistance to certain aspects of Freud's theories, she did have an acknowledged intellectual interest in his ideas, as the notebooks which record her reading demonstrate. For example, she noted that she had read or wanted to read Freud's *The Future of an Illusion* as a 'preliminary study to her final work on the androgynous person'.[39] On the other hand she vociferously criticized analysis as a form of treatment of psychological disturbances.

After all, Freud encroached directly on one of the most sensitive parts of her private life, namely her marriage. She consistently rejected explanations of emotional difficulties which involved the unconscious. Thus when Freud, after a therapeutic session with Karl, suggested that Karl felt overpowered by his dominant wife, that indeed he unconsciously hated her, Rosa responded:

> Freud's basic mistake is that he confuses the psyche of the neurotic person with that of the healthy person and uses the processes in the former to explain those in the latter – instead of the other way round ... He makes side-effects into causes; and in addition he does not notice that there are no limits to his brilliant art of interpretation. Indeed the virtuoso in interpretation excels by far the scientific observer in him.[40]

This comment of February 1916 seems uncompromising. But eight years later she indirectly admitted what was behind her opposition. For when Karl made it clear that he saw himself merely as the 'husband of Rosa Mayreder', she confessed that if she had to admit that Karl did suffer under her personality, that would provide 'confirmation of Freud's opinion'. But if she accepted this, it would mean 'the complete loss of all that made our life together of value'.[41] What she did not confess was that such a personal loss would also mean for her the loss of one of the pillars of her feminism. For the strong, intellectual woman was the precondition for her vision of a new humanity in which man and woman could be equal partners and in which married love was to be paramount. Freud's diagnosis impinged just too painfully both on Mayreder's feminist theory and on her personal life.

The responses of early Viennese feminists to Freud and psychoanalysis were thus rather ambivalent. They openly used his theories as legitimation for their own ideas and as support for their criticism of the status quo. And it was above all their moral demands, different though they were, which they saw as being substantiated by it. However, psychoanalysis was seen as a handmaid, not a master. Thus while acknowledging Freud's courage, Meisel-Hess clearly states that the 'great' movement for sex reform emerged from women's own endeavours.[42] A hierarchy of innovation is clearly established. Freud figures not as a mentor, but as a supporter. Similarly, Schlesinger-Eckstein uses psychoanalysis as confirmation, not inspiration. Her ideal of a morality of compassion was with her long before she came into contact with Freud's ideas. Psychoanalysis was merely to provide scientific support. Of the feminists mentioned, only Eckstein seems to have used Freud's ideas in a more substantial way, not only as support but also as a directive. These women were also highly selective in their reception of psychoanalysis. Freud's negative attitudes to femininity and the women's movement were not critically confronted at this stage. The early alliance between feminism and psychoanalysis was to remain pragmatic and partial.

Notes

I gratefully acknowledge the support provided by the Fonds zur Förderung der wissenschaftlichen Forschung in Österreich for my research on Austrian feminism 1890–1914, only one aspect of which is dealt with in the present article.

1. See Carol Hagemann–White, 'Die Kontroverse um die Psychoanalyse in der Frauenbewegung', *Psyche*, 32 (1978), 732–63; also Wolfgang J. A. Huber, 'Der junge Freud und die "Frauenfrage"', in *Unterdrückung und Emanzipation. Festschrift für Erika Weinzierl*, ed. Rudolf G. Ardelt, Wolfgang J. A. Huber and Anton Staudinger (Vienna, 1985), pp. 39–54.
2. Rosa Mayreder, *Tagebücher 1873–1937*, ed. Harriet Anderson (Frankfurt, 1988), p. 161.
3. Therese Schlesinger–Eckstein, 'Strafjustiz und Erziehung', *Der Kampf*, 22 (1929), 415–18 (p. 418).
4. Grete Meisel–Hess, *Das Wesen der Geschlechtlichkeit: Die sexuelle Krise in ihren Beziehungen zur sozialen Frage und zum Krieg, zur Moral, Rasse und Religion und insbesondere zur Monogamie* (Jena, 1916), p. XVII.
5. See 'Protokolle der Enquete betreffend die Reform des osterreichischen Eherechts', *Mitteilungen der Kulturpolitischen Gesellschaft*, 4 (1905); John Boyer, 'Freud, Marriage, and Late Viennese Liberalism: A Commentary from 1905', *The Journal of Modern History*, 50 (1978), 72–102.
6. *Mutterschutz und Sexualreform. Referate und Leitsätze des 1. Internationalen Kongresses für Mutterschutz und Sexualreform in Dresden*, ed. Max Rosenthal (Breslau, 1912), p. 134.
7. See Jeffrey Masson, *The Assault on Truth: Freud's Suppression of the Seduction Theory* (New York, 1984), pp. 233–50.
8. See Annie Urbach, 'The Federn Family', *Journal of Clinical Psychology*, Monograph Supplement 32 (Jan. 1972), 12–17.
9. Mayreder, *Tagebücher*, p. 221.
10. Ibid.
11. Hedwig Schulhof, 'Heilen und Bilden', *Neues Frauenleben*, 16 (1914), 195–6 (p. 195).
12. See *Minutes of the Vienna Psychoanalytic Society*, ed. Herman Nunberg and Ernst Federn, vol. 2 (New York, 1967), p. 499.
13. Meisel–Hess, *Das Wesen*, pp. XVII–XVIII.
14. Grete Meisel–Hess, *Die Sexuelle Krise* (Jena, 1909), p. 400.
15. Ibid., p. 384.
16 Grete Meisel–Hess, *Die Bedeutung der Monogamie* (Jena, 1917), p. XIV.
17. Ibid., p. XV.
18. Emma Eckstein, *Die Sexualfrage in der Erziehung des Kindes* (Leipzig, 1904), p. 13.
19. See ibid., p. 14.
20. Ibid., p. 15.
21. See ibid., p. 17.

22. Therese Schlesinger-Eckstein, 'Strafjustiz und Psychoanalyse', *Der Kampf*, 23 (1930), 34–40 (p. 38).
23. Schlesinger-Eckstein, 'Strafjustiz und Erziehung', 418.
24. Meisel-Hess, *Die Sexuelle Krise*, p. 384.
25. See ibid., p. 382.
26. Ibid., pp. 162–3.
27. See Therese Schlesinger-Eckstein, 'Zur Psychologie der Geschlechter', *Der Kampf*, 18 (1925), 225–9 (226).
28. See Schulhof, *Neues Frauenleben*, 16 (1914), 196.
29. Meisel-Hess, *Das Wesen*, p. XVIII.
30. Ibid.
31. Rosa Mayreder, *Geschlecht und Kultur: Essays* (Jena, 1923), pp. 67–8.
32. See Theodor Reik, 'Die Krise der Vaterlichkeit', *Imago*, 10 (1924), 353.
33. See for example Erich Fromm, *Greatness and Limitations of Freud's Thought* (New York, 1980), pp. 30–2.
34 See Boyer, *Journal of Modern History*, 50 (1978), 92.
35. See ibid., 88–90.
36. Therese Schlesinger-Eckstein, 'Ein Volksbuch über die Freudsche Lehre', *Der Kampf*, 20 (1927), 191–5 (p. 193).
37. See ibid., 194.
38. See Rosa Mayreder, *Zur Kritik der Weiblichkeit: Essays* (Jena, 1905), pp. 102–38.
39. These are part of the Rosa–Mayreder–Nachlass which is kept at the Manuscripts Department, Vienna City Library, Zuw. Prot.–Nr. 264/51–3.
40. Mayreder, *Tagebücher*, p. 160.
41. See ibid., p. 226.
42. See Meisel–Hess, *Das Wesen*, p. XVII.

Otto Rank and the *Doppelgänger*

Andrew Webber

Foreword: The Strange Case of Dr Rank and Herr Rosenfeld

Otto Rank occupies an ambivalent position in the history of psychoanalysis: ambivalent, one is tempted to say, in the psychoanalytic sense of the term. The strategy of returning to Freud by turning his own positions back on him is of course by now commonplace, in particular in terms of the feminist critique of Freudian ideology. Much post-Freudian debate has taken the form of the two-way traffic of variations on what Freud identifies, in the case of Dora, as a primary vehicle of psychic defence: returning criticism by way of the 'Retourkutsche' (Freud VI, 112; cf *SE* 7: 35).[1] For theoretical purposes, the domestic scenes around the psychoanalytic couch have been largely superseded by sophisticated variations on this technique of discrediting critics of psychoanalysis.

The 'case' of Otto Rank, which was recorded only after the event in the casebook of the Freudian establishment, was one of the earliest and least auspicious instances of such trafficking. Strongly bound to his mother, rejecting his father, the young Otto Rosenfeld exchanged his Judaic patronymic for that of a character from Ibsen's *A Doll's House* who suffered from congenital syphilis. Rank's imagination was visited by Ibsenesque ghosts of the father's sins (as doubtless also by the real-life spectre of Austrian *fin-de-siècle* anti-Semitism). In terms of the power structures of the Freudian circle, he gravitated from the role of the master's fostered son, secretary, and lieutenant, to that of a heretic with no clinical training. The prodigal son was even deemed a suitable case for analysis by the more zealous champions of Freudian orthodoxy. The construct of the Oedipus complex proved particularly amenable to being returned on the renegade, whose 'psychosis' was diagnosed by the fathers of the Freudian academy as being rooted in a pathological 'Vaterablehnung' ('rejection of the father').[2]

When Rank during his American exile sketched out a brief history of psychoanalysis, he challenged the received idea of Freud the founding father in a telling rewriting of the 'family romance' of the psychoanalytic movement. He named Breuer as father and claimed that psychoanalysis 'found a tender and loving foster-mother in the person of Sigmund Freud' (Lieberman, p. xxvii). Encoded in this transsexual subversion is not merely a challenge to the primacy of Freud, turned from progenitor into surrogate nurturer, but also an indication of a key element in Rank's 'Oedipal revolt': his objection to the phallocentric strain of psychoanalytic theory. In an unlikely way Rank, the Nietzschean and erstwhile admirer of Weininger, thus adumbrates the feminist critique of the patriarchal constructions of Freudianism. This latter-day Oedipus threatened the authority of 'the father' precisely by denying the totemic primacy of the Father and the phallus as inscribed in the founding Oedipal myth. By asserting, in his *Trauma der Geburt* ('Trauma of Birth', 1924), the pre-Oedipal separation from the mother at birth as the primal psychic trauma, Rank rendered the fear of castration at the hands of the prohibitive father (for Freud the crux of the primal scene) a secondary effect.[3] The revolt, which cost him his Freudian licence, anticipates the shift towards the side of the mother in the Kleinian wing of post-Freudian analysis (not least in terms of Rank's desire to emancipate the effects of maternal transference in the analytic situation). The theoretical revival around Lacan, on the other hand, has tended to revert to the phallocentric bearing of Freudian orthodoxy. The trauma of parturition is typically derived anachronistically from that of the separation of the 'supreme signifier' or 'kingpin' of the Symbolic order that is the phallus.[4]

It is only recently that the role of Rank, the prodigal son in the family romance, has begun to be rehabilitated, and this very much from the side of the American analytic establishment (where he eventually found a successful exile) rather than the French. The charge of 'Vaterablehnung' levelled by such Freudian patriarchs as Ernest Jones has been refuted (along with those of paranoia, narcissism, and excessive masturbation). Indeed it may be seen to be emasculated in a preemptive way by a basic plank of Rank's position: the rejection of the overriding principle of paternal transference.

If this account was introduced by the word 'ambivalent', then this involves the sort of love-hate dialectic which abounds in Freud's Oedipal triangle. And 'filial love' was certainly the first term of the double-bind; in the first instance, Rank's work is clearly bound to that of his mentor. Where it departs from Freud it is less in outright antagonism than by shift of emphasis; the scandalous schism was primarily an effect of personality cults and clashes. The principal difference, though, lies in Rank's disposition and training. Unlike Freud, the scientific practitioner, Rank applies his analysis mainly to culture and its effects rather than to the personal psyche and its traumas. From the outset his work tended to privilege the phylogenetic perspective over the ontogenetic, and to seek its material in myths and their textual workings. Such work as he did on personal cases was piecemeal, operating very much within the parameters laid out by Freud in his praxis, and tending always towards the side of ego- rather than id-psychology. And it was the accommodation of Freudian models too, above all that of dream-work, which sustained Rank's mythopoeic readings of texts. If he claimed that 'Art is life's dream interpretation' (Lieberman, p. 25), then it is because he saw art as 'working out' the collective desires, violence, and traumas which are the stuff of myth. The onus is on the *work* of art, that is, the way in which it transforms the prime term of Freudian dream theory – 'Wunsch' – by the work of the 'Wille'. The Nietzschean principle of willed individuation enters into play here to temper the primacy of the instinctual. Rank's writing is accordingly informed by a vitalistic spirit, one which is able to affirm the creative agency of the ego, not least where it is contingent upon the power of illusion (in religion and art). The paradigm is given by Rank's assertion that aesthetic creativity is a sublimated form of narcissistic investment, allowing the artist to renounce "'the egoistic principle of self-perpetuation in one's own image" and substitute for it "the perpetuation of the self in work reflecting one's personality"'.[5] The aesthetic working of mythical experience is thus in the first place a reworking of the myth of Narcissus, seen by Rank as the 'real inventor of painting', converting the passive, self-absorbed projection of an image into an active recreation of the self. The aesthetic act is thus akin to the 'creative act of the person' (Lieberman, p. xxviii) as rebirth.

For Rank dream-life was also the product of narcissistic creativity, and he set out to align the means of production in dream, myth, and art. In his *Psychoanalytische Beiträge zur Mythenforschung* (1919), the principles of Freud's 'Traumdeutung' are applied extensively to the psychological structures of myth.[6] As Freud had distilled essential mechanisms of dream production out of multifarious material, so Rank's analytic mythology organizes the variety of mythical narrative according to a series of topoi. The recurrent scenarios of mythical experience are correlated with Freud's system of psychic rites of passage. As dreams narrate personal fantasy in strategically distorted forms, so myths are read by Rank as the distorted vestiges of the collective fantasy of whole nations: 'die entstellten Überreste von Wunschphantasien ganzer Nationen' (R 4). Myth works out desires repressed when they met prohibition in the 'childhood' of their respective cultures, but in a compromised and substitute form as 'Ersatzbefriedigung' ('surrogate satisfaction'). The development of myth and fairytale is seen as 'ein *Negativ der Kulturentwicklung'* ('a *negative of cultural development*', R 380), representing, that is, what culture denies or inhibits but also serving to sustain the development of culture as 'positive'. This dialectic is only possible by dint of dissimulation. 'Myth-work' is produced by analogy with the 'Entstellung' of Freudian dream-work: 'Wir finden in der Mythenbildung die aus dem Traumstudium bekannten Mechanismen der Verdichtung, der Affektverschiebung, der Personifizierung psychischer Regungen und ihrer Spaltung oder Vervielfachung, endlich auch die Schichtenbildung wieder' ('In the formation of myths we encounter mechanisms familiar from the study of dreams: condensation, the displacement of affect, the personification of psychic motions and their splitting or multiplication, and finally the stratification', R 5).

The key function of myth-formation for present purposes, however, runs counter to this scheme of things. For it is a consequence of the narrative extrapolation of mythical scenarios that the condensation which operates in the dream economy is offset by the story-telling principle of attenuation. The essentialized mythical structure is complicated by the counterpoint of repetition, above all in terms of the duplication of character, motif, and action. The creation of myth and legend obeys a general principle of 'spinning out a simple schema' (R 231) through the doubling of various components. While dreams tend to condense their drama and dramatis personae into overdetermined configurations, which duly have to be spun out in the service of interpretation, this process is both reflected and reversed in the case of myth. Here, Rank notes 'daß die Doublettierung, manchmal auch Vervielfältigung einzelner mythischer Figuren in der Regel mit der Verdoppelung oder Vervielfachung ganzer Sagenepisoden einhergeht, die man erst wieder zur Deckung, man möchte sagen zur Verdichtung zu bringen hat, die ihnen im unbewußten Phantasieleben zukam' ('that the doubling, sometimes also the multiplying, of individual mythical figures is accompanied as a rule by the duplication or multiplication of whole episodes of legends, so that one has first to restore the coextension, one might say the condensation which characterized them in unconscious fantasy-life', R 17). This counter-movement indicates that Rank is working at a further remove from the original locus of the psyche. If Freud's work on dreams involved processes of discursive transcription of the essential 'stuff of dreams', interpreting that is by way of dilution, Rank works on structures which are more radically inseparable from the extensive weave of their narrative forms and from the cultural consciousness in which these circulated. But there is also a potential for these forms to reflect analytically on their origins. This is the conclusion drawn from the case of 'Der Doppelgänger' (1914), in terms of the foregrounding of the erotic element in the latter-day literary workings of the mythically conceived figure: 'mit besonderer Betonung der in der Urgeschichte noch nicht so deutlich hervortretenden libidinösen Faktoren, die jedoch einen Rückschluß auf die undurchsichtigeren Urphänomene gestatteten' ('with particular stress on the libidinal factors, which did not emerge so clearly in the original story, but might afford insight into the opaque original phenomena', R 349).

Rank's study of the *Doppelgänger* as mythical archetype and literary motif exemplifies the difference between the two directions of psychoanalytic work, as it works both ways, recreating and undoing condensation. At the same time it shows up the problematics of applying an essentializing mythological imagination to the variegated narrative workings and reworkings of the archetype. Rank's assertion that the doubling of character operates in tandem with a doubling of narrative structure indicates a perception of the *narratological* implications of his enterprise, but, as we shall see, this is not generally borne out in his readings in the case of the *Doppelgänger*.

The Case-history of the *Doppelgänger*

The *Doppelgänger* may be said to be intrinsic to psychoanalysis and its origins. In the theories of mesmerism and magnetism which circulated around the turn of the eighteenth century, the double was seen as an embodiment of the 'nocturnal side' in the Romantic science of the self, and duly appeared as such in contemporary fiction. The main source is Schubert, who, as Rank notes, disseminated the idea of the somnambulist or dream-self as double (R 300). Having gone underground during the hegemony of nineteenth-century positivism, the *Doppelgänger* made its return in the theories of such as Dessoir, deriving in part from the renewed psychiatric interest in the power of hypnosis.[7] The second self of Dessoir's 'Doppel-Ich' is a potential other within, the

'Unterbewußtsein' ('subconscious') as manifest in dreams, hypnotic trance, mystical ecstasy, madness, and poetry. This other self is potentiated and projected in the act of creative writing as 'Externalisation'. The double is thus conceived both as a hypostatic forerunner of the psychoanalytic unconscious and as figuring the 'other self' of aesthetic creation.

It is Todorov's contention that Rank's theoretical appropriation of the double did away with its literary potential, that the *Doppelgänger* returned at the beginning of this century only to die a definitive death.[8] With reference to Rank, Kittler certifies the death of the Romantic double but suggests that it found new haunts as the ultimate in 'Filmtricks' on the cinema screen.[9] In fact, the literary double is a stubborn revenant and duly returns after the event of Rank's essay, where it arguably eludes the exorcism of comprehensive analysis anyhow. The *Doppelgänger* which returns to fictional life in Musil's *Man without Qualities*, for instance, may be cast ironically between Romantic fantasy and its denial, but then the classic *Doppelgänger* of E. T. A. Hoffmann are no less dialectically complicated.[10] The certifications of death are premature as long as Realism may still be predicated on magic.

Rank begins his account with something of a pre-text. His aim is to operate a parallel reading of the *Doppelgänger* motif in myth and modern literature, that is, to locate the literary treatment within its ethnological origins. But the first 'text' is perceived as being more thoroughly dislocated from those origins: the populist narrative of an early film, Ewers's Romantic drama *Der Student von Prag* ('The Student from Prague'). The 'banal' point of access by means of 'eines so sehr auf äußerliche Wirkungen angewiesenen Schaustückes' ('a spectacle so dependent on external effects', R 267) might nonetheless have the potential of partaking in the master narrative of psychoanalysis. The new form may in fact be closer to the originary myth than the more sophisticated literary versions, and the modern means of representation paradoxically simulate the most original form of psychic text, the dream. What will elude discursive means may be recuperated in the 'sinnfällige Bildersprache' ('palpable pictorial language', R 268) of film. As Freud, in his *Interpretation of Dreams*, transcribes the pictographic narrative of dream into discursive form, so Rank is no less bound by considerations of representability. Discursive transcription of the scenario will capture the 'schattenhaft flüchtigen ... Bilder' ('images as fleeting as shadows', R 268), and in the process start the work of interpretation. As is invariably the case with *Doppelgänger* stories, the *Student von Prag* is a tale of *flight* from *shadows*. The flight of shadowy images in filmic representation is all the more apposite when the fugitive is pursued by the shadow, the projected image, of himself (Figure 1). The most modern medium thus rejoins the earliest, the magic lantern as projector of alter egos in the first *Doppelgänger* tales of the Romantic era.

The 'spectacle', far from being too 'pictorial', points to the first principle of doubling from its Gothic heyday onward: the double is spectre and spectacle, a visually compelling figure which above all represents the power of the *imaginary* to enthral or to terrorize. The *Doppelgänger* hero has the terrible faculty of the 'zweite Gesicht', or 'second sight', in its original sense of seeing

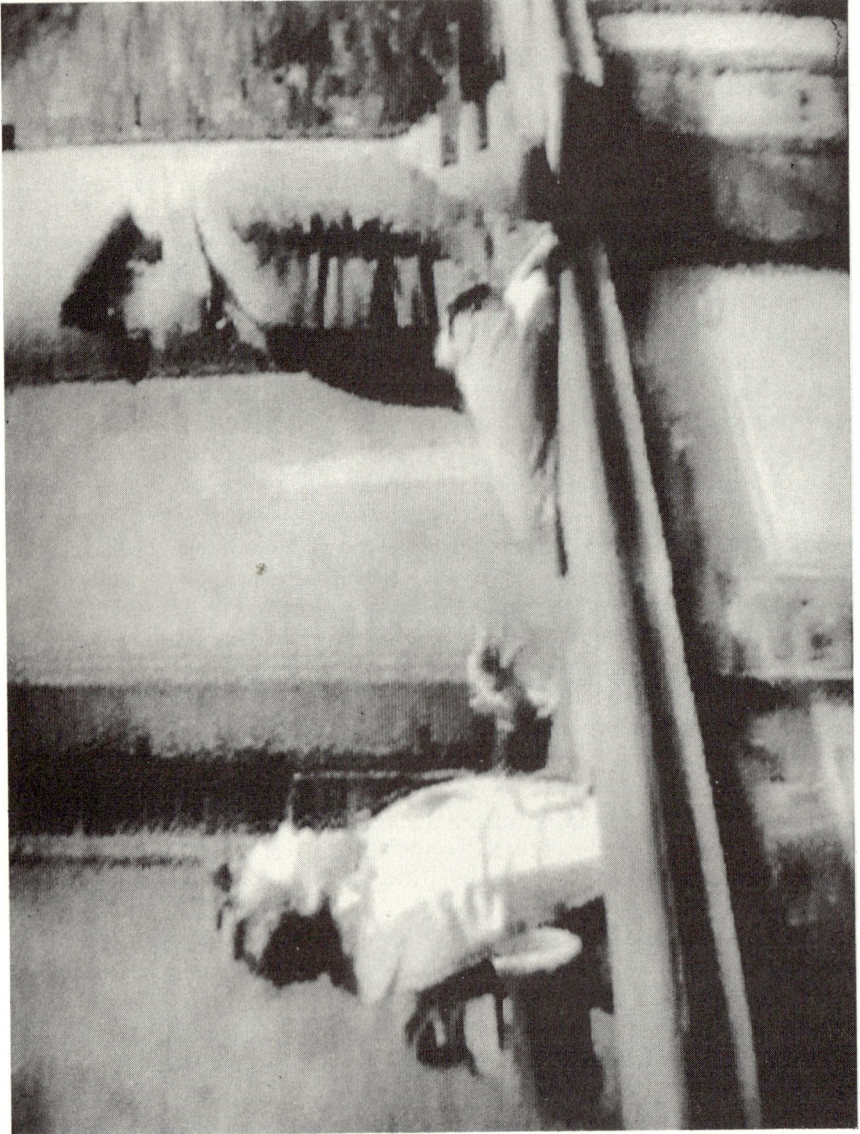

Figure 1. The student (Paul Wegener) is visually terrorized by his *Doppelgänger* (also played by Paul Wegener).

Figure 2. The *Doppelgänger* interrupts the embrace of the student and the countess (Grete Berger) in the Jewish Cemetery.

the self twice (R 315), as in Jean Paul's *Hesperus,* cited by Rank, where the double mortifies the beholder 'wie mit einem Basiliskenblick' ('as if by the gaze of a basilisk', R 301). This power, still inhibited in the *Student von Prag,* an early costume-drama film, comes fully into play in the classic 'Gothic revivals' of Expressionist cinema. If the early film, in its mutism, foregrounds 'das Urproblem des Ich' ('the primal problem of the self', R 271) by lending it such a powerful visual language, then this revives what Rank elsewhere defines as the primary motor of myth, 'Schaulust' or scopophilia. Rank follows Freud in taking the 'Urszene' – the primal arena of 'Schaulust' – as setting the scene for the interplay of interdiction and transgression in myth (R 231). He also emphasizes the spectacular principle of drama (and cinema, one might add, *a fortiori*) as 'Schauspiel' (R 85). In the *Doppelgänger* myth the scopophiliac drive of the primal scene is diverted onto the self, which beholds itself auto-erotically as other. And as Rank points out, from its anthropological origins as shadow, the double is invested with the sort of ambivalence which attaches to the taboo object.

Given that it is autoscopic desire which motivates the 'Schauspiel' of so many of the double's classic literary appearances, Rank might have clinched the tripartite focus of myth, literature, and film by pursuing the question of visual mediation in each form. As it is he limits himself to a survey of the literary manifestations and the anthropological sources of the motif, glossing texts in pursuit of a rather basic typology. The main functions derived from the *Student von Prag* are, firstly, that the double stands allegorically for past experience and, secondly, that the alter ego typically intervenes to frustrate the desire of his host (Figure 2). At least implicitly there is also a recognition that the narrative operates according to the principle of 'doubling' ('Doublettierung') which Rank identifies in mythical narratives. He does not, however, note the fact that the doubling is reflexive in character: thus, the enigmatic gypsy girl Lyduschka follows both the student and his beloved as a double shadow, and the student is both pursued by his *Doppelgänger* and rehearses its motions, emerging from behind the tombstone and from behind the tree bearing the double's murder-weapon as his 'shadow' had before him. These reflexive projections indicate that the priority of self over other self is radically at issue. Accordingly, flight and pursuit collapse in the final sequence; the student flees desperately in a coach only to discover that he is being driven in his flight by his *Doppelgänger*. As is so often the case in the *Doppelgänger* scenario, the return home involves dispossession from it, as the 'unheimlich' ('uncanny') is shown to be resident there; it was after all from the domestic mirror that the uncanny double was produced. The coach proves to be a sort of 'Retourkutsche', doubling the attempt at defence back on itself. Freud characterizes the mechanism as a projection, whereby an original is 'doubliert' (Freud VI, 112; cf. *SE* 7: 36). As the student restores himself to his home and his mirror-image, shooting the interloper, it transpires that the murder-shot in self-defence has also been returned. This reflexiveness anticipates what will be Rank's essential proposition: what might be called the '*double*-bind'. By asserting that the repressed returns through the process of repression ('Wiederkehr des Verdrängten im

Verdrängenden', R 340), Rank anticipates Freud's thesis of the dialectic involvement of the domestic and the uncanny in *Das Unheimliche* (1919).

It is worthwhile to read intertextually between *Der Doppelgänger* and *Das Unheimliche* (Rank notes Freud's essay in his 1919 edition, and Freud refers to Rank as a precedent). In either case the main recourse is to the master of the uncanny tale, E. T. A. Hoffmann. While Rank glosses a number of Hoffmann's *Doppelgänger* stories, Freud focuses on a reading of *Der Sandmann* ('The Sand-Man'). This controversial reading has been one of the most popular points of return to Freud; a series of post-Freudian critics have reread the case of the *Sandmann* with and against Freud. The major point of contention has been Freud's selective reading and reduction of the tale's uncanny effects to the castration complex. Rank, the anti-Oedipal son, on the other hand, works rather on the side of narcissism and death. An optimal study of the uncanny potential of doubling would integrate the two tendencies. While Freud is arguably reductive in his readiness to take the eye for the phallus, his discussion of the scenes of spectral enthralment and optical exchange would be eminently applicable to a whole series of Rank's cases.

Both accounts are marred by a naive grasp of narrative form. While Rank seems to take the question of form and reader response for granted, Freud takes issue with formal strategies in a way which underscores the discrepancy between his radical challenge to received ways of reading stories for their content and his readerly conformism on the level of narrative means. One of the key arguments of Freud's essay, taking its cue from Rank, is that repetition is a common denominator in the repertory of uncanny effects. On the one hand replication is associated with traumatic loss on the model of the castration complex: 'Die Schöpfung einer solchen Verdopplung zur Abwehr gegen die Vernichtung hat ihr Gegenstück in einer Darstellung der Traumsprache, welche die Kastration durch Verdopplung oder Vervielfältigung des Genitalsymbols auszudrücken liebt' ('The creation of such a doubling in defence against destruction has its corollary in a mode of representation of the language of dreams which tends to express castration through the duplication or multiplication of the genital symbol', Freud, IV 258; cf. *SE* 17: 235). The correlation points to Rank's resistance to the castration dogma, even as he identifies the shadow as symbolic stand-in for virility (in 'Stellvertretung für die männliche Potenz', R 320), and its lack with the threat of impotence (R 322). Characteristically, Rank has equal regard for the double as agent of paternal authority, operating in the image and/or the name of the father (R 319), and the derivation of its erotic and mortal double aspect from the 'mother complex' (R 336). Though Rank does not pursue the point, the classic *Doppelgänger* narratives of Hoffmann and Jean Paul are informed by just such a double agency. The pursuit of self-identity is divided between matriarchal and patriarchal instances, and the doubling of the self is a function of the doubling of the parents as anti-mother and anti-father.

Repetition is also associated by Freud with the ambivalent desire for return to the womb as the primordial object of homesickness. Once more the bearing of his argument is Oedipal. While Rank's birth trauma asserts the priority of the loss of the primal 'home', Freud stresses the erotic, giving priority to the genital accessing of the intra–uterine fantasy (Freud, IV 266; *SE* 17: 244). In Freud's account the site of birth is thus only traumatized *a posteriori* (as if by the retrospective, psychic principle of 'Nachträglichkeit').

Freud's appeal to castration symbolism underpins a general, paradoxical principle of repetition as representing loss defensively. He looks forward here to *Beyond the Pleasure Principle* and the drive beyond pleasure of the repetition compulsion. Yet his reading of Hoffmann's *Elixiere des Teufels* ('The Devil's Elixir') abides very much on the near side of the pleasure principle. In his readerly displeasure Freud gives the text and its serial repetitions short shrift. There is no sense here that the 'beständige Wiederkehr des Gleichen' ('the constant recurrence of the same', Freud, IV 257; *SE* 17: 234) may actually serve the uncanny purposes of the narrative. What textual 'Doublettierung' does here is to operate as *mise-en-abyme*, projecting the master narrative back into itself, and thereby questioning the whole idea of narrative mastery. If Freud registers the mixture of readerly pleasure and terror in being made to view things through the perspective of the 'demonic optician', in *Elixiere des Teufels* the perspective of double and multiple vision is trained very much on the spectacle of compulsively recurrent violence.

Rank is more sympathetic in his account of the *Elixiere*, granting Hoffmann the 'poetic licence' for his multiple doublings. He also notes the fetishistic investment of the desired image: 'die Erotomanie, die sich an das nur flüchtig geschaute Bild der Geliebten knüpft' ('the erotomania which attaches to the fleetingly glimpsed image of the beloved', R 277). No less than in the *Sandmann*, the image and other simulacra come to take the place of the object of desire; in either case the *Doppelgänger* is integral to a circuit of potent optical illusions. At the same time the *Doppelgänger* thematics of the *Elixiere* turn on what Rank sees as the fundamental conflict of subjectivity, that between 'individuation' and 'generation' (Lieberman, p. 199). The characteristic haunting of revenant doubles represents the regeneration of past guilt and disorder in terms of congenital identifications. As the origins of identity are displaced from the self onto its originators, so the self is constituted as double.

The common lack of regard for the narrative potential of repetition is all the more counter-productive, given the fact that the *Doppelgänger* embodies for both Rank and Freud the dialectic between the drives of narcissistic self-preservation and of mortal aggression. Rank characterizes the double in its origins as entelechy: the soul in the image of the bodily self, affirming the idea of its metaphysical presence. But as the shadow as psyche takes its form from the mortal body, so it marks the body out for death. The original ambivalence which attaches to the totemic power of the shadow and surrounds it with the prohibitions of taboo is borne out in the literary manifestations of the double as shadow, mirror-image, or portrait. The traumatic loss of the other self, which is so often the subject of *Doppelgänger* narratives in the mould of Chamisso's *Peter Schlemihl*, is frequently turned into paranoiac pursuit. The exalted narcissistic investment of images of the self is seen to lend these a pathological power over the self when they assert their autonomy as the self's primal lack: 'So erklärt sich der scheinbare Widerspruch, daß der Verlust des Schatten- oder

Spiegelbildes als Verfolgung durch dasselbe dargestellt werden kann' ('This explains the apparent contradiction, that the loss of the shadow or mirror-image may be represented in terms of being pursued by it', R 340).

The derivation of paranoia from narcissism is Freud's, and for both Freud and Rank narcissism, conceived as a primary magic circle of infantile fantasy, is of key significance. Not only can the resources of its 'Allmacht' ('omnipo-tence') be reflexively revisited on the self through its crazed projections, but the part which narcissism has in every investment of libido ensures that its ambivalence is always in play in the operation of desire. Narcissism is thus the linchpin for Freud's triangle of dialectic relations between the drives of Eros, death, and the ego. The myth of Narcissus furnishes the model for the confused rivalry of drives on this ternary model. And as the avatar of the *Doppelgänger*, Narcissus also stands as model for the self-reflexive fantasies of the *Doppelgänger* heroes in Rank's account. In this sense the double can be regarded in psychoanalytic terms as the figure of this triangular double-binding. Rank accounts for the pathological exertion of the fear of death in the *Doppelgänger* host, by the component of 'verdrängter Libido' ('repressed libido', R 345) involved in the narcissistic disposition.

The key psychic reality at stake in the *Doppelgänger* game is desire. If Rank diagnoses 'Erotomanie' as operating in tandem with paranoiac fantasies in Hoffmann's *Elixiere des Teufels*, then this is part of the psychosexual problematics which invariably afflict hosts to the literary *Doppelgänger*. The main bearing of Rank's interpretation of the *Student von Prag* is the way in which the double interrupts the hero's desire. The interruption is redoubled by Lyduschka as the shadow of the countess: 'und beide Doppelgänger stellen sich zwischen das Heldenpaar, um es zu entzweien' ('and both doubles intervene between the hero and heroine to bring them apart', R 271).

Rank's argument is that the disturbance of the *Doppelgänger* hero is narcissistic, and that this is bound to resist the self's 'Aufgehen in der Geschlechtsliebe' ('absorption in sexual love', R 345). The apparently antago-nistic agent might thus serve the subliminal desire of the self to defer consummation. It is also Rank's contention (citing the case of Dorian Gray) that the narcissistic resistance is bound up with repressed homosexuality (an intrinsically narcissistic 'condition' for early psychoanalysis).[11] Most recently, Elaine Showalter has pursued this argument in relation to the patriarchal shadow-world of *Jekyll and Hyde*.[12] It is certainly true that the *Doppelgänger* is an almost exclusively male preserve, but it is an unreliable double agent in the service of male pleasure.

For the purposes of Rank's pathographic reading, *Doppelgänger* are sympto-matic of narcissistically determined disorders in the authors who created them. The third section of the essay is a sketchy case-book of such personality disorders. The mottoes at the head of the section set out the principle that, in Schlegel's terms, '"Dichter sind doch immer Narzisse"' ('"Every creative writer is a Narcissus"', R 299). The writer is seen as making a self-reflexive fiction or a play of himself. The most catastrophic examples of the motif are duly seen to be scripted by the gravity of the author's disorder. While Rank sees aesthetic creativity as continuous with neurosis, the compulsive return of the *Doppelgänger* under its dark aspect is symptomatic of authorial neurosis beyond the necessary 'measure' (R 300).

A lone example of such measure is given: the eminent case of Goethe and the well-known instance from *Dichtung und Wahrheit* ('Poetry and Truth') where he encounters a double as he leaves Friederike in Sesenheim: 'Da überfiel mich eine der sonderbarsten Ahnungen. Ich sah nämlich, nicht mit den Augen des Leibes, sondern des Geistes, mich mir selbst, denselben Weg, zu Pferde wieder entgegenkommen' ('Then I was surprised by a most bizarre intuition. For I saw, not with the eyes of my body, but with those of the spirit, my very self, coming back the same way towards me on horseback', R 304). However bizarre, Goethe's encounter is anything but uncanny; the strange 'illusion' rather affords him 'reassurance' in the moment of parting. This is something of a sanitized anti-double, viewed retrospectively as a harbinger of love's restoration, without any uncanny confusion of real vision and the illusory projection of the psyche. The double returns not as ghastly revenant or erotic rival but as a figure of prospective recuperation of lost experience in a more successful guise. This as it were represents the double in its original benevolent aspect, as 'protective spirit' and narcissistic supplement to the self's wishes. In its secondary form, common to almost all the texts under Rank's scrutiny, the double is rather a supplement in the sense that Derrida gives to the word, not so much fulfilling the self as marking its deficiency. It is thus afflicted by the same, frequently terminal, discrepancy between plenitude and lack as is its host. If the double enters into rivalry with the self, it is because it too suffers from lack, even as it imitates the self's bravado gestures of potency. This is the real implication of Lucka's point that the shadow is deficient as a duplication by virtue of its lack of sight ('das Fehlen des Blickes').[13] In fact, the essential deficiency is designed to reflect upon the impaired vision of the original from which it is cast.

Such examples as that from *Dichtung und Wahrheit* are grist to the mill of Kittler in his essay on Rank and the *Doppelgänger*, where he sets out to debunk the psychoanalytic appropriation of the figure as psychosexual fantasm. He has to read rather tendentiously in order to tailor the myriad manifestations of the Romantic double to his theory that it is essentially a 'Schreibtischgespenst', visiting the writer at his desk and thereby displacing the creative act. It is certainly the case that, to customize Kittler's words, there is both more and less to the double's appearances than is dreamt of in psychoanalytic theory, and his emphasis on their social and textual production is useful. Indeed, the argument could be extended to the level of intertextual reproduction, given that the double returns not only within texts but also from text to text. Such key permutations as the hapless Schlemihl figure (R 273) and the sinister magus (in the mould of Coppola) recur throughout the literature and are revived in early cinema (in their intertextual life they in a sense return to their original status as myth). On the other hand, Kittler's focus on technical reproducibility diverts from a more general phenomenon in which it has part: the fact that the *Doppelgänger* not only doubles vision, but also discourse. The beguiling image of Narcissus is accompanied by the voice of Echo. Thus, what Rank calls the 'Amphitryonmotiv'

(R 278), the playing of a part to the end of erotic usurpation, also takes the form of vocal mimesis in the novels of Jean Paul.

If the double is indeed (*pace* Lucka) 'lacking' as a sentient being, the trauma of self-recognition may be said to reside as much in the failure to see or hear the self as in hearing or seeing another in its place. Thus, in Rank's discussion of Maupassant (R 286), the terror of the double's anagnorisis is twofold. The initial terror lies in being unsighted to the mirror-image, as it is blanked out by the intervening negative of the double's invisible and yet 'impenetrable body'; but this terror is tellingly compounded when the image of the self does indeed emerge, mediated by the disappearance of the *Doppelgänger*. The double-bind is such that there is terror both in the absence of the self-image and in its re-presentation. Hence also the dilemma of Dostoevsky's Mr Golyadkin, who can assert his difference from his *Doppelgänger* only by expressing his own essential alterity in the identical form of a doublet: '"Er ist ein anderer Mensch, Ew. Exzellenz, und auch ich bin ein anderer Mensch!"' ('"He is a different person, Your Excellency, and I too am a different person!"', R 297).

In such encounters alterity and identity collapse. They illustrate most forcefully the unresolved dialectic at the core of Rank's theory of the *Doppelgänger*. In conclusion Rank returns to his thesis of the reversion of the repressed through the mechanism of repression. In many of the *Doppelgänger* stories this is shown to take the form of a pre-emptive suicide. The doubles' compulsive return paradoxically represents the eternal prospect of no return for their dispossessed hosts ('ihres ewigen, ewigen Nichtmehrwiederkommens', R 345); and suicide, as the only means of forestalling the fateful imposition of death, closes the circle of repressive self-defence catastrophically back upon itself. This 'strange paradox' is commensurate with that which constitutes the *Doppelgänger* figure in the conclusion to Rank's account:

> Auf der anderen Seite kehrt aber in denselben Phänomenen der Abwehr auch die Bedrohung wieder, vor der sich das Individuum schützen und behaupten will, und so kommt es, daß der die narzißtische Selbstliebe verkörpernde Doppelgänger gerade zum Rivalen in der Geschlechtsliebe werden muß oder daß er, ursprünglich als Wunschabwehr des gefürchteten ewigen Unterganges geschaffen, im Aberglauben als Todesbote wiederkehrt. ['On the other hand the threat against which the individual wants to protect and assert himself returns in these same phenomena of defence; so it is that the *Doppelgänger,* which embodies narcissistic self-love, must come to be a rival in sexual love, or that, in spite of its original conception as a wishful defence against the feared eternal oblivion, it returns in superstition as a harbinger of death', R 354.]

However rudimentary his textual glosses may be, Rank isolates a fundamental dialectic here. And through its anticipation of analogous double-binds in subsequent Freudian and post-Freudian theory, Rank's case-book makes a crucial contribution to psychoanalysis in its cultural context.

Notes

1. References in the form 'Freud VI, 112' give the volume and page number of the Sigmund Freud *Studienausgabe,* ed. Alexander Mitscherlich, Angela Richards and James Strachey, 11 vols (Frankfurt, 1972). Translations are my own, but references are also given to *The Standard Edition of the Complete Psychological Works of Sigmund Freud* (identified as *SE* followed by volume and page number).
2. Ernest Jones in a letter quoted in E. James Lieberman, *Acts of Will: The Life and Work of Otto Rank* (New York, 1985), p. 223.
3. Otto Rank, *Das Trauma der Geburt und seine Bedeutung für die Psychoanalyse* (Leipzig and Vienna, 1924).
4. See for instance: Anika Lemaire, *Jacques Lacan* (London, 1977), p. 145.
5. Otto Rank, *Beyond Psychology* (New York, 1958), p. 99.
6. Otto Rank, *Psychoanalytische Beiträge zur Mythenforschung* (Leipzig/Vienna, 1919); includes reprint of 'Der Doppelgänger' (pp. 267–354); henceforth referred to in text as R.
7. Max Dessoir, *Das Doppel-Ich* (Leipzig, 1890).
8. Tzvetan Todorov, *Introduction à la littérature fantastique* (Paris, 1970), pp. 168–9.
9. Friedrich Kittler, 'Romantik – Psychoanalyse – Film: Eine Doppelgängergeschichte' in J. Hörisch and G. C. Tholen (eds), *Eingebildete Texte: Affairen zwischen Psychoanalyse und Literaturwissenschaft* (Munich, 1985), pp. 118–35.
10. For further discussion of the 'Doppelgänger' in Musil, see my *Sexuality and the Sense of Self in the Works of Georg Trakl and Robert Musil,* MHRA Texts and Dissertations, vol. 30, Bithell Series of Dissertations, vol. 15 (London, 1990).
11. See Rank's own 'Beitrag zum Narzissismus', *Jahrbuch der Psychoanalyse,* 3 (1911), 401–26.
12. Elaine Showalter, *Sexual Anarchy: Gender and Culture at the fin de siècle* (New York, 1990).
13. Emil Lucka, 'Verdoppelungen des Ich', *Preußische Jahrbücher,* 115 (1904), 54–83 (p. 67).

Freud, Musil and Gestalt Psychology

Hannah Hickman

In the years following the rediscovery of Musil's work after World War II, a lively debate arose concerning his possible indebtedness to Freud. His first novel for instance, *The Confusions of Young Törless*(1906), was seen by some scholars as a classic example of the Oedipus complex.[1] Harry Goldgar describes it as 'probably the earliest novel [...] to show specific Freudian influence', assuming as he does that Musil would have read Freud's early works immediately upon publication.[2] Annie Reniers on the other hand points out that at the time of writing Musil does not mention Freud in his notebooks, whereas other writers on human and animal psychology are discussed.[3] Certain features of the novel are shown to be already present in Musil's early sketches entitled *M. le vivisecteur,* probably written at the same time as the publication of Freud's *The Interpretation of Dreams* (1900); thus it would be preferable to speak of affinities rather than influence.

Karl Corino examines Musil's life and work from the psychoanalytical point of view, but agrees that direct influence is unlikely.[4] It appears probable that Musil knew Weininger's *Sex and Character* (1903). In a letter written in 1906, long after completion of the novel, he mentions 'French psychiatrists', perhaps Janet and Charcot, whose works he may have read by then.[5] The debate concerning *Törless* and Freud continues: in a recent paper Andrew Webber considers the novel in the light of Freudian and post-Freudian psychoanalysis, with particular reference to Lacan.[6]

While psychoanalytical interpretations are illuminating, it may be argued that they do not give a complete view of the work: by focusing attention through a particular frame of reference, they divert attention from two essential features. One of these is Musil's epistemological preoccupation with questions of perception and expression, which was to lead him to study experimental psychology in Berlin from 1903, that is, during the time he was writing the novel. The other is the poetic use of imagery as an integral part of the text, to express the principal themes of perception and expression, of growth and of the role of emotion.[7]

Imagery is again vitally important for the narrative of 'The Perfection of a Love', the first of the two novellas Musil published in 1911 under the title *Unions*.[8] However, it is the second novella, 'The Temptation of Quiet Veronica', which according to Corino documents Musil's increasing knowledge of psycho-analytical theory.[9] After comparing successive versions of the text, he concludes that the author had probably read Freud and Breuer's *Studies in Hysteria*, and Bleuler on ambivalence. In his view, changes were made in the final version to remove any appearance of Freudian influence.[10] Jacqueline Magnou shows that Musil knew works by Janet, Binet and Ribot, and his unpublished papers include excerpts on personality disorders as well as on apperception and the psychology of emotion.[11] David Midgley, in a recent paper, draws attention to the significance of metaphor in this novella, which he interprets as a deliberate attempt by the author to transcend the limitations of 'conceptual ordering of psychopathological (and other intellectual) insight [...] what the literary text itself is expressing through its dynamic sequence of metaphors is a perception of psychic activity which is at once stimulated and repelled by such fixed concepts.'[12]

In 1911, the same year as the novellas, Musil published the essay 'Obscenity and Disease in Art' as a contribution to a current public debate on censorship. He argues that if a writer chooses subject-matter which may be described as obscene or diseased, he presents it in its relations to other phenomena in order to make the reader or spectator understand it both intellectually and emotionally. This is not so very different from the methods of science, where understanding is also based on establishing analogies and connections. Art, like science, seeks knowledge; it presents that which is obscene and diseased in its relationships with that which is decent and healthy, and so increases understanding of the latter. This process in the artist's mind must then be echoed in the mind of the recipient, who, by receiving this artistic whole, will benefit from the purifying effect of art, which lifts the original subject-matter into a higher, more general sphere. Art, if it has any value, reveals things hitherto only seen by a few.[13] Not only *Törless* and the two novellas, but also Moosbrugger, Clarisse and other figures in *The Man without Qualities*, may be regarded in this light.

Thus by 1911 Musil had probably read some works by Freud and other authors in this field. In addition we find references to or excerpts from Konstantin Oesterreich on psychiatric case-studies, and Ernst Kretschmer.[14] Musil kept himself informed in this as in other areas of scientific enquiry, since he insisted on basing his creative work on knowledge, if relevant knowledge was available. Once the preparatory work had been done, the process of creative writing took over, as he describes in the essay of 1911. Yet his personal comments on psychoanalysis were always guarded, to say the least. He was certainly prepared to acknowledge that it had lifted the previous taboos on discussion of sexuality which had blighted many lives: 'that is its immense civilizing achievement' (GW II, p. 832). On the other hand he condemned the uncritical acceptance of psychoanalytical theories by many creative writers, who conversely paid no attention to academic psychology because they were ignorant of its possible uses (ibid., p. 1221).

In *The Man without Qualities* he presents psychoanalysis and Marxism ironically as opposites:

'Over there is one of those Marxists, [explains the general] he maintains [...] that man's economic basis entirely determines his ideological superstructure. And he is contradicted by a psychoanalyst; he maintains that the ideological superstructure is entirely a product of his instinctive basis' (GW I, pp. 1019–20).

In Musil's last published book, *Legacy in My Lifetime* (1936), he includes a satirical sketch: 'Oedipus in Danger'. Here, he begins by praising psychoanalysis, apparently in good faith, for restoring to the individual time to be himself in the midst of the daily rush. Where? On the analyst's couch. Then he considers the significance of the Oedipus complex, the little boy's desire to return to the warm nest of his mother's lap. But where, asks Musil, is the lap nowadays? Not in a ski outfit and certainly not in a bathing costume. Soon Oedipus will be homeless: shall we then have Orestes instead?[15]

Some critics may regard such persiflage as mere self-defence against possible Freudian interpretation of Musil's own life. Be that as it may, there can be no doubt of his opposition to the *'psychologia phantastica'* of Klages, Freud and Jung, his 'instinctive enmity: because they are pseudo-poets' (TB I, p. 787). He felt himself and his work threatened by the widespread acceptance of a body of writing that was not science, in his rigorous understanding of the term, nor yet literature, but which nevertheless claimed the status of eternal truth.

Musil's Studies in Berlin

Musil had good reasons for his dismissive comments about psychoanalysis, for he had found in Mach and Gestalt psychology more fruitful lines of enquiry which directly contributed to his own conception of the form-giving function of literature. Musil was a qualified engineer trained to make exact observations and precise discriminations. When in 1903 he gave up his engineering post at the Technological University of Stuttgart, he moved to the University of Berlin to enrol as a doctoral student at the Institute of Psychology, also reading philosophy, physics and mathematics.

The choice of philosophy and psychology as principal fields of study naturally follows the direction of his reading over the preceding years. In Notebook 4, in 1902, he mentions Kant, Nietzsche, and Ernst Mach's *Popular Scientific Lectures* (1896), as well as three studies of animal psychology.[16] This notebook also contains a series of sketches, probably dating from 1900, entitled *M. le vivisecteur*. The term vivisection in the sense of psychological investigation was used by Nietzsche, Dostoevsky and Strindberg, whose work Musil knew. In the first piece, 'Pages from the Night Book of M. le vivisecteur', the writer looks out from his window at night: he sees nothing but white spaces and feels isolated, as if under a thick layer of ice, or like a mosquito imprisoned in rock crystal. He begins to analyse his own reaction. At night, in contrast to the day, he can be honest with himself: he can act as his own historian or become the researcher observing himself as an organism under the microscope (TB I, pp. 1–3).

In 'The Street' this becomes more specific. If he sets himself a logical problem, his mind functions normally; but as soon as he turns to that strange part of his mind which functions not logically but by fits and starts, that which is called the life of the spirit, or the nerves, or by other names, then he is startled. He sees through things and through people, and senses the mysterious processes of a secret life (ibid., pp. 8–10).

Musil's notebooks bear witness to his life-long interest in the workings of the human mind. At this time the study of psychology was still closely linked to philosophy. Ever since the publication of Wilhelm Wundt's *Contributions to the Theory of Sense Perception* (1858–62), perception had been an important focus of research. Carl Stumpf, Musil's professor, had previously concentrated on the perception of sounds; after his appointment to the chair at Berlin his laboratory expanded into a large and important institute. He was joint founder of the Berlin Society for Child Psychology, and set up with Erich von Hornbostel (whom Musil knew) the gramophone archives for records of primitive music.[17]

E. G. Boring traces the development of two opposing approaches in this new science, whose leading centres were Leipzig and Berlin. Wundt, at Leipzig, developed 'an introspective psychology of sensory elements that enter into associations and other combinations [...] and may be characterized as the psychology of *content*'.[18] The other school, led first by Franz Brentano and then by Stumpf, gave primacy to psychical *acts* such as sensing, imagining, judging, perceiving, recalling, and the phenomena of loving and hating (Boring, p. 351). Stumpf later accepted both act and content as a part of perception. Edmund Husserl meanwhile developed what he called phenomenology, a discipline that deals with pure consciousness by a method of immanent inspection. His book *Logical Investigations* (1900), dedicated to Stumpf, influenced the latter's views. In 1907 Stumpf set out his theoretical position as follows (Boring, pp. 357–60):

> 1. First there are the *phenomena*, sensory and imaginal data like tones, colors and images.
> 2. Then [...] the *psychical functions* [*acts* for Brentano]: perceiving, grouping etc.
> 3. Thirdly the *relations* [within or between phenomena, e.g. relations of coexistence, of sequence or of difference]
> 4. Finally [...] Stumpf created a special class for the immanent object of the functions, and called these objects *formations* [*Gebilde*].

In this way Stumpf brought phenomenology into psychology, and soon his pupils began experimental work leading to a new departure in psychology, substituting the term 'Gestalt' for Stumpf's 'Gebilde'.

'Gestalt' may be translated as configuration, pattern, form, structure or shape, but is used in psychology in a special sense. The concept Gestalt means that out of the spatial or temporal association of sense data something new can arise, which cannot be explained by reference to the separate elements alone. Musil's definition of the term in his last essay, 'The Writer and Literature' (1931), gives as examples the four sides of a square or the notes of a melody. He emphasizes:

their unique relationship to one another, which is indeed what makes the Gestalt, and which possesses an expressive force that cannot be explained by the expressive possibilities of the separate elements [...] One might also say that they form a whole, but it must be added that they do not make a cumulative whole, but at the moment of coming together they produce a special quality that is different from that of their elements.[19]

Before examining the implications of Gestalt psychology in more detail, it may be useful to look at Musil's Notebook 24 (1904-5), which records his studies in Berlin. Visual perception was at the centre of his experimental work in the laboratory. He states a theory by Helmholtz relating to the psychology of colour vision, the relationship of stimuli and the possibility of additive combination, and proceeds to work out the implications mathematically (pp. 121–3, 126). Much space is devoted to discussion of Husserl's *Logical Investigations*: probability, causality and logic; perception of colours and spatial relationships, particularly of a drawn figure bounded by six parallelograms, which may come to be perceived in three dimensions as a 'hollow box'. The British philosopher David Hume is also mentioned.[20]

Aldo Venturelli, in his book *Robert Musil and the Project of Modernism*, points out that since the pioneers of Gestalt psychology were working at the institute at the same time as Musil, Notebook 24 provides useful pointers to the topics being debated there.[21] Musil concentrates above all on Husserl's central problem, the relationship between logic and psychology:

The question is first of all: Is logic to be treated psychologically? Or metaphysically? Or is there a third possibility?
The characteristic feature of logic in my sense would be that while admittedly it does not operate with definite values, yet it has a tendency to do so, i.e.behaves as if...[22]

On the whole, Musil reacts critically to Husserl; where Husserl makes categorical statements concerning the validity of logical laws, Musil concludes that truth is not objective, but relative to the context. The relationship between truth and this context can therefore be investigated experimentally, at least in visual perception.[23] He also considers Husserl's investigation of 'Expression and Meaning', whose theme is that the logic of our language determines the conceptual expression of our thinking. Musil starts from the multiplicity of meanings of every statement. For example, the sentence 'A. travels' can have various meanings according to the nature of A. and the type of travel. Once all these factors are known, their reciprocal interaction determines the meaning of the statement. He concludes: 'In other words, the judgement is not a third factor separate from the reciprocal modification'.[24] However, he accepts Husserl's view that logical laws cannot be based on simple associations of feelings, rather they are extremely complex acts of thinking (Venturelli, p.124). In notes on Sigwart's *Logic*, Musil again considers the relationship between the whole and the parts, this time with regard to language:

The word requires its completion in the sentence, the sentence in the paragraph, the paragraph in the whole. It is a continuous connected impression, probably individually varied according to the whole.

Certain sequences of thoughts are only possible because each [part] points beyond itself.[25]

Musil's experiments included sessions with the tachistoscope, an apparatus that allows a researcher to test the attention span of a subject by showing sequences of letters for short, exactly controlled periods (TB I, p.125). He also constructed another test apparatus for his friend Johannes von Allesch, later professor of psychology at Göttingen. This was a chromatometer or colour wheel: two coloured discs, each of which is slit along one radius, are mounted on a motor-driven rotating axle in such a way that the coloured surfaces relate to one another in the desired ratio. The wheel is then set in motion, and as soon as the rotation speed is high enough, the eye perceives the intended colour mixture. Musil's chromatometer was a great improvement on the one previously in use, since in contrast to the latter it was made entirely of metal and equipped with numbered scales for exact setting. It was subsequently manufactured by a firm in Göttingen and used in all European psychological research laboratories.[26]

Musil's doctoral thesis, *A Contribution to the Assessment of Mach's Theories*, was completed in 1908. Mach, who had contributed since the 1860s to experimental psychology, was a leading positivist thinker. His book, *The Analysis of Sensations and the Relation of the Physical to the Psychical*, was not widely noticed in 1886; between 1900 and 1902, however, it was published in three new editions. Originally a physicist, Mach argues that things, bodies, materials cannot be perceived except through the complexes of colours, sounds etc. by which they strike the senses; analysis of the sensations received from the outside world is thus the only way to gain knowledge of phenomena. For him, all phenomena of the inner and outer world consist only of a small number of similar elements; the supposed entities, 'body' and so on are therefore only tools or concepts we invent to help us during the process of orientation. In the same way the self is only a concept invented as a tool for thinking purposes; in reality it has no separate existence.[27]

These theories attracted widespread attention. The problem of the relationship between body and mind seemed to have been solved at a stroke: there was no mind! Musil now undertook a systematic examination of Mach's position. At the beginning of the thesis he sets out Mach's theories. Mach argues that the laws of nature do not imply necessity but only relationships. In future science should be seen in the light of evolutionary theory, providing concepts to help human beings adapt to their environment. The problem of the connection between physical and psychical aspects of life is now irrelevant.[28]

While Musil concludes that Mach's theories cannot be generally accepted, he welcomes them as a clear exposition of modern scientific thought. He supports the evolutionary approach and the use of mathematical and inductive methods (Thesis, pp. 13, 19, 31). However, he refuses to accept Mach's definition of mind as nothing but a concept. If there is no mind, who or what does the thinking? According to Musil, the case for monism has not been proved: therefore the mind survives (ibid., pp. 118–20).

There can be little doubt that Musil had to respect the views of Stumpf, who firmly upheld the distinction between mind and matter and emphasized psychical functions. In fact, Stumpf declined to accept the thesis on first submission and only accepted it in 1908 after revision.[29] After graduation Musil was offered an assistant lectureship at the foremost Austrian institute for experimental psychology at the University of Graz. For an academic career this would have provided a splendid beginning, but after three weeks of intense reflection he decided in favour of becoming a full-time writer, a decision he later questioned on more than one occasion (TB II, pp. 893–4).

The Development of Gestalt Psychology

The idea of Gestalt in the psychological sense was anticipated by Mach. In 1886 he investigated sensations of space, of vision, of time and of sound, pointing out that two short but different melodies may have the same rhythm, a likeness that we sense immediately. The same applies in sensations of space, for instance with two circles identical in size but of different colour. The two circles have the same shape in space, whereas the two melodies have the same shape in time. Later he uses the example of a melody which, transposed into different keys, still remains the same melody, and describes the two versions as sound structures having the same sound shape.[30]

Four years later Christian von Ehrenfels raised the question whether the sound shape of a transposed melody was merely a combination of separate elements, that is, the notes, or something new. Was the whole different from the sum of the parts? He concluded that it was indeed something new, and called this new factor Gestalt-quality.[31] Ehrenfels had worked in Graz under Alexius von Meinong. Notebook 24 includes an excerpt from Stephan Witasek, also in Graz; Musil remarks that the principle of Gestalt-quality is accepted as proved. The notes show that the act of perception is here understood as a *process* (TB I, pp. 131–2; II, pp. 75–6).

It was this conception of the mind not as a passive recipient of sensations, but as actively engaged in psychical functions that led to the establishment of Gestalt psychology. Max Wertheimer (whom Musil knew personally) undertook in 1912 an investigation of perceived movement. Wolfgang Köhler and Kurt Koffka were the principal observers; all three were pupils of Stumpf. Later, Köhler described the experiment:

> When a visual object, for example a line, is shown briefly in one place and almost immediately afterwards a second [...] line appears in a second place, not too distant, an observer does not see two objects appearing in quick succession at their two places; rather he sees one object moving rapidly from the first to the second place.[32]

Wertheimer investigated the conditions under which this apparent movement appeared. In his book Köhler also refers to the cinema. The objects shown in a film never move while the individual pictures are shown; thus the film consists of a sequence of many different pictures at rest. The movements seen by the audience are therefore all apparent movements (ibid., p. 39).

It is worth remembering here a passage in Musil's *Törless*, written at the same time as Notebook 24. Numerous images in the text use the inadequacy of surface vision to perceive the whole of outer reality, to represent the discrepancy between our conscious awareness and unconscious aspects of our being. Törless, watching Basini, experiences

> a restlessness and uneasiness [...] such as one feels in front of a cinematograph, when, beside the illusion of the whole, one still cannot shake off a vague perception that behind the picture one receives, hundreds of – essentially quite different – pictures are flitting past. (GW I, p.91)

Wertheimer, Köhler and Koffka declared that the movement observed in experiments must be regarded as a Gestalt and not as a 'bundle' of sensations. The concept of wholeness is the cardinal principle of Gestalt psychology: '[it is] a unitary structure, in which the change of any part changes the whole, and conversely' (Boring, p. 578). This principle was repeatedly stated by Musil with regard to language, and also with reference to human life: 'Utopia means that experiment in which we observe the possible modifications of an element and the consequences these modifications would have for the composite phenomenon that we call life'.[33]

Köhler (originally trained as a physicist) spent the years 1913–17 studying the psychology of apes. In 1920 he published *Physical Gestalten at Rest and in the Stationary State*, in which he demonstrates the existence of Gestalten in electrostatic structures, going on to argue for the existence of Gestalten in the psychological domain.[34] Another finding of Gestalt research is that when groups of similar objects are observed, they increasingly appear simple and symmetrical to the observer. Köhler links this phenomenon with known facts concerning the behaviour of materials and forces within a *physical* system or field when it approaches a state of equilibrium (Köhler 1969, pp. 55–62).

Musil mentions Köhler's book of 1920 in the essay 'The Helplessness of Europe' (1922), an attempt to take stock after the horrors of World War I and to plead for a new, realistic outlook based on science. Commending the book, Musil writes that such a work, starting from a factual basis, is able to suggest solutions to ancient metaphysical problems.[35]

Köhler, Koffka and Wertheimer all emigrated to the United States of America after Hitler came to power; as a result their later works are written in English. However, Köhler had already published an English-language introduction to Gestalt psychology, to demonstrate its advantages both over introspectionism and over behaviourism (founded in 1913). He attacks Descartes's view of the human organism and its functions as mechanical, asserting that dynamic interaction plays an essential part in sensory processes. He discusses sensory organization, for instance, the way in which, in vision or sound, the brain distinguishes significant patterns or figures against their background. Another chapter considers the properties of organized wholes.[36] Köhler's last book, *The Task of Gestalt Psychology* (1969), contains a particularly clear exposition of the thinking process. He stresses the importance of relationships not only in visual perception but in all problems with which we may be confronted. Sometimes we cannot solve a problem without discovering *new* relations. Once the material has been restructured by the brain, a solution presents itself, often quite suddenly. It is remarkable that such insights, sought without success during periods of active work, tend to occur at moments of extreme mental passivity, in 'the Bus, the Bath and the Bed'.[37]

Musil intended to include in Book II of *The Man without Qualities* a short treatise on the psychology of emotion; although this plan was later abandoned, the excerpts made in preparation are illuminating. Authors represented include Koffka, Freud (two pages of notes on *Civilization and its Discontents*), Jung, William Stern, Kurt Lewin and others, as well as numerous titles (TB II, pp. 583–4). In addition, he always kept Köhler's book of 1920 to hand. Stern is known as the founder of personalistic psychology. Lewin was a pupil of Stern and in his work expanded the concept of Gestalt into a field theory of human behaviour. Another application of the theory was in the area of education, whereby learning came to be understood not as a mechanical process of passively absorbing impressions from outside, but rather as a process of actively structuring in the mind information as it is acquired.[38]

Such theories may clearly be applied to everyday life. A baby learns to stand: she pulls herself up, holds on to the furniture, lets go and stands for a second; the whole process is repeated over and over again for several weeks. It may take months before she has learnt this sequence; after that the action becomes intuitive, or in other words, it becomes a Gestalt. The child has no need to think about it any more; she uses a mental formula, described by Mach as an economical aid in adapting to one's environment. Such a formula therefore helps us to cope with life. At a higher level we find more complex skills in sport, in playing instruments or for instance in driving a car. The exact sequence of actions required, changing gear and so on, is in fact a Gestalt; once you have mastered it, you execute it automatically. Indeed, it can then be confusing to think about it too much or to explain the separate steps to a learner.

In *The Man without Qualities* Arnheim uses the example of playing a shot at billiards for such a complex action which, if you try to analyse it while carrying it out, is bound to go wrong (GW I, p. 570). In preparatory notes for this chapter Musil criticizes the indiscriminate use of the word 'intuition' by contemporaries, asking sarcastically: 'Is it therefore my soul that plays billiards?' He draws a careful distinction between true intuition and complex motoric skills that must be amenable to the intellect and are clearly envisaged in terms of Gestalt theory (TB II, pp. 1163–9). When Arnheim concludes: 'The decisive processes of life occur beyond the intellect. The greatness of man is rooted in the irrational', the author's irony is aimed at contemporaries who will not make the effort to think clearly. His distinction between the irrational and what he calls the 'non-rational' domain of personal relationships, religion, mysticism and art is set out in many essays.

Musil's Application of Gestalt Psychology to Life, Language and Literature

According to Gestalt theory, the brain organizes external phenomena into ordered structures. Language fulfils a similar function. Musil refers to the ancient belief that possession of the magic word affords protection against the untamed wildness of things 'out there'; myth and fairy-tale abound in examples (GW I, p. 1088). Words help us to cope with life: 'what appears immense and alien while our words reach out to it from afar, becomes simple and loses its disturbing aspect as soon as it enters the active sphere of our life', he writes in *Törless* (GW II, p. 65). Indeed one of the central themes of the novel is the essential need for all human beings to find expression for their deepest concerns, although the converse, that certain experiences cannot be put into words, is given equal weight. Young Törless only reaches maturity when he learns to achieve a balance between these two aspects of life.

Musil considers the making of mental formulas with regard to language, similar to those employed in performing complex actions, and finds them in intellectual as well as emotional language behaviour. We make up formulas for ourselves, often to save time and effort, sometimes to avoid distressing thoughts. The term 'war' for instance does not begin to describe what actually happens in a war. He speaks of the importance for every person of 'shaping' his or her life content. Neurotics are often incapable of structuring their mental contents, or of devising their own life-saving formulas (GW II, pp. 1219-21). Several of the characters in Musil's fiction suffer from profound difficulties in expressing themselves to others or even in organizing their own thoughts, sometimes with tragic consequences. The worst case is that of the psychopath Moosbrugger in *The Man without Qualities*. Moosbrugger, a murderer, is defenceless against the outside world because he cannot think clearly himself, much less understand the language of the lawyers and psychiatrists in charge of his case. He is quite incapable not only of abstract thought, but even of understanding the conventional phrases of everyday life (GW I, pp. 253–42).

A very different figure is Claudine in 'The Perfection of a Love', who at first seems entirely normal, but whose life, in the course of three days, undergoes a profound and unexpected crisis (GW II, pp. 156–94). In notes made at the time of writing, Musil discusses in psychological terms the relationship between perception, emotion and the individual's sense of self-worth, which he defines as a state of equilibrium between emotionally coloured inner and outer worlds. This equilibrium is a vital ingredient of personality, if alienation is to be avoided. Claudine's crisis arises from the sudden emergence of just such a feeling of alienation, as Musil predicts, if the equilibrium is disturbed. Her agonizing sense of isolation and of lack of meaning in her life is vividly conveyed (TB II, pp. 927–34).

Field theory has been identified as an integral part of Gestalt theory: the relationship of observed phenomena to one another and to the background; in terms of language, the significance of context. Musil's early comments on the relative nature of truth recur later: 'There are truths but no truth' (GW I, p. 1835). Ulrich, in *The Man without Qualities,* surveys his world, suspecting that its order is not as solid as it pretends to be:

The value of an action or a quality, indeed their intrinsic nature seemed to him to depend on the circumstances that surrounded them, the goals that they served, in a word on the whole of which they formed a part, constituted now in this way, now in that. (GW I, p. 250)

He speaks of a field of force in which all moral events derive their meaning from its constellation: a murder may be seen as a crime or an heroic deed, according to the circumstances, and so on. In this infinite system of interacting connections, a human being is envisaged as the embodiment of his or her possibilities rather than as a settled character. In the same way Ulrich regards accepted morality not as something rigid, but as a 'dynamic equilibrium' that requires constant effort to keep it in balance (GW I, p. 252).

Thus Musil uses the idea of dynamic interaction in describing Ulrich's revolutionary view of life and society. At the same time he is very much aware of the significance of Gestalt theory for writing. Words irradiate one another, he states in 1925.[39] He frequently reflects on his aims as a writer, and it is the determination to shape his material, to find the appropriate form, which makes the artist. The writer's task is for him an ethical one: even at the age of nineteen he notes: 'To stylize is to see and teach others how to see' (TB II, p. 813).

In 1931 he analyses the way a poet operates, choosing an example from Goethe and comparing it with an earlier version, to demonstrate how the poet arrives at the final result (GW II, p. 1212). For English-speaking readers we may take an example from Blake: 'Tiger, tiger, burning bright / In the forests of the night'.[40] A prose version might read: 'The tiger has flame-coloured fur and prowls through dark forests.' But the poet conveys his meaning by a simple rhythm, by using rhyme, and most of all, here, by choosing a graphic metaphor, 'burning bright', and thus renders his vision of the tiger unforgettable.

Musil shows that in arriving at the perfect version, the poet instinctively chooses that arrangement of words which will most vividly convey his meaning. The musical rhythm and the actual sound of the words are all essential parts of this whole. Once the final version is found, none of the individual details may any longer be changed. None of them counts on its own, any more than one side of a square would do. But 'from all of them together and from their interaction with one another, the whole evolves in a way that remains mysterious.' After reading first the preliminary and then the perfect version, we find:

> that the quite tangible contraction which these sentences show at the moment of the right arrangement of words, that the unity and form which takes shape almost at a stroke in place of the diffuse earlier version, is not so much a sense experience as a change of meaning beyond the realm of logic.

He points out that this change of meaning is the central element in all writing, whether prose or verse. It may be seen as an axis round which all details are arranged, or the focus of a circle round which the whole revolves. Musil always thinks in terms of a whole, a structure, but one which must never be inflexible:

'The structure of a page of good prose is [...] not anything rigid, but the swinging of a bridge that changes the further you go' (GW II, pp. 1212–13).

Shaping the meaning or structuring the content is essential to all writing: 'form and content have a unity that cannot be completely dissected' (ibid., p. 1218). Marie-Louise Roth, in her book *Robert Musil. Ethik und Ästhetik,* quotes Musil's term 'gestaltendes Denken', which may be translated as creative thinking, from notes on visual art.[41] There is no space here to list the many other references in his work to the ideas of Gestalt psychology, whether in respect of writing or of the wider implications.

In 'Theoretical Aspects of the Life of a Writer' (1936), he considers several areas of a writer's work (GW II, pp. 965–74). He seeks to distinguish between psychology in writing on the one hand and academic psychology, as well as psychoanalysis, on the other, defining the relationship between the two domains: 'Literature does not convey knowledge [...] But: literature makes use of knowledge [...] And in fact of the inner world [...] just as much as of the outer one'. Recalling the intense effort of writing *Unions,* he finds in himself at that time a turning away from realistic or naturalistic writing to truth, from psychology to something different. Truth is relative. 'The task of literature is not to depict what is, but what ought to be; or what might be, as a partial realization of what ought to be.' What are the distinguishing features of genuine literature? A closely-woven texture, purity of the Gestalt, avoidance of all superfluous elements, and greatness of language: we recognize a poet on the very first page (ibid., pp. 970–1).

Musil's ethical purpose in all his writing becomes clear from reading his notebooks and essays. When he writes of depicting what might be, as a partial realization of what ought to be, we recall Notebook 24, where he describes his own logic as based on the 'as if' principle. When Ulrich defines a human being as an embodiment of his or her possibilities, we recall the young Musil's study of how a definite judgement, a Gestalt, is reached out of the multiplicity of possible meanings. The poetic Gestalt created by the writer expresses a new meaning, whether in the actual arrangement of words, or in the organized structure of poem, novel or drama. Literature can show us new possibilities and suggest new possible solutions to human problems. Jeanette Winterson, a novelist of our time, writes: 'The story builds a bridge from incoherence to order [...] Art doesn't impose an order where there is none, rather it often suggests an order we have overlooked.'[42] For Musil, creative thinking implies 'organization in depth', and literature 'gives meaning. It is interpretation of life' (GW II, p. 970).

Notes

1. Robert Musil, *Die Verwirrungen des Zöglings Törleß, Gesammelte Werke,* ed. Adolf Frisé (2 vols, Reinbek, 1978), II, 7–140. Further references will be to GW I or GW II.

2. Harry Goldgar, 'The Square Root of Minus One: Freud and Robert Musil's *Törleß'*, *Comparative Literature,* 17 (1965), 117–32 (p. 118).

3. Annie Reniers, 'Törleß: Freudsche Verwirrungen?', in *Robert Musil. Studien zu*

seinem Werk, ed. Karl Dinklage (Reinbek, 1970), pp. 26–39 (pp. 27–9).

4. Karl Corino, 'Oedipus oder Orest? Robert Musil und die Psychoanalyse', in *Vom Törleß zum Mann ohne Eigenschaften*, eds. Uwe Baur and Dietmar Goltschnigg, Musil-Studien, vol. 4 (Munich-Salzburg, 1973), pp. 123–235.

5. Ibid., pp. 156-7. Letter of 21 December 1906.

6. Andrew Webber, 'The Beholding Eye. Visual Compulsion in Musil's Works', in Hannah Hickman (ed.), *Robert Musil and the Literary Landscape of His Time* (Salford, 1991; obtainable from the editor, Dept. of Mod. Langs., University of Salford, M5 4WT, England).

7. See also Hannah Hickman, *Robert Musil and the Culture of Vienna* (London and Sydney, 1984), pp. 28–54.

8. *Vereinigungen*, GW II, pp. 156–223; 'Die Vollendung der Liebe', pp. 156–94.

9. Ibid., 'Die Versuchung der stillen Veronika', pp. 194–223.

10. Corino, 'Oedipus', pp. 174–80.

11. Jacqueline Magnou, 'Grenzfall und Identitätsproblem (oder die Rolle der Psychopathologie) in der literarischen Praxis und Theorie Musils anhand der Novellen "Vereinigungen"', in *Sprachästhetische Sinnvermittlung. Robert Musil-Symposion, Berlin 1980*, ed. Dieter Farda and Ulrich Karthaus (Frankfurt, 1982), pp. 103–13 (p. 109).

12. David Midgley, 'Writing against Theory: Musil's Dialogue with Psychoanalysis', in *Musil and the Literary Landscape*.

13. 'Das Unanständige und Kranke in der Kunst', GW II, pp. 977–83.

14. Robert Musil, *Tagebücher*, ed. Adolf Frisé (2 vols, Reinbek, 1976), I, 180–1, 785; II, 115–17, 565–6. Further references will be to TB I or TB II.

15. *Nachlaß zu Lebzeiten*, GW II, pp. 471–562, 'Der bedrohte Oedipus', pp. 528–30.

16. TB I, p. 13. The authors mentioned are G. J. Romanes, K. Groos and K. Lange.

17. E. G. Boring, *A History of Experimental Psychology* (New York and London, 1929), pp. 354–6.

18. Ibid., pp. 377, 423–4.

19. 'Literat und Literatur', GW II, pp. 1203–25 (p. 1218).

20. TB I, pp. 119-21; Edmund Husserl, *Logische Untersuchungen* (2 vols, Halle/Saale, 1900-1), 1, Chs 4, 7 and 9.

21. Aldo Venturelli, *Robert Musil und das Projekt der Moderne* (Frankfurt, Bern, New York, Paris, 1988), p. 117.

22. TB I, p. 127; Husserl, p. 68.

23. TB I, p. 121; Venturelli, pp. 120–4.

24. TB I, pp. 127–9; Venturelli, pp. 121–2.

25. TB I, p. 127; Christoph Sigwart, *Logik* (2 vols, Tübingen, 1873), I, 40–1.

26. GW II p. 942-5; photo on p. 943.

27. Ernst Mach, *Die Analyse der Empfindungen und das Verhältniss des Physischen zum Psychischen*, 2nd edn (Jena, 1900).

28. Robert Musil, *Beitrag zur Beurteilung der Lehren Machs* (Berlin, 1908); reprinted (Reinbek, 1980).

29. See Karl Corino, *Robert Musil. Leben und Werk in Bildern und Texten* (Reinbek, 1988), p. 142.

30. Mach, *Analyse*, pp. 5–21.

31. See Boring, pp. 434–5.

32. Wolfgang Köhler, *The Task of Gestalt Psychology* (Princeton, NJ, 1969), p. 35.

33. GW I, 246. Quoted by Jacques Le Rider, 'Between Modernism and Postmodernism', *Austrian Studies*, 1 (1990), 9.

34. Köhler, *Die physischen Gestalten in Ruhe und im stationären Zustand* (Braunschweig, 1920). Cf. Venturelli, pp. 145–9.

35. 'Das hilflose Europa', GW II, pp. 1075–94 (pp. 1075–82, 1085).

36. Köhler, *Gestalt Psychology* (New York, 1929), pp. 103–47.
37. Köhler, *Task of Gestalt Psychology* (1969), pp. 133–64, esp. pp. 154–64.
38. *Nachlaß-Mappe* VI/1: long excerpts from a work by Koffka, and Lewin: 'Untersuchungen zur Handlungs- und Affektpsychologie I. Vorbemerkungen über die psychischen Kräfte und Energien und über die Struktur der Seele'; 'Untersuchungen [...] II. Vorsatz, Wille und Bedürfnis', in *Psychologische Forschung*, VII (1926), pp. 294–329, 330–85 (N/M VI/1, pp. 135–48). Cf. TB II, pp. 1213–16. Venturelli (pp.160–9) relates these to chapters 52, 54, 55 of *Der Mann ohne Eigenschaften*, Bk. II. A letter of 28 October 1936 establishes the date of the Lewin notes; similar handwriting is found in all excerpts (including those from Freud's *Civilization and its Discontents*; Nachlaß-Mappe VI/I, pp. 156–7), so all probably belong to this period. Other references to Lewin in TB I, pp. 801, 873, 914.
39. 'Ansätze zu neuer Ästhetik', GW II, pp. 1137–54 (p. 1147).
40. William Blake, 'The Tiger', *Oxford Book of English Verse* (Oxford, 1939), p. 577.
41. Marie-Louise Roth, *Robert Musil. Ethik und Ästhetik* (Munich,1972), pp. 217–30, 426.
42. Jeanette Winterson, *The Guardian*, 29 September 1990, p. 11.
Note Translations from Musil's works and notebooks are my own.

Acknowledgements

I would like to express sincere thanks for photocopies of *Nachlaß* papers and transcriptions to the following research centres:

Arbeitsstelle für Robert-Musil-Forschung, University of the Saarland, Saarbrücken; Robert-Musil-Archiv, Klagenfurt. Parts of this article are based on preliminary studies presented at the International Robert Musil Sommerseminar, Klagenfurt, 1985.

Between Freud and Nietzsche

Canetti's *Crowds and Power*

Ritchie Robertson

Canetti's relationship to Freud is complex and ambivalent. His familiarity with Freud's work is unquestionable: from his autobiography we learn that in 1920s Vienna Freud so dominated the intellectual landscape that the uncovering of Freudian slips was part of everyday conversation.[1] So in 1925, when Canetti began the study of crowd phenomena that was to issue 35 years later in *Crowds and Power* (*Masse und Macht*, 1960), he naturally began with Freud's essay 'Group Psychology and the Analysis of the Ego' ('Massenpsychologie und Ich-Analyse', 1921). He tells us that, finding Freud's approach unsatisfactory, he made Freud into the antagonist whose opposing views provided him with intellectual stimulus. Only much later did he realize that he also needed Freud as a model, inasmuch as Freud had shown that it was possible for an individual to inquire into the fundamental laws governing human life. 'It was clear to me', says Canetti, 'that I needed him as an adversary. But the fact that he served as a kind of model for me – this was something that no one could have made me see at that time.'[2]

This is a revealing passage. First, it shows that, for Canetti, intellectual inquiry was agonistic, a struggle against an opponent. No wonder that some of the most arresting pages of *Crowds and Power* deal with the satisfaction of surviving. Second, it reveals the scope of Canetti's ambitions. Even if Canetti thought Freud mistaken in some ways, Freud had revolutionized the understanding of human nature, and Canetti intended no less. It is appropriate that his book culminates in an interpretation of the paranoid fantasies of Daniel Paul Schreber, for these fantasies owe their fame not only to Schreber's own book, *Memoirs of my Nervous Illness* (*Denkwürdigkeiten eines Nervenkranken*), but to Freud's interpretation of it in the essay 'Psycho-analytic Notes on an Autobiographical Account of a Case of Paranoia (Dementia Paranoides)' (1911). Canetti's study of Schreber may be seen as a re-writing of Freud's.

Although *Crowds and Power* was written to confute Freud, Freud's name does not occur in the text.[3] Neither does that of Nietzsche. In putting forward an interpretation of crowd phenomena different from Freud's, however, Canetti fell back on another tradition of crowd psychology, that associated with Nietzsche, and I shall point out various ways in which Freudian and Nietzschean strands mingle in Canetti's book. Its dual indebtedness (not to mention, of course, Canetti's vast reading in anthropology and mythology) makes *Crowds and Power* a rich but also a bewildering book. Sometimes Canetti seems to be interested in *origins*, in tracing civilized behaviour back to that of primitives and even animals. At other times he seems to be interested in *meanings*, in disclosing the unconscious significance of ritual and myth. Schematizing for the sake of clarity, I should like to discriminate between the biologistic (Nietzschean) side and the hermeneutic (Freudian) side of Canetti's enterprise.

Two Traditions of Crowd Psychology

The title of Freud's essay, 'Group Psychology and the Analysis of the Ego', is doubly misleading. Firstly: unlike William McDougall, one of the earlier thinkers whose work he acknowledges, Freud does not postulate a 'group mind'.[4] Instead, he is concerned with the changes undergone by each individual mind in a crowd; the crowd, for him, is no more than the sum of its parts. Secondly: in the course of the essay, Freud transfers his attention from the psychology of the mass ('Masse' is his word; Strachey's translation 'group' is hardly satisfactory) to the psychology of leadership. He takes it for granted that a crowd requires a leader, and argues that each member of the crowd is attached to the leader by libidinal bonds, regarding him as an unattainable object of love. The leader exercises a kind of hypnotic influence over the crowd, and this collective hypnosis enables members of the crowd to identify with one another. The crowd therefore represents a regression to the emotional structure of the supposed primal horde, in which a band of brothers were united by their ambivalent attachment to their father. Freud betrays his interest in leadership by illustrating the structure of groups ('Massen') from the Church and the army. These are highly inappropriate examples, since, instead of absorbing individuals into a relatively undifferentiated mass, the Church and the army separate them by rank and ritual, locating them within a system formed by actual and symbolic spaces.[5]

Freud's interest in leadership indicates the political origins of his interest in mass psychology. He is indebted to a conservative tradition of thought which saw the crowd as irrational and dangerous and as the motive force behind modern revolutionary upheavals.[6] The Paris Commune brought fears of a second Reign of Terror and encouraged the view that the violence of the crowd was the greatest danger to modern civilization. The crowd had to be brought under control, and the first step was to treat it as a medical problem. A number of thinkers elaborated a psychopathology of the crowd, and their theories were popularized by Gustave Le Bon, in a book which Freud cites extensively and with undeserved respect. Le Bon maintains that crowds have a collective mind, which resembles that of a hypnotized subject; that they are violent, fickle, incapable of reason, prone to collective hallucinations; in short, they display the qualities which 'are almost always observed in beings belonging to inferior forms of evolution—in women, savages, and children, for instance.'[7] The dominance of crowds since the French Revolution convinces Le Bon of the ineluctable decline of the race.

Canetti's own experience of crowds did not chime with Freud's or Le Bon's descriptions. According to his autobiography, he was first provoked into reflecting on crowd psychology by a demonstration in Frankfurt in 1922 protesting against the murder of Walther Rathenau. Canetti records two findings. One was that in joining the crowd he underwent a complete change of consciousness. The other was the physical attraction exerted by the crowd. These findings were confirmed and expanded by his experience of the riot outside the Palace of Justice in Vienna on 15 July 1927. This riot was provoked by a miscarriage of justice: some members of a right-wing paramilitary organization, accused of shooting a forty-year-old Socialist and a young boy during a political confrontation in a border village earlier that year, were tried and acquitted on 14 July by a slender majority of the jury. On the following morning, protest demonstrations were held in Vienna. The demonstrators were forced by mounted police away from Parliament into the square outside the Palace of Justice. The police fired from inside the building into the crowd, which eventually succeeded in forcing an entrance and setting fire to the building. Ordered by their chief to clear the square, the police continued to shoot into the crowd (thus also preventing firemen from saving the building, which was burnt to the ground). This incident, together with sporadic disturbances the next day, resulted in ninety deaths and over a thousand injuries. From his participation, Canetti concluded that a crowd did not, as Freud claimed, require a leader; he recognized the importance for a crowd of rhythm, and of destruction; and he saw how the fire kept the crowd in being by providing it with a focus.[9] All these features appear in the description of the open crowd at the beginning of *Crowds and Power*.

Besides criticizing Freud's essay for misrepresenting crowd experience, Canetti disagreed with its political assumptions and with its theoretical structure. While recognizing that Freud was writing in a political tradition of conservative hostility to the crowd as such, Canetti was inclined to take a more positive view of the crowd. Ernst Fischer tells us that in the early 1930s Canetti used to identify power with death, and to advocate 'return to the masses ['die Masse'], the absorption of the individual by the mass as a reprieve from death, as the principle of immortality'.[10] This dissolution of the individual into the crowd, according to Canetti, would be made possible by Communism, and would begin from Asia rather than Russia. As Fischer notes, Georg Kien maintains similar views in *Die Blendung (Auto-da-Fé)*.[11] Given the young Canetti's left-wing sympathies, it would seem that he saw mass existence as a way of overcoming the isolation of bourgeois society. *Auto-da-Fé* offers a despairing view of individual existence: most of its characters are locked in their private fantasies, incapable of communicating with one another. Although crowds are also shown in the novel to be dangerous (one of the characters is torn to pieces by a crowd), mass existence might well seem to offer the only prospect of redemption from solitude. Moreover, while Freud describes the crowd as hierarchical, subordinated to a leader, Canetti sees the crowd as a body of equals. The equality of the crowd's members is of such fundamental importance that 'one might even define a crowd as a state of absolute equality'.[12]

Canetti's theoretical objection is that Freud failed to recognize crowd experience as something elemental. Instead, Freud treated it as a problem in individual psychology and tried to analyse it away. For Canetti, however, the primary, elemental character of crowd experience was the insight that underlay all his work on the subject. He tells us how he suddenly realized 'that there is such a thing as a crowd instinct, which is always in conflict with the personality instinct, and that the struggle between the two of them can explain the course of human history'.[13] This conception of two opposed primary urges is basic to *Crowds and Power*. The book begins by describing fear of physical contact as a basic human trait, which produces the strict taboos against the violation of personal space, and gives a defensive character to houses and walls. But the spaces that separate people also imprison them, and the crowd offers a welcome release from such confinement. Therefore Canetti sees the urge to be separate, and the urge to join a crowd, as complementary and fundamental human impulses.

Although this construction separates Canetti from the Freud of 'Group Psychology', it does bring his theoretical structure close to the Freudian model of the mind, which assumes a conflict between two powerful 'instincts' or 'drives' ('Triebe'). In Freud's earlier work the principal conflict is between the sexual instincts and the ego-instincts or instincts of self-preservation. In 'Beyond the Pleasure Principle' (1920) Freud replaces this with a new dualism, that of the life-instinct and the death-instinct. Canetti's argument has the same structure, opposing a crowd instinct to a personality instinct (a version of Freud's ego-instinct). Despite its antagonism to Freud, therefore, *Crowds and Power* does not altogether escape from the Freudian framework.

Nevertheless, it should be stressed that Canetti is writing within a tradition of crowd psychology different from the conservative tradition of Le Bon and Freud. Canetti's distance from the Le Bon tradition has recently been emphasized by J. S. McClelland, who does not, however, locate Canetti within an alternative school.[14] This other tradition – no less problematic in its assumptions than the Le Bon school – includes Nietzsche and the English psychologist Wilfred Trotter, whose book *Instincts of the Herd in Peace and War* is cited in the bibliography of *Crowds and Power*. Nietzsche is important for his remarks on 'herd instinct' in the section of *Beyond Good and Evil* that offers a 'natural history of morals'. Nietzsche affirms that man is an animal; that man's behaviour is based on primitive instincts and drives ('Triebe') which are developed or distorted by civilization; and that the conventional morality of modern Europeans is simply an expression of the herd instinct.[15] The problem with these assertions is their ambiguous status. Is Nietzsche simply using bold images to continue the polemic against the German bourgeoisie that he began in *Untimely Meditations*? Or is he invoking modern biology in order to give his polemics the authority of science? Nietzsche's ambiguous use of metaphor has been defended as a cognitive instrument.[16] When one considers, however, how his quasi-scientific rhetoric was later taken literally and developed perniciously by theorists of race, it is difficult not to feel that Nietzsche's ambiguity is irresponsible.

Similar problems arise from Trotter's work. Trotter was the brother-in-law and close friend of Ernest Jones; from 1905 to 1908 Jones and Trotter were partners in a medical practice in Harley Street; and it was from Trotter that Jones first heard of Freud. However, Trotter's intellectual allegiance was to Nietzsche, under whose influence he became, according to Jones, 'the most extreme, and even blood-thirsty, revolutionary in thought and phantasy that one could imagine, though there was never any likelihood of this being expressed openly'.[17] *Instincts of the Herd* is in part a polemic of Nietzschean brilliance against 'the great class of normal, sensible, reliable middle age, with its definite views, its resiliency to the depressing influence of facts, and its gift for forming the backbone of the State'.[18] According to Trotter, conventional morality is an expression of the herd instinct. Individuals sensitive enough to resist it are condemned to isolation and mental instability. It is, however, dangerously anachronistic for this simple mental type to be in charge of complex modern society, and Trotter thinks it necessary for man to progress towards 'a gregarious unit informed by conscious direction', in which man's social instincts can be developed towards altruism and social cohesion.[19] He leaves the reader in no doubt that he is literally applying biological principles to human society. He criticizes Freud for accepting 'the human point of view' instead of founding psychology on biology.[20] In the part of the book written during World War I, he approaches absurdity by equating English society with the socialized gregariousness of the beehive and German society with the aggressive gregariousness of the wolf-pack. 'When I compare German society with the wolf pack, and the feelings, desires, and impulses of the individual German with those of the wolf or dog,' he tells us, 'I am not intending to use a vague analogy, but to call attention to a real and gross identity.'[21] Yet it remains possible, and indeed likely, that what Trotter calls an identity is no more than an analogy between human and animal behaviour, and that, less cautious than Nietzsche, he has been ensnared by his own metaphors.

There is no need to stress the harm that has come from the abuse of biological analogies. Vast numbers of people have been categorized as 'pests', 'parasites' or 'foreign bodies' and treated accordingly; while delusions about eugenic breeding have a perennial appeal. Jones tells us that Trotter, under Nietzsche's influence, toyed with the notion of breeding an improved race. Less harm, but considerable intellectual confusion, has come from modern sociobiology. Much popular sociobiology rests on a mistake similar to Trotter's. Animal behaviour is described by metaphors taken from human experience, such as 'aggression' or 'territoriality'; these metaphors are then applied once more to human behaviour and mistaken for statements of identity.[23] These confusions may be illustrated from the popular work of one of the founders of sociobiology, the Austrian Konrad Lorenz. His widely-read *On Aggression* is full of metaphorical statements presented as literal: geese fall in love, animals practise rituals and ceremonies, a jackdaw colony forms a circle of old friends.[24] The popularity of *On Aggression* seems to be a phenomenon similar to the popularity of Le Bon's *The Crowd* at the end of the last century. In both books, simple master concepts ('the crowd', 'aggression') give readers the illusion of understanding events which are bewildering and alarming. Vivid detail serves to obscure the dubiety of the arguments and analogies used. Both are works of cultural pessimism: Le Bon thinks that civilizations pass through cycles of growth and decay, and that the appearance of crowds signals an extreme stage of decline; Lorenz is indebted to Spengler for similar assumptions and thinks that modern democracy is a symptom of decay. Moreover, Lorenz illustrates the connection between biological analogies and sinister social policies. During the Nazi period, despite his professed indifference to politics, he strongly supported programmes of improving the race by eradicating alien and inferior elements.[25] In 1943 he explicitly advocated a scientifically based racial policy to arrest the degeneration of civilized man.[26]

Canetti must have been acutely sensitive to the possibilities of abusing biological analogies. In comparing his procedures to those of Lorenz, Dagmar Barnouw rightly points out how much more tentative Canetti is, and how anxious he is not merely to reduce human behaviour to manifestations of animal instincts.[27] Any writer in the Nietzsche-Trotter tradition, however, has to strike a very fine balance in order to retain the suggestive power of his analogies without slipping into biological reductiveness, or encouraging his readers to do so. If Canetti is more successful than either Nietzsche or Trotter in striking this balance, the reason may be that he is able to combine their tradition with that of Freud. Canetti's position between Nietzsche and Freud has implications both for the overall organization of *Crowds and Power* and for his detailed interpretations of his material.

Crowds and Power: Plots and Methods

The organization of *Crowds and Power* is elusive. Canetti is anxious not to reduce the richness of his material by squeezing it into a system. By his own admission, he did not want to arrive at any conceptual summation of his material.[28] Although the book's first two sections classify many different types of crowd and pack, with ample and detailed illustrations, the remainder tends to concentrate on examining particular ceremonies, practices, historical events, and myths, without making it clear what general thesis is being advanced – except the rather vacuous thesis that crowd phenomena and the will to power are virtually omnipresent in life. Canetti has largely chosen to renounce formal argument as a means of organizing his material. The other method of structuring and interpreting such diverse material is what Hayden White calls 'emplotment', that is, giving it a narrative form which produces both readability and 'explanatory affect' – the sense that, in being structured, the material has also been explained.[29] A number of plots could probably be discerned in *Crowds and Power:* I shall single out two, a Nietzschean plot and a Freudian plot.

The Nietzschean plot takes the form of a genealogy. As Nietzsche, in *The Genealogy of Morals,* professes to derive Christian ideals of virtue from the morality of ancient slaves, or the sense of guilt from the position of the debtor, so Canetti explains the modern crowd as an expansion of the primitive pack. In this procedure, a phenomenon found in modern society is equated with, and derived from, one found in earlier and arguably more primitive societies. It is a suspect procedure, because it depends on transforming an analogy between two phenomena into a historical derivation of one phenomenon from the other. It relies on presenting an analogy so bold and striking that the reader will be distracted from enquiring about the historical connections between the earlier and the later phenomena. Beyond that, the genealogy relies on a historicist explanatory paradigm in which tracing the origins of something is felt to be equivalent to explaining it. This underlying paradigm gives words like 'origin' and 'derived' their rhetorical force. Canetti employs this rhetoric when he derives the modern crowd from the primitive pack. The pack may have several functions – hunting, warfare, mourning, or increase – and Canetti sees it as the origin of various types of religion. How the mourning pack developed into the rituals of Christianity or Shi'a Islam, however, is something Canetti does not and could not explain. As an explanatory narrative, the genealogy is grandiose but hollow.

The Freudian plot is a dialectical one, and here the obvious comparison is with Freud's speculative historical narrative, *Civilization and its Discontents*. Setting out to explain why the advance of civilization does not make people happier, Freud conjectures that civilization is founded on instinctual renunciation. Instead of needing to be controlled by external authority, man sets up an authority within the mind, known as conscience; and it is a more terrible dictator than any external power, because it does not distinguish intentions from actions, and punishes both by the feeling of guilt. The advance of civilization means a steady increase in self-control, guilt, and unhappiness.

This dialectical scheme is final and compelling in a way that Canetti dislikes. He speaks in *The Human Province* of dialectic as a 'kind of false teeth'.[30] Nevertheless, one can reconstruct from *Crowds and Power* a speculative history of mankind which is likewise dialectical. The two parts of *Crowds and Power* correspond to the two concepts theorized by Canetti in opposition to Freud: the first part explores the 'mass drive' or 'crowd instinct' which impels man to form crowds; the second explores the 'personality drive' which impels man to protect his solitude. Both are rooted in basic human needs. Primitive man, small in numbers and vulnerable to enemies, invented ceremonies and myths as a symbolic means of becoming more numerous; and these ceremonies were performed by the increase pack which Canetti finds to be at the origin of religious ceremonies such as communion. Power, however, is even more basic to humanity: grasping, eating, and digesting are interpreted as primordial acts of power. And power brings with it the need to preserve one's solitude, the 'personality drive'. Civilization depends on finding a balance between the two: on controlling the dangerous open crowd by making it into a stable closed crowd; and Canetti stresses the achievement of the great religions in doing this. Control, however, means power, and so the history of civilization becomes a dialectic between the need to increase and the need for control. In the twentieth century, Canetti suggests, this dialectic has led to mass destruction. The 'crowds' part of his book ends with the German inflation, in which the currency was so devalued that sums of millions lost their meaning, and what Canetti sees as its necessary counterpart, the Holocaust, in which the Jews were so degraded that they could be destroyed in millions. The 'power' part ends with paranoiacs: the case of Schreber (who will concern us later) and the Mogul Sultan Muhammad Tughlak, who killed vast numbers of his subjects and planned huge campaigns of conquest. The parallel between Muhammad Tughlak and Hitler hardly needs mention. The book ends bleakly by contemplating the possibilities for mass destruction that the nuclear age has placed in the hands of the ruler.

The great strength of *Crowds and Power*, however, is not its overall construction but its specific interpretations. Here too a Nietzschean mode of interpretation may be distinguished from a Freudian one. The Nietzschean method is to interpret apparently harmless or benevolent activities in such a way as to disclose an underlying will to power. This is most apparent in the section on the survivor. Canetti's reflections on the pleasure of surviving other people are repugnant but persuasive, and place him among the great moralists – La Rochefoucauld, Hobbes, Kraus, and of course Nietzsche and Freud – who have analysed the more unpleasant side of human nature. They remain valid even if one rejects the biologistic assumptions on which they are founded. Consider only one brief passage, headed 'Cemeteries', in which Canetti describes and analyses the melancholy sensation experienced in churchyards. 'A cemetery very soon induces a special state of mind. We have a pious habit of deceiving ourselves about this mood. In fact, the awe we feel, and still more the awe we exhibit, covers a secret satisfaction.'[31] The nature of this satisfaction emerges as Canetti, by inducing the reader to accept his description of walking round a churchyard examining the gravestones, solicits acceptance also of his interpretation: that one takes pleasure in reflecting that one has already lived longer than some of the people buried there, that one has a good chance of rivalling the older ones, and that in any case all of them are dead - the longer ago, the better - while one is still alive with some of one's life before one. Moreover, the dead are prostrate in a single mass, while the visitor is still upright; and here, without explicitly making the connection, Canetti shows that the mind of the innocent churchyard visitor contains a grain of the will to power that animates the paranoid dictator.

A different mode of interpretation is employed when Canetti deals with symbols, myths, ceremonies, and ritual action. His interpretations are Freudian in the loose sense that he is concerned with the unconscious meanings of such actions. On the whole, however, he is not dealing with the personal unconscious of the actors; one of the few exceptions is his account of the presumable significance of fire for an elderly pyromaniac described by Kräpelin (and reminiscent of Peter Kien in *Auto-da-Fé*).[32] More typical are his sections on the symbolic meaning of the Pueblo Indians' rain-dance or of Roman Catholic ceremonies. Here Canetti is dealing with shared systems of meaning, and his method is to move gradually from a surface description of the ceremonies to an account of their unconscious symbolism. With the Pueblos' rain-dance, his description brings out how the dance imitates the action of rain and suggests a symbolic equation of the shower of rain-drops with the ancestors of the tribe. Dealing with Catholic services, he interprets them as a highly effective form of crowd control, separating each communicant from the rest of the congregation, and representing, by their slowness and solemnity, a kind of mummified lament.[33]

In such passages the biological analogies are fortunately distant. Rather than making analogies of questionable scope between human and animal behaviour, Canetti is concerned with what is specifically human about human behaviour: not its purpose or its function, but its meaning. He treats human activities as cultural activities, located within systems of meaning. I have argued elsewhere that in such passages as his account of Catholic ceremonies Canetti is practising what later came to be called 'thick description', a description of actions that brings out their unconscious as well as conscious meanings.[34]

The Schreber Case

The final section of *Crowds and Power*, dealing at some length with the Schreber case, deserves special attention, for it is written in implicit opposition to Freud's account. Canetti supplies a more Nietzschean interpretation. His study of Schreber comes immediately after his account of the tyrannical Sultan of Delhi, Muhammad Tughlak, based on contemporary reports by the Arab traveller Ibn Batuta. Schreber's system of paranoid delusions is described in his *Memoirs*. The juxtaposition of an actual ruler and a man who excogitated his system in the isolation of a padded cell is meant to shock, and, by disclosing the homology between Tughlak's actions and Schreber's fantasies, to show how deeply rooted megalomania is in the human mind. In Tughlak, we see the paranoiac from outside, while Schreber's fantasies are taken as a revelation of the paranoiac's inner world – and hence of the inner world of the paranoid autocrat.

Canetti goes back beyond Freud to Schreber's own testimony, and it will be necessary to report Schreber's ideas in some detail. Schreber, a prominent Saxon lawyer, suffered his first attack of 'nervous illness', as he called it, in the autumn of 1884. He attributed it to mental overstrain resulting from his candidacy for the Reichstag. From December 1884 to June 1885 he was in Professor Flechsig's clinic. He was released, to all appearances cured. However, soon after his appointment as Senatspräsident (presiding judge to the Dresden appeal court) in June 1893, Schreber felt overwrought because of pressure of work. Later he remembered feeling, while in bed early one morning, that it would be nice to be a woman enjoying sex. In November he was readmitted to Flechsig's clinic. From February 1894 onwards he had cosmic fantasies and constructed a system in order to explain the universe. According to this system, the soul is contained in the nerves, and God, who consists entirely of nerves, communicates with man through the nerves. It is, however, dangerous for God to remain too long in contact with any human being, since he may be unable to detach himself. This had happened with Flechsig: God, unable to extricate himself from Flechsig, had entered into an alliance with him against Schreber. Its purpose was 'soul murder': to take possession of Schreber's soul, as in the Faust legend. Schreber's soul was to be given to some other person, who would then sexually abuse

Schreber's body and finally leave it to rot. At first Schreber thought that Flechsig and God were opposed, with God on his side; only later did he conclude that the two were in league. He also came to think that he himself was becoming so attractive to God that God could only attain freedom by destroying him. In the conflict between himself and God, Schreber was finally victorious.

Schreber was persecuted for years by God's rays. They spoke to him, continually uttering nonsensical phrases or incomplete sentences which he was forced to complete. They wrote down everything he said or thought. They compelled him to think absurd thoughts. They stood around on his head in the form of little men. Sometimes they removed his internal organs: for example, in the middle of a meal his stomach would be miraculously removed, so that he felt his food falling into his legs. Insects were continually created *ex nihilo*, in order to annoy him. Eventually Schreber interpreted the most trivial everyday events as resulting from miracles: for example, every time he wanted to use the lavatory, his tormentors ensured that somebody else was occupying it. Schreber also entertained fantasies of world destruction. At one time he thought he was receiving news of successive planets and constellations being overrun. At another, he frustrated a plan to destroy the earth and transfer the sun to other planets. He also imagined the downfall of the Aryan race, since one of the future reincarnations foretold to him was that of a Mongol prince. While confined in a cell, Schreber even thought that he was the only surviving human being, and that the doctors and attendants were mere phantasms which dissolved on leaving his presence.

These fantasies were fitted into Schreber's cosmogonic system. He thought it probable that God was in the habit of destroying worlds which had become irremediably corrupt, as had happened on a small scale with Sodom and Gomorrah, and of saving one person who would then propagate a new race. This fantasy was nourished by scientific speculations about periodic catastrophes as well as by the Bible and the Germanic myth of the Twilight of the Gods. Schreber came to think that he was such a person, and that God intended to turn him into a woman in order to copulate with him and beget a new race; on two occasions he felt his penis disappearing, and he thought that female nerves were being implanted in his body. Given this divine mission, the sufferings he underwent seemed worthy to be compared to Christ's.

Gradually Schreber came to accept his transformation into a woman, since he felt it to be part of his sublime destiny as the greatest spirit-seer of all time. Feminization seemed a reward for his persecutions, for he associated femininity with voluptuous pleasure. In his opinion, women could feel pleasure on every part of their bodies, but men only in the genital region. Towards the end of his account he describes himself as frequently experiencing intense pleasure similar to that which a woman feels during sex, and as being man and woman simultaneously. His sensations approach the incessant enjoyment for which souls are destined in heaven. He is convinced that if he suffered a fatal accident, God would restore him to life, and that he is the only person in whom God is interested. He insists that nothing happens anywhere without reference to him.[35]

Freud's approach to Schreber's fantasies is genetic. He tries to trace them back to Schreber's family history. As he has only the *Memoirs* to go on, this involves conjecture, though of an ingenious and often plausible kind, and a selective reading of the text. He chooses two aspects of the text that seem at first only contingently related - Schreber's fantasy of being transformed into a woman, and his conception of God - and uncovers an essential connection between the two. From Schreber's dream of enjoying copulation as a woman, Freud concludes that he must have had repressed homosexual inclinations. Such inclinations, Freud says, are the usual cause of paranoia. Schreber's lack of a son - his wife had had six miscarriages - deprived him of a standard outlet for homosexual libido. His homosexual desires were directed towards Flechsig, and when his wife ceased to visit him, these desires became powerful enough to generate his fantasy-world as a defence-mechanism. The paranoid, Freud explains, denies his homosexual fantasies by saying, in effect: 'It is not true that I (a man) love him (a man); on the contrary, I hate him, and I hate him because he is persecuting me.' The persecution was ascribed to Flechsig and to God, both of whom were versions of Schreber's father.

From an article on Schreber senior published in 1908, Freud knew of him as a public figure who had published many educational textbooks. Had he read them, he might have hesitated to surmise that 'in real life the later years of his relationship with an excellent father had probably been unclouded'.[36] His genetic explanation of Schreber's fantasies has since been developed and modified by investigations of Schreber's upbringing. Dr Schreber senior, a specialist in orthopaedics, wrote some twenty books and pamphlets on how to bring up children. He recommended correcting their posture by encasing them in machines that would force them to sit and stand upright; he invented such machines, and used them on his children. He recommended recording all a child's misdemeanours on a board fixed in the nursery, and examining them monthly. The constant surveillance and the physical pain to which Schreber junior felt himself subjected by God's rays can plausibly be traced back to the God-like authority of his father. In Flechsig's clinic, moreover, he was placed for several years in solitary confinement in a padded cell, which must have helped to encourage his delusions of being the only person left alive.[37]

Canetti's approach to the Schreber case is wholly different from Freud's, and is composed almost explicitly in opposition to Freud. In *Crowds and Power* Freud is not named, except in an end-note that appears only in the English translation; in the text, Canetti refers only to 'a well-known attempt to find the origin of [Schreber's] particular illness, and of paranoia in general, in repressed homosexuality'.[38] This, Canetti says (without citing evidence), is completely mistaken. Anything can give rise to paranoia; what is important is not the origins of the delusion, but its structure and content. A little later he turns Freud's arguments against Freud by maintaining that the search for causal explanations is itself characteristic of paranoia. The thought-compulsion inflicted on Schreber forced him at one time to ruminate on the causes of everything. This, says Canetti, is typical of the paranoiac, who cannot bear the existence of anything other than himself, and therefore tries to trace the unfamiliar back to its origins in the familiar. The paranoiac always wants to unmask, and behind the mask he always finds a person (and, by implication, a person familiar to himself). Canetti applies this to Schreber by recalling how Schreber, briefly transferred to a small private sanatorium, identified all the patients as acquaintances. By implication, however, this is also a criticism of Freud, who traced Schreber's delusions back to a personal origin in Schreber's father.

While Freud is interested in the origins of Schreber's delusions, Canetti is interested in their systematic character. He therefore presents them synchronically, as a system essentially unchanged by time. This system is to be understood politically, as disclosing the mental world of the ruler ('Machthaber'). By emphasizing the political character of Schreber's fantasies, Canetti certainly scores over Freud, who entirely ignores this very striking aspect of the *Memoirs*. Schreber was convinced that the Germans were God's chosen people, that God had helped them defeat France in 1871, and that God himself spoke German. When he imagined God as divided into two, he thought that the higher God was concerned with the blonde races (the Aryan nations) and the lower God with the brown-haired races (the Semites). However, as a Saxon Protestant, he also believed Germany to be threatened by Catholics, Jews, and Slavs, and in his delusions he projected these threats on to the cosmos. Many Catholic souls assailed him; on one occasion 240 Benedictine monks entered his head, only to perish there. Another soul, that of a Viennese nerve doctor, wanted to use Schreber in order to make Germany Slavic and simultaneously to bring it under Jewish domination. Even the scorpions placed inside his head were divided into 'Aryan' and 'Catholic' scorpions; Schreber explains in a footnote that the souls used the word 'Aryan' as a synonym for 'German nationalist'. Sometimes he thought himself the chosen champion of the German people.[39]

As Canetti points out, Schreber imagined God to be likewise a political figure, ruling over provinces, practising amoral power-politics, and entering into alliances with other potentates such as Flechsig. God is not imagined as a moral being, but as in a political dilemma: Schreber's attraction threatens God's autonomy, yet an increase in Schreber's happiness would enhance God's power. Thus Schreber imagined both God and himself as rulers. Canetti therefore justifies himself for placing his account of Schreber immediately after his chapter on Muhammad Tughlak. While Muhammad Tughlak reveals the paranoia of the despot, Schreber reveals that despotic fantasies are part of paranoia. Both believed themselves to be surrounded by enemies (rightly, in Muhammad Tughlak's case) who must be exterminated. Both enjoyed the consciousness of being the sole survivor: Muhammad Tughlak when he surveyed the deserted expanse of Delhi from which he had evicted the inhabitants; Schreber when he thought himself the last surviving human being, chosen by God to give birth to a new race. The paranoiac and the ruler do indeed seem to be homologous: in fact, Canetti says, the former is more impressive because his fantasies are invulnerable to incursions from reality.[40]

Canetti says very little about Schreber's fantasy of being transformed into a woman, which for Freud is the most important aspect of the *Memoirs*. In emphasizing the themes of politics and power, Canetti gives a more complete account of Schreber's fantasies than Freud does. However, his presentation of these fantasies as a coherent and synchronic system leads to some distortion. It prevents him from examining the changes in Schreber's fantasies—notably the elaboration of fantasies which followed his wife's absence; the change from conceiving Flechsig and God to be fighting over him to supposing them to be leagued against him; and, above all, his gradual acceptance that it was his destiny to become a woman. Since this fantasy remained constant, but was regarded by Schreber in very different ways, there is good reason to see it, as Freud does, as central to his delusions. Because of the changes it underwent, however, Canetti cannot properly deal with it. It does not fit into the synchronic portrayal of Schreber's fantasies which Canetti is determined to provide.

The least persuasive feature of Canetti's account is his attribution to Schreber of a fascination with crowds. Certainly, Schreber thought himself assailed by large numbers of souls. He also thought that souls after death gradually lost their individual consciousness and were absorbed into a single unit. Canetti represents this as 'the merging of all souls into a single crowd'.[41] In fact, however, it is the opposite of a mass phenomenon: it is the reduction of a mass to a single unit. Canetti also makes much of Schreber's power over souls, pointing out that as they approached him they grew smaller and he was able to absorb them. As a whole, however, Schreber's narrative does not suggest that he had much power over souls: rather, it took him years of unremitting effort to resist their attempts to deprive him of his reason.

Canetti ends his account of Schreber by emphasizing his sense of solitude and his megalomania. He could have supplied further justification for this emphasis, however, if he had paid more attention to Schreber's fantasies about being transformed into a woman. Near the end of his account, Schreber describes how, being exempt from the moral constraints that apply to other people, he spends as much time as possible in vivid and highly enjoyable sexual imaginings which, he insists, do not involve masturbation. In these he is simultaneously man and woman:

> Um nicht mißverstanden zu werden, muß ich hierbei bemerken, daß ich mit der mir sozusagen zur Pflicht gewordenen Pflege der Wollust *niemals eine geschlechtliche Begehrlichkeit gegenüber anderen Menschen* (Frauenspersonen) *oder gar einen geschlechtlichen Umgang* mit solchen meine, sondern mich selbst als Mann und Weib in einer Person, mit mir selbst den Beischlaf vollziehend, vorzustellen, mit mir selbst irgendwelche auf geschlechtliche Erregung abzielende – vielleicht sonst als unzüchtig geltende – Handlungen vorzunehmen habe u. s. w., wobei natürlich jeder Gedanke an Onanie oder dergleichen ausgeschlossen ist.
>
> [In order not to be misunderstood, I must point out that when I speak of my duty to cultivate voluptuousness, I *never mean any sexual desires towards other human beings (females) least of all sexual intercourse*, but that I have to imagine myself as man and woman in one person having intercourse with myself, or somehow have to achieve with myself a certain sexual excitement etc. – which perhaps under other circumstances might be considered immoral – but which has nothing whatever to do with any idea of masturbation or anything like it.][42]

This forms an appropriate conclusion to Schreber's story. He has now vanquished both Flechsig and God. God, as he tells us in the very next paragraph, is indissolubly bound to him by the superior attractive power of his nerves. Now that he has God at his mercy, God is no longer so important as before. The prospect of being turned completely into a woman is now spoken of as a remote possibility. Instead, Schreber is half-man, half-woman, in a state of complete sexual self-sufficiency (like the primordial beings in Plato's *Symposium*). Narcissism could hardly go any further. And so Schreber's sexual fantasies turn out to tend in the same direction as his political fantasies – to complete independence of other people. The theme of autonomy, which C. Barry Chabot has discerned running through the *Memoirs*, here reaches its consummation.[43]

Canetti's account of Schreber is perceptive and enlightening, as is Freud's. The two studies are conducted by different methods, for different purposes, and emphasize different aspects of Schreber's fantasies. Each is inadequate, in symmetrically opposed ways. Freud focuses on Schreber's sexual and familial fantasies, ignoring their political aspect; Canetti focuses on their political aspect, ignoring the sexual and familial ones. Each misses significant evidence that could have strengthened his conclusions. Canetti's strength is that he is interested, not only in crowds, but also in power. His Nietzschean readiness to look for a hidden will to power gives a political edge to his productive disagreement with Freud.

There is much more to be said about the intellectual context of *Crowds and Power*, and indeed about the book itself. Its current reputation is low, and it has been described as hibernating.[44] The way to arouse it from its slumbers is, I suspect, to show how to read it; and that means coming to understand its construction and its rhetoric, and uncovering its semi-suppressed dialogue with Freud, Nietzsche, and a host of other writers absorbed by the polymath Canetti.

Notes

1. Elias Canetti, *The Torch in My Ear,* tr. Joachim Neugroschel (London, 1989), pp. 119–20.
2. Ibid., p. 122.
3. Canetti does criticize Freud by name in a note which appears only in the English translation, *Crowds and Power,* tr. Carol Stewart (London, 1962), p. 481, and in the essay 'Power and Survival' in *The Conscience of Words,* tr. Joachim Neugroschel (London, 1987), pp. 25–6.
4. William McDougall, *The Group Mind* (Cambridge, 1920). Freud's essay is to be found in *The Standard Edition of the Complete Psychological Works of Sigmund Freud,* ed. James Strachey, 24 vols (London, 1953–74), 18: 69–143.
5. See Paul Connerton, 'Freud and the Crowd', in Edward Timms and Peter Collier (eds), *Visions and Blueprints: Avant-garde Culture and Radical Politics in Early Twentieth-Century Europe* (Manchester, 1988), pp. 194–207.
6. See J. S. McClelland, *The Crowd and the Mob: From Plato to Canetti* (London, 1989).
7. Gustave Le Bon, *The Crowd* (London, 1896), p. 17.
8. Canetti, *The Torch in My Ear,* pp. 79–80.
9. Ibid., p. 251. For accounts of these events and responses to them, see Winfried R. Garscha and Barry McLoughlin, *Wien 1927: Menetekel für die Republik* (Vienna,

1987); Gerald Stieg, *Frucht des Feuers: Canetti, Doderer, Kraus und der Justizpalastbrand* (Vienna, 1990).

10. Ernst Fischer, *An Opposing Man*, tr. Peter and Betty Ross (London, 1974), p. 205.

11. Canetti, *Auto-da-Fé*, tr. C. V. Wedgwood (London, 1946), pp. 410–11.

12. Canetti, *Crowds and Power*, tr. Carol Stewart (London, 1962), p. 29.

13. Canetti, *The Torch in My Ear*, p. 123.

14. See McClelland, *The Crowd and the Mob*, p. 300.

15. Friedrich Nietzsche, *Beyond Good and Evil*, tr. R. J. Hollingdale (Harmondsworth, 1973), pp. 102–3.

16. See J. P. Stern, 'Nietzsche and the Idea of Metaphor', in Malcolm Pasley (ed.), *Nietzsche: Imagery and Thought* (London, 1978), pp. 64–82.

17. Ernest Jones, *Free Associations: Memories of a Psycho-Analyst* (London, 1959), p. 101.

18. Wilfred Trotter, *Instincts of the Herd in Peace and War* (London, 1953), pp. 36–7; this is a reprint, with new index and chapter-headings, of the 1919 edition which Canetti lists.

19. Ibid., p. 129.

20. Ibid., p. 57.

21. Ibid., p. 154.

22. Jones, *Free Associations*, p. 130.

23. See Steven Rose, R. C. Lewontin, and Leon J. Kamin, *Not in Our Genes: Biology, Ideology, and Human Nature* (Harmondsworth, 1984), esp. Ch. 9. Cf. the cogent Marxist critique by Ernst Fischer, 'Bemerkungen zu Elias Canettis *Masse und Macht*', *Literatur und Kritik*, no. 7 (Oct. 1966), 12–20.

24. Konrad Lorenz, *On Aggression* (London, 1966).

25. See Benno Müller-Hill, *Murderous Science: Elimination by Scientific Selection of Jews, Gypsies, and Others, Germany 1933-1945* (Oxford, 1988), esp. pp. 14, 56, 183–4; Rose, Lewontin, and Kamin, *Not in Our Genes*, p. 30.

26. Lorenz, 'Die angeborenen Formen möglicher Erfahrung', *Zeitschrift für Tierpsychologie*, 5 (1943), 235–409, quoted in my review of Lorenz's *The Waning of Humaneness* in *Austrian Studies*, 1 (1990), 207–8. From the revealing account of Lorenz's authoritarian upbringing in Norbert Bischof, *Gescheiter als alle die Laffen: Ein Psychogramm von Konrad Lorenz* (Hamburg, 1991), his social thinking can be seen as a compromise-formation reconciling 'masculine' aggressiveness with a 'feminine' escape into unbridled fantasy.

27. Dagmar Barnouw, 'Masse, Macht und Tod im Werk Elias Canettis', *Jahrbuch der Deutschen Schiller-Gesellschaft*, 19 (1975), 344–88 (p. 367).

28. Quoted ibid., p. 365.

29. Hayden White, *Metahistory* (Baltimore, 1973), p. 12.

30. Canetti, *The Human Province*, tr. Joachim Neugroschel (London, 1985), p. 256.

31. *Crowds and Power*, p. 309.

32. Ibid., pp. 79–80.

33. Ibid., pp. 135-7, 154-8.

34. For 'thick description' see Clifford Geertz, *The Interpretation of Cultures* (New York, 1973); I have applied this to Canetti in 'Canetti as anthropologist', in Adrian Stevens and Fred Wagner (eds), *Elias Canetti: Londoner Symposium 1989* (Stuttgart, 1991).

35. Daniel Paul Schreber, *Denkwürdigkeiten eines Nervenkranken*, ed. Peter Heiligenthal and Reinhard Volk (Frankfurt, 1985), p. 180; *Memoirs of my Nervous Illness*, tr. Ida Macalpine and Richard A. Hunter (London, 1955), p. 197.

36. 'Psycho-analytic Notes on an Autobiographical Account of a Case of Paranoia (Dementia Paranoides)', *Standard Edition*, XII, 78. Freud's source was an article published on the centenary of the elder Schreber's birth in *Der Freund der Schreber-Vereine* for October 1908; this journal was concerned with allotments, known in German as 'Schrebergärten' by an accidental connection with Schreber senior. The

source is identified in Han Israëls, *Schreber: Father and Son*, tr. H. S. Lake (Madison, CT, 1989), p. 264.

37. See Morton Schatzman, *Soul Murder: Persecution in the Family* (London, 1973); William G. Niederland, *The Schreber Case: Psychoanalytic Profile of a Paranoid Personality* (New York, 1974); Roy Porter, *A Social History of Madness: Stories of the Insane* (London, 1987), Ch. 8. The work of Niederland and Schatzman is critically examined in Israëls, *Schreber: Father and Son*.

38. Canetti, *Crowds and Power*, p. 449.

39. On Schreber's nationalism, and his membership of *Burschenschaften* (which reappear in distorted form in his *Memoirs*), see Israëls, *Schreber: Father and Son*, pp. 133-6, 159-62.

40. For a comparison between the paranoid fantasies of Schreber and Hitler, see Wolfgang Treher, *Hitler, Steiner, Schreber: Ein Beitrag zur Phänomenologie des kranken Geistes* (Emmendingen, 1966).

41. *Crowds and Power*, p. 437.

42. Schreber, *Denkwürdigkeiten*, p. 194; *Memoirs*, p. 208.

43. C. Barry Chabot, *Freud on Schreber: Psychoanalytic Theory and the Critical Act* (Amherst, 1982), p. 136.

44. Serge Moscovici, quoted in Stieg, *Frucht des Feuers*, p. 9.

*Part Two
Review Articles*

Current Freud Research

Sander L. Gilman

Sigmund Freud, *Jugendbriefe an Eduard Silberstein 1871-1881*, ed. Walter Boehlich (Frankfurt: Fischer, 1989), x + 252 pp., DM 42.

Edith Kurzweil, *The Freudians: A Comparative Perspective* (New Haven and London: Yale University Press, 1990), xii + 371 pp., £25 / $42.

Ken Frieden, *Freud's Dream of Interpretation*, SUNY Series in Modern Jewish Literature and Culture (Albany, NY: State University of New York Press, 1990), xii + 159 pp., $10.95.

Bernd Nitzschke (ed.), *Freud und die akademische Psychologie: Beiträge zu einer historischen Kontroverse* (Munich: Psychologie Verlags Union, 1989), 197 pp., DM 38.

Jakob Hessing, *Der Fluch des Propheten: Drei Abhandlungen zu Sigmund Freud* (Rheda-Wiedenbrück: Daedalus, 1989), 350 pp., DM 38.

Larry Wolff, *Postcards from the End of the World: An investigation into the mind of fin-de-siècle Vienna* (London: Collins, 1989), x + 275 pp, £15.00.

Peter Homans, *The Ability to Mourn: Disillusionment and the Social Origins of Psychoanalysis* (Chicago: University of Chicago Press, 1989), xiv + 390 pp., £27.95 / $40.25.

The study of Sigmund Freud and his times has become big academic business, rivalling and surpassing the Joyce industry which seemed to have control of the publishing market a decade ago. And rightly so. For so very long Freud was a specialist's dish – a bit too spicy, too sweet, too heavy for more than the *cognoscenti*. Now Freud has become the academic's McDonalds, where everyone can find something quickly.

In the eyes of academics Sigmund Freud is one of the most important bell-wethers for the opening of the century which is now closing. How did we get to where we are now? – let's ask Freud. And we have here a number of questions and answers, some of them more satisfying than others.

Let me begin with one of the more important collections of Freud letters to be published during the past decade. With the complete Fliess correspondence now out (at least in German; the Harvard version is still incomplete in spite of its title), we now have the major letters of the middle period. We are still awaiting the Andreas-Salomé, Ferenczi, and Jones letters to complete the late period (and we have been promised these soon, a promise which in one case is over two decades old!). Now we have the major collection of letters from Freud's youth (to add to the letters to Emil Fluss): Freud's letters to his school-friend Eduard Silberstein. Bits of these had already appeared in the 1960s, and William McGrath used them well in manuscript for his book *Freud's Discovery of Psychoanalysis* (1986).

This very litany of dates, of promises, of things seen but unpublished, is an indication of what is still wrong with Freud scholarship. Much of it is based on incomplete access to materials which are hidden or locked away. Here we have a first-rate, unprejudiced edition (unlike Masson's English edition of the Fliess letters) undertaken by an independent scholar of high repute, Walter Boehlich, who understands the late nineteenth century and who has done a solid job in reconstructing these letters. And they are well worth reconstructing. Written in a strange mixture of pidgin Spanish and schoolboy German – the secret language of the boys' fantasies – they reflect the high school and university years of both men very clearly. What we see is Freud's extraordinary sense of his own self, his enthusiasm for the high science of his day, heard in the lecture halls of Vienna, and for his reading – Cervantes, of course, but also Lichtenberg whom he discovers at University. This is a mine of materials and reflects the sort of primary scholarship which needs to be done on Freud.

The secondary studies on Freud and his impact are a more mixed bag. Edith Kurzweil, professor of sociology at Rutgers University, has presented the best overview to date of the social and historical implications of psychoanalytic theory. This is a social and intellectual history of psychoanalysis (of the Hannah Decker type) which, however, attempts to cover the entire field. The book is divided into three parts. The opening surveys the rise and spread of psychoanalytic theory before 1945; the middle section covers the infiltration of psychoanalytic theory into medicine, education, feminist psychology, and cultural studies; the final section deals with the impact of psychoanalysis after 1945. Kurzweil surveys the function of psychoanalysis in England, the United States, Germany, Austria and France. Her survey is clear, spare, and clean. She provides the necessary cross-cultural ties – showing, for example how the pattern of German and Austrian emigration during the 1930s and 1940s to Britain, France, and the United States provided different contexts for the various schools and different, often amazing, turns in their development. This is a handbook as well as a monograph, for Kurzweil has interviewed extensively and she is able to integrate memory into the world of her history. This is by far the best book of its kind and will be widely used.

Ken Frieden's study of Freud returns to the model laid out by David Bakan in the 1950s – find something within 'Jewish' interpretive tradition (that is, the tradition of Rabbinic Judaism) and see how Freud's work parallels it. Frieden undertakes this in terms of the tradition of dream interpretation in the Babylonian Talmud and shows how Freud's approach is similar – and yet different. Relying heavily on the work of scholars such as Susan Handelman and

Sanford Budick, Frieden makes a case for the 'Jewishness' of Freud's method of reading. The biggest problem of this is that it assumes a discontinuous tradition of reading – Jews in the early Near East; Jews in the Christian Middle Ages; then Freud. There is, of course, a complex hermeneutic tradition present in nineteenth-century German Jewry (one can think of Samuel Raphael Hirsch as a classic example) which relies on European hermeneutic traditions, such as those of Schleiermacher and the Romantics. Suddenly one doesn't really need all this discussion of the Talmud, which Freud certainly did not know. Even in the religious instruction to which he would have been exposed as a pupil, there was no reading of the Talmud. What Frieden shows is that the old, post-Shoah model of acculturated Jews needing to understand 'Judaism' as a religious experience (for example Bakan) has not vanished. What Frieden also shows, in his various readings of the overt and covert Jewish components in the dreams which Freud presents and analyses, is that there is indeed a strong 'day residue' of acculturated Jewish imagery, much of it negative, and stemming from his own time. Frieden's discussion of the linguistic component of these dreams would have benefited rather strongly from a reading of my own work on Jewish self-hatred. He almost has it right, but then misses the full implication of Freud's sublimated use of 'Mauscheln', that is, speaking with a Jewish accent and intonation.

Bernd Nitzschke's compact volume on Freud and academic psychology is much more uneven. He intends to serve a valuable purpose. Except for the first volume of the multi-volume German-language encyclopedia of psychology published during the 1970s, there has been little attention paid to Freud's relationship with the academic psychology of his day nor with Freud's impact on modern ('post-Freudian') academic psychology. Here we have essays on Freud and Brentano, Fechner, Wundt, Stern, Lewin, Piaget, Luria and Vygotski. Sadly, however, these essays are not very sophisticated. They are all very 'psychology-internal' in their approach. They look at 'influence' as if it were directly traceable and pay little attention to the culture of science in which Freud lived. For example, Christfried Tögel's short essay on Wundt ignores the rich web of associations shared by Freud and Wundt concerning the meaning of memory and of racial consciousness (where a reading of the anthropologist Boas could have provided a further answer to Wundt). Nothing is here, except a replaying of Freud's citations of Wundt and a statement that this is important. It is important, but why? Here is an essential topic which needs the sophistication of an Edith Kurzweil.

Jakob Hessing's book treads much the same path concerning Freud's cultural identity taken early in the 1960s by Dennis Klein and Marthe Robert. Freud's Jewish identity haunts the background of this beautifully written and reasoned book. It is indeed the curse of the prophet, the 'disease which is Judaism', to paraphrase Heine, which marks Hessing's reading of three aspects of Freud's thought: the rise of psychoanalytic theory in Vienna and Paris, the introduction of the death drive, and the rediscovery of Freud's Jewish roots in the writing of *Moses and Monotheism*. It is the return of the repressed which for Hessing marks these central turnings in Freud's thought, and he links them all to traditional Jewish texts. Again the question of what kind of a Jew was Freud must be raised. Klein's book *Jewish Origins of the Psychoanalytic Movement* (1981) made it clear that if Freud knew this tradition as well as some people assumed, he was a lot better educated in matters Jewish than his training would have allowed. Is it merely 'a common mental construction' (to use Freud's own phrase) which relates Freud and these older, Jewish texts? This may have sufficed at the turn of the century as an explanation, but in our age of nurture rather than nature it no longer does. Hessing's book is readable and interesting and adds much detail to a portrait of an aspect of Freud's thought which many may wish to find, but which may in fact be a reflection of the writer, not an aspect of his subject.

This too may be said of Larry Wolff's study of child abuse, battering, and murder in *fin-de-siècle* Vienna. Wolff focuses on a series of cases of child murder during the late 1890s in Vienna and reports – elegantly and intensely – on the reception of these cases in the media. Indeed, this is the major source for all of his material, and he regards the fictionalization of these cases as exemplifying the treatment of child murder as 'atavism' at the turn of the century. Wolff's point is that child abuse is a universal of human activity and that in the late nineteenth century it was seen as an anomaly. He cites the 1962 paper of Kempe, Silverman, et al., on 'child abuse' as the first moment when an awareness of the all-pervasiveness of abuse becomes evident. And he projects the refusal to see this problem back into the late nineteenth century. Wolff's villain is Sigmund Freud. He picks up the thread of Masson's *Freud: The Assault on Truth* (1984) and blames Freud's refusal to deal with the reality of child abuse on the escapism of his work.

Freud, like all physicians of his time, understood and recognized that child abuse occurred. He underestimated (as did the epidemiologists in the 1960s) the extent of the problem. But his focus was not only on the individual's course of life but also on the universals of human development which were altered by that course of life. The conflict with the parent is different when one has a physically abusive parent. And this he recognized and stated.

Wolff tells a complicated story but misses many major points. First, child abuse was investigated and uncovered by a number of the reformers of the day. Harry Graf Kessler's account of the poverty in Berlin working-class districts saw the poverty of the parents as a clue to the abuse of the children. This is a theme in much of the classic literature of German middle-class life: what else is the Gretchen tale in *Faust* all about? Infanticide is a literary topos which was understood as an anomaly, but also as a result of social conditions. Even in our age of the fetishization of child abuse (see the discussion in my *Sexuality: An Illustrated History* [1989]), child abuse is still an exception and is most often the reflection of direct or indirect psychosocial conditions (not necessarily only those of the working class). That it is much more frequent than people knew in the late nineteenth century may well have to do with our redefinition of child abuse. One of the cases which Wolff reports dealt with a parent who used what he thought were appropriate standards of discipline; the court agreed. Those standards today would be unacceptable. But was he wrong or have the standards changed?

Can we blithely project back into time our sense of self-correctness or should we ask what were the constructions of childhood, of abuse, of acceptable behaviour of the time and try to understand them rather than condemn them? It is clear from the cases reported that physical damage to the child was actionable in Vienna a hundred years ago, as it is today. But this is clearly not Wolff's point. He wants to draw attention to the malevolent fantasies about child abuse which preoccupied Freud's Vienna for the proverbial fifteen minutes. I would suggest that he spend some time reading the newspaper reports, novels, and non-fiction works which have been recently written about the Joel Steinberg child abuse case and see whether, in our enlightened age, they are that much different from those of the *Neue Freie Presse* in Vienna. This is not to defend Moriz Benedikt but to suggest that other factors, such as the development of the modern newspaper, the creation of a specific type of popular reading public, the concerns with 'broader' social problems such as poverty and disease have also altered the meaning of 'child abuse' from time to time and from culture to culture.

Without a doubt the most important book to appear on Freud and the culture of his time in the past decade is Peter Homans's study of 'disillusionment and the social origins of psychoanalysis'. One cannot praise this book highly enough. It is sober and well thought through. Starting from the sort of approach one wished that Cuddihy had taken in *The Ordeal of Civility* (1974), Homans uses the Bowlby model of mourning to understand how Freud worked through his identification with various individuals and what they represented. His discussion of Freud's Jewish identity in regard to his father, to Breuer and to Fliess is on a par with the best interpretive work of Didier Anzieu.

Homans presents a compelling case for Freud's disillusionment not only with the values and standards of his time, but also with the changing meaning of these standards as the twentieth century rushed toward the Shoah. The only quibble one could have with Homans's approach is that while he is completely independent in his reading of Freud and his works, his reliance on the social historians of Vienna (especially Marsha Rozenblit) does not always serve him well. The assumption many critics and readers make is that there is a 'history' out there which supplies the background and context for the written word. Homans also makes this assumption. When one reads Rozenblit side-by-side with, let us say, Wistrich or Beller, it becomes clear that history too is the selection and organization not of facts but of opinions about what facts should be. But Homans manages to balance the discussion of what Judaism means for Freud with many equally complex questions about the framing of an identity in times of stress. His approach is well balanced (as we know from his work on Jung) and extremely careful. One can rarely argue with either his premises or his conclusions.

Freud is and will remain a challenging topic. His work provides such an elaborate introduction to any number of questions to which we still lack answers, but which reflect on our sense of who we are and why we are the way we are. And Freud, his works, his person, his impact, provide us with clues – not answers.

Freud and Antiquities

S. R. F. Price

Lynn Gamwell and Richard Wells (eds), *Sigmund Freud and Art: His Personal Collection of Antiquities* (London: Thames and Hudson, in association with State University of New York and Freud Museum, London, 1989), 192pp., £18.95; £14.95 in paperback from the Freud Museum.

Christfried Tögel, *Berggasse-Pompeji und zurück: Sigmund Freuds Reisen in die Vergangenheit* (Tübingen: Diskord, 1989), 176pp., DM 34.

The interest of Freud in antiquity is clear to any reader of his works, in which archaeology often serves as a metaphor for the process of psychoanalysis. 'The Aetiology of Hysteria' (1896) draws an analogy between the investigator of hysteria who probes deeper than the statements of the patients themselves and the explorer of a little-known region who does not rest content with the surface remains and the traditions of the area, but undertakes a thorough excavation (*SE* 3: 192)[1]; while *Civilization and its Discontents* (1930) includes a long analogy between the mind and the different levels of civilization of the city of Rome (*SE* 21: 69–71).

Freud also made use of this metaphor in the actual process of analysis. The Wolf Man later recalled that Freud told him: 'The psychoanalyst, like the archeologist in his excavations, must uncover layer after layer of the patient's psyche, before coming to the deepest, most valuable treasures.'[2] To the Rat Man, Freud

> made some short observations [...] upon the fact that everything conscious was subject to a process of wearing-away, while what was unconscious was relatively unchangeable; and I illustrated my remarks by pointing to the antiques standing about in my room. They were, in fact, I said, only objects found in a tomb, and their burial had been their preservation: the destruction of Pompeii was only beginning now that it had been dug up. (1909, *SE* 10: 176).

This collection of antiquities, which eventually filled his consulting-room and study, was of major importance to Freud. In his seventy-fifth year he wrote to correct an idealized portrait by an admirer:

Your description does not tally with the fact ... that despite my much vaunted frugality I have sacrificed a great deal for my collection of Greek, Roman, and Egyptian antiquities, have actually read more archaeology than psychology, and that before the war and once after its end I felt compelled to spend every year at least several days or weeks in Rome, and so on.[3]

The antiquities are the subject of the beautifully presented *Sigmund Freud and Art,* which publishes (mainly for the first time) sixty-seven objects from Freud's collection brought by Freud to London in 1938. These objects were displayed at seven museums in the United States, and the book began life as the exhibition catalogue (as featured in *People Magazine,* 27 November, 1989). There are framing essays by Peter Gay, 'Introduction', Lynn Gamwell, 'The Origins of Freud's Antiquities Collection', Donald Kuspit, 'A Mighty Metaphor: The Analogy of Archaeology and Psychoanalysis', Ellen Handler Spitz, 'Psychoanalysis and the Legacies of Antiquity', Martin S. Bergmann, 'Science and Art in Freud's Life and Work', and Wendy Botting and J. Keith Davies, 'Freud's Library and an Appendix of Texts related to Antiquities'. To supplement this volume, Freud's travels, including trips to Rome and other classical sites, are meticulously documented and interestingly analysed in Tögel's *Berggasse-Pompeji und zurück.*

There are two major difficulties in analysing the relationship of Freud to antiquity: uncertainties over the evidence, which are often quite unnecessary; and a tendency to psychoanalyse Freud himself, rather than first to set his interest firmly in his own cultural context.

Various matters of fact remain obscure. How many antiquities did Freud possess? Sadly, the catalogue Freud himself produced in 1914 does not survive. *Sigmund Freud and Art* (p. 21) says he had more than 2000 objects, but according to M. Lobner of the Sigmund-Freud-Gesellschaft in Vienna, he amassed around 3000.[4] This difference of opinion is underlined by the fact that the London volume does not refer to the sixty objects returned to Vienna by Anna Freud in 1974, details of which were subsequently published.[5] No criteria are stated for the selection of the sixty-seven objects published in the London volume, nor are we given a full list of the pictures that hung on the walls. *Sigmund Freud and Art* (p.31, n.31) merely refers to approximately fifty prints owned by Freud, 'many of which depict archaeological sites, including an intaglio [i.e..engraved] map of ancient Rome, an eighteenth-century etching by Piranesi from the *Vedute di Roma,* and a nineteenth-century engraving of the Acropolis at Athens.'[6] The book tacitly assumes that the objects and pictures were all specifically chosen by Freud himself, but overlooks the point that some were given to him by colleagues and friends.[7] And the list of archaeological books unfortunately excludes Freud's books on ancient history and Greek, for which one must turn to a previously published list of Freud's non-psychoanalytic books.[8] Finally, in relation to Freud's travels, only thirteen of approximately four hundred letters Freud wrote to his family while travelling have been published (Tögel, p. 16).

More important is the issue of how to interpret Freud's passion for collecting antiquities. Some associations of individual objects were purely private: we happen to know of two antiquities broken by Freud as a symbolic gesture to ward off worse trouble concerning a daughter and a friend *(The Psychopathology of Everyday Life, SE* 6: 169–70. These examples were added in 1907). Such associations can generally not be recovered by the historian. The best way to begin is to locate Freud in his contemporary cultural context, though the tendency, all too common in work on Freud, is to ignore this in favour of Freudian psychoanalysis. The problem is seen clearly in the catalogue of *Sigmund Freud and Art*. Experts from the British Museum and Cambridge present the objects in the normal academic manner; juxtaposed, for some objects, are psychoanalytic comments by researchers from the Freud Museum. And, with the exception of p. 23, no time is spent in discussing how normal Freud's collection was in the Vienna of his day.

An interest in Greek and Roman antiquities might seem not to be surprising. Freud was a star product of the Gymnasium education, which meant that throughout his school career he spent more time on Latin and Greek than on any other subject.[9] When Freud was fifty-eight he wrote in a Festschrift for his Gymnasium that there he had seen 'my first glimpses of an extinct civilization (which in my case was to bring me as much consolation as anything else in the struggles of life)' (1914. *SE* 13: 241). Also, since student days, he had been a close friend of the scholar Emmanuel Löwy: he had twelve of his books and articles on Greek art, nine presented by the author (Tögel, pp. 31–2; *Sigmund Freud and Art*, p. 190, includes only the books).

So far this might seem like predictable bourgeois taste. And yet only five of several hundred Viennese dealers sold only antiquities, and of fifty-two private collections catalogued in Vienna in 1908 only six included antiquities; the remainder were mainly collections of Renaissance, Baroque and Biedermeier.[10] Thus Freud's collecting, which started in 1896, also began with Florentine art and only moved to antiquities in the early years of this century.[11] By 1910 he was corresponding excitedly with his friend Sándor Ferenczi in Budapest about the purchase of Roman objects from an 'excavation' in Hungary (*Sigmund Freud and Art*, p. 29, n. 14).

Freud clearly had an intensely personal attachment to antiquity. He had to break a major psychological barrier in order to visit Rome: he himself analysed the situation in terms of the relationship of the Jewish outsider to Catholic Rome, an issue which was connected to Freud's relationship with his father (*SE* 4:193–8; Tögel, pp. 54–5). Once the barrier was broken he went to Rome six more times. Freud also visited Athens only by accident, as he himself explained in later life (*SE* 22: 239–48).

The problematic nature of Freud's travels also invites study of the meanings for Freud of at least some of the objects in his collection. That one should look principally at his professional persona is suggested by the fact that the antiquities were located only in the consulting-room and study and not in the domestic quarters of the house, which had perfectly conventional decor. Athena was of particular importance to Freud. A bronze figurine was selected by him as the sole piece of his collection to be smuggled out of Austria when he feared he might lose the whole collection (*Sigmund Freud and Art*, pp. 11, 110–11). The Freud Museum commentary on this piece focuses on Freud's own discussion of the sexual symbolism of the head of Medusa and of Athena (1922, *SE* 18: 273–4). This commentary epitomizes the shortcomings of trying to establish one-to-one correspondences between Freud's text and particular objects (a problem noted on pp. 154–5). Psychoanalytic discussion of female sexuality does not explain why this was his most prized possession. Surely the answer lies not in Freudian psychoanalysis, but in ordinary classical scholarship: Athena was the symbol of wisdom and rationality – an appropriate mentor for Freud's quest.

Oedipus and the Sphinx also demand attention. Freud had a number of representations of the Sphinx, of which *Sigmund Freud and Art* catalogues a terracotta figure (pp. 92–3), a fragment of a Roman wall painting (p.113), and a vase of Oedipus and the Sphinx (pp. 94 –5; cf. p. 159 for another vase). These objects had multiple resonances for Freud: his own role as the solver of riddles, and in particular his formulation of the Oedipus complex. As a young man he had fantasized that his own bust, adorned with a line from Sophocles' *Oedipus Rex*, 'Who knew the famous riddle and was a man most mighty', would one day be displayed in the University of Vienna; on his fiftieth birthday he was dumbstruck when his friends presented him with a medallion with the line and his own portrait on one side, and Oedipus and the Sphinx on the other. His private symbolism had become common knowledge among his colleagues and pupils.

But the classical objects and images were in fact outnumbered by Egyptian items (*Sigmund Freud and Art*, p. 21); indeed the Sphinx was not only Graeco-Roman but also Egyptian, and Freud had a print of the famous Egyptian statue on his wall (p. 27). The dominance of Egyptian, and Near Eastern and Oriental, objects raises sharply the problem of personal meanings. The interest in Egypt was not a product of his Gymnasium education, which was mainly classical,[12] and the balance of his collection was eccentric among contemporary Viennese private collections: only one of the fifty-two collections catalogued in 1908 had a significant number of Egyptian antiquities (approximately two hundred and fifty, and they were the result of extensive travels in the East and Egypt (see above, note ten). But on his desk, besides Athena in the centre, were numerous 'exotic' figures, including the Egyptian baboon god Thoth (*Sigmund Freud and Art*, pp. 56–7), the sage Imhotep (p. 27), a Chinese sage and a Chinese table screen (pp. 128–9). Each morning he would stroke Thoth and greet the Chinese sage (p. 27; cf. illustrations on pp. 1–2, 28). Egypt and the Orient clearly had profound resonances for Freud. Tögel (p. 32) claims that Emmanuel Löwy was responsible for this interest of Freud's, but Löwy was in fact interested principally in Greek art, and in any case this could not be a proper explanation. Nor was Freud's interest in Egypt simply the result of the discovery of the tomb of Tutankhamun in 1922 (although he did own the three-volume publication on the tomb by Howard Carter and Arthur Mace). His books on Egypt go back to 1895; when on holiday in 1904 he visited the Schloss Miramare with its fine collection of Egyptian antiquities whose catalogue he possessed (Tögel, pp. 113,

153); in 1907 he had recently acquired 'a handsome glazed Egyptian figure' (*SE* 6: 170) and by 1914 he already had several Egyptian pieces on his desk (etching by Max Pollack illustrated in *Sigmund Freud and Art*, p. 152).

Sigmund Freud and Art (pp. 18-19, 21, 58, 155-9) advances the theory that this aspect of Freud's interest is explicable by his ambiguous relation to Judaism. Certainly, Freud is said to have remarked occasionally that one of his mummy portraits had 'a nice Jewish face' (Bernfeld, p. 110); and in an unpublished letter to Sándor Ferenczi in 1922 he wrote that 'strange secret longings' were rising up in him, 'perhaps from the heritage of my ancestors from the Orient and the Mediterranean' (*Sigmund Freud and Art*, p. 18). Freud himself, late in his life, argued in *Moses and Monotheism* that Moses was an Egyptian, and that Jewish monotheism was derived from that of Akhnaten, but this identification of Judaism and Egypt, though taken as obvious in *Sigmund Freud and Art*, is extremely peculiar. It runs parallel, as Freud will have known, to Graeco-Roman polemic against the Jews, which identified them as renegade Egyptians; indeed Jewish friends urged him in 1938 not to publish the work in order not to aid Goebbels' propaganda machine. Surely in addition to a purely psychological explanation one should also seriously consider Freud's study of Egyptian hieroglyphics and the uses he made of this knowledge in his work, and the fact that probably all his Egyptian objects came from tombs, an origin which, as we have seen, was for Freud analogous with the human unconscious.

When Freud was seventy-eight he wrote: 'None of us has ever lost his longing for the Mediterranean' (unpublished letter, quoted in Bernfeld, p. 112). As Peter Gay notes (*Sigmund Freud and Art*, p. 19), we still do not understand 'the full meaning of Freud's antiquities for him'. We cannot hope to recover the purely private evocations of objects; what is needed is further work on the Viennese context and a full study of the whole range of objects collected by Freud. A cursory examination of the objects suggests that they fall into two main groups: plain vases, lamps and other small objects without much decoration; and figurative representations on vases and figurines. The common factor in the second group is perhaps not the idealized human form created by the Greeks, but multiform and part-animal figures. One might speculate about a parallelism here with Freud's own rejection of classical models of the psyche in favour of the disturbing realities of the subconscious. Further study on these lines would significantly advance our understanding of this fascinating and hitherto largely neglected aspect of Freud's thought.

Notes

1. *SE* refers throughout to *The Standard Edition of the Complete Psychological Works of Sigmund Freud*, ed. James Strachey, 24 vols (London, 1953–74).
2. *The Wolf-Man and Sigmund Freud*, ed. Muriel Gardiner (London, 1972), p. 139.
3. To Stefan Zweig. *Letters of Sigmund Freud*, ed. E. L. Freud (New York, 1960), pp. 402–3.
4. Carina and Heinz Weiss, 'Ein Blick in die Antikensammlung Sigmund Freuds', *Antike Welt*, 16 (1985), 43–52 (p. 43).

5. See H. and W. Jobst in *Sigmund Freud-House Catalogue.* ed. Sigmund-Freud-Gesellschaft (Vienna, 1975).

6. A much fuller account of the collection and its origins is given by Heinz and Carina Weiss, 'Eine Welt wie im Traum – Sigmund Freud als Sammler antiker Kunst-gegenstände', *Jahrbuch der Psychoanalyse,* 16 (1984), 189–217; see also their 'Dem Beispiel jener Forscher folgend ... Zur Bedeutung der Archäologie im Leben Freuds', *Luzifer-Amor,* 3 (1989), 45–71.

7. H. Jobst, 'Freud and Archaeology', *Sigmund Freud House Bulletin,* 2.1 (1978), 46–51 (p. 48).

8. Harry Trosman and Roger Dennis Simmons, 'The Freud Library', *Journal of the American Psychoanalytic Association,* 21 (1973), 646–87.

9. S. C. Bernfeld, 'Freud and Archaeology', *American Imago,* 8 (1951), 107–28 (112–13); Tögel, pp. 29–31.

10. *Österreichische Kunsttopographie 11. Die Denkmäler der Stadt Wien (XI-XXI Bezirk)* (1908), pp. xxviii–xxix, 525, 532, cited in *Sigmund Freud and Art,* p. 29, n. 9.

11. *Sigmund Freud and Art,* pp. 23–5 and 31, nn. 26–7. He already had a statuette of Venus by 1905: *SE* 6: 169.

12. R. Hornich, 'Österreichisches Schulwesen', in W. Rein (ed.), *Encyklopädisches Handbuch der Pädagogik,* 2nd edn (1907), VI, p. 449: history focused on Greece, Rome and the Austro-Hungarian Empire.

The Sciences in Exile

J. M. Ritchie

Friedrich Stadler (ed.), *Vertriebene Vernunft: Emigration und österreichische Wissenschaft*, 2 vols (Vienna and Munich: Jugend und Volk, 1987 and 1988), 584 and 1117 pp., 498 and 980 Sch.

Perhaps it should be said at once that volumes of this kind might be issued with a health warning. Their very bulk makes it impossible either to hold them in one hand without breaking a wrist, or to grasp in any way satisfactorily the implications of the masses of material and of the hundreds of names and individual fates charted. Perhaps the worthwhile cause of exile research would have been better served by more rigorous editing. Printing every word spoken at the original series of lectures devoted to the problems of exile from Austria, plus all the papers delivered at the subsequent symposium from 19 to 23 October 1987, inevitably results in a certain degree of overkill and intellectual indigestion. Reluctance to prune and cut may derive, however, from feelings of guilt and bad conscience. After all, it has taken nearly fifty years for such a survey to be conducted. Not surprisingly, the name of Waldheim is mentioned early, and the fact that emigration from Austria involved so many Jews obviously meant facing up at last to the ugly history of Austrian anti-Semitism. In addition, the realization that Exile Studies in East and West Germany have made great strides, while Austria apparently has hardly made a start, is constant cause for regret and embarrassment.[1] Nevertheless, the sheer size of the present volumes and the meticulous record of the debates which did take place between older and younger generations is evidence enough that the problems are (at last) being tackled, and that support is forthcoming from the highest levels.

Fortunately, one helpful feature of these collections of lectures and papers is that, from the start, the heavier, more academic offerings are leavened by testimony from so-called 'Zeitzeugen', so that, instead of constantly having to hack through theoretical abstractions or statistical analyses, the reader can occasionally relax with personal reports from individuals who explain why and when they decided to go into exile, where they went, and what they subsequently experienced. Such excursions not only make the discourse more lively, but also make the reader aware of one important fact, namely that exile could have almost global consequences. The Austrian going into exile did not automatically land in England or North America; departure from Austria could mean arrival in Singapore or South-East Asia. In addition, these volumes record just how much Austria lost by forcing out the best talents in the land; they also reveal the sheer gain for the countries which eventually became the Austrian exiles' place of permanent residence. Expressing such vast sociological changes in terms of profit and loss may seem simplistic, but where so many scientists are involved, it has become common practice for scores to be kept, for example, in terms of Nobel Prize winners. Looked at in this way, it is indeed possible to measure the extent of the brain drain. Austrian prize-winners residing in North America can easily be counted, highlighting by contrast present-day Austria's poorer record. Crude calculations of this kind take no account of the personal and social damage done by forcibly evicting such a large section of the population. Nevertheless, statistics can be very revealing, as for example in those sections of these volumes which attempt to calculate the number of Austrians involved in these population shifts. Staggering figures of many thousands are reached.

A variation on the statistical approach to Austria's professional classes in exile is that adopted by those researchers who do not accept divisions into subject areas such as psychiatry, sociology, law, chemistry, but look rather at the country of exile. One potential danger of this approach may be that the selective reader will be interested only in his or her own country. It is certainly clear how much Britain gained from the waves of émigrés arriving from German-speaking lands, both before and after the Anschluss. Opera in England was immediately revitalized by Busch and Ebert who staged Mozart in German at Glyndebourne, dance by Rudolf von Laban, Kurt Joos and Sigurd Leeder at Dartington Hall in Devon. Their influence radiated to almost every aspect of life, as for example when Laban's theories of movement were put into practice to make the lives of factory workers not only easier but also more productive. The arrival of the Warburg Institute in London could not have had such a dramatic effect, but the addition of the Vienna school of Art History, especially in the person of Sir Ernst Gombrich, was clearly significant. Other names which spring to mind are Wittgenstein and Freud, but with them it has to be realized that, whatever their individual greatness, they brought with them not merely their own personal thoughts or idiosyncrasies, but also whole schools of Viennese thought.

After general sections on emigration, oral history and theoretical approaches to exile studies, *Vertriebene Vernunft* vol. I provides a survey of the emigration of the Vienna Circle. Exactly who belonged to this Circle of logical positivists has for some time been a matter of confusion, but certain steps in the disintegration and dissolution of the group are fairly clear, following the departure of Carnap for Prague as early as 1931, the murder of Schlick in 1936, and the Anschluss in 1938. If one restricts the circle to Gustav Bergmann, Rudolf Carnap, Herbert Feigl, Philipp Frank, Kurt Gödel, Hans Hahn, Viktor Kraft, Karl Menger, Otto Neurath, Olga Hahn-Neurath, Moritz Schlick and Friedrich Waismann, then a very powerful group of thinkers is already adumbrated. Most were to make their way to the United States, where Gödel, in particular, was to enjoy such success as a mathematician. Neurath and Waismann, however, came to England, bringing logical positivism with them; they could rely on a well-disposed A. J. Ayer, who had studied in Vienna. The relationships between Neurath, Waismann, and Wittgenstein are a matter of record, though Wittgenstein never liked to think of himself as a refugee, given his family fortune, his residence in England before 1933, and his block-house in Norway.

Accounts here of the departure of the Vienna school of psychoanalysis correspond with similar accounts from other quarters. Despite their familiarity with anti-Semitism in Vienna and elsewhere, Sigmund and Anna Freud refused to consider leaving until it was too late, and had to rely on special measures on their behalf to escape from Vienna to London. Since psychiatry was denounced by the Nazis as a Jewish science (just as physics was to be because of Einstein), there was no possibility of the Wiener Psychoanalytische Vereinigung continuing to exist, and nearly all its members had to go into exile. Of the fifty or so ordinary and extraordinary members, nearly twenty are listed as having Great Britain as place of exile in the first instance, including Dr Eduard Bibring (Secretary) and Otto Sakower. Erwin Stengel became Professor of Psychiatry at the University of Sheffield. Despite this Austrian presence in Britain, the impact of the emigration of the Vienna Psychoanalytic Society was to be far greater in the United States, where many Viennese doctors had already settled. Indeed, psychoanalysis was destined to become a deeply ingrained part of American culture.

Studies of other areas of academic expertise show the same general tendency. The social sciences were almost as unpopular with the Nazi authorities as the psychological sciences: not only were they suspected of being populated by Jewish scholars, they were also accused of being left-wing. Of the thirty-eight Austrian university social scientists who were removed from their posts, thirteen went to America and three to Great Britain. As far as the legal profession was concerned, the proportion leaving for America as against Great Britain was even greater, namely 13 to 1. In this case, the peculiarities of English law, and the difficulties of European scholars in adapting, may have been a complicating factor. As for the medical profession, Austrian doctors forced abroad also encountered difficulties. To a certain extent they could rely on medical organizations to help with such matters as the recognition of qualifications and certification, but here again the general climate seems to have been more favourable in North America than in Great Britain. Austrian doctors in Great Britain encountered some reluctance from conservative quarters to grant admission to foreign (Jewish) competitors. Such doctors were, at first at least, granted only 'temporary registration' which allowed them to practise medicine only during wartime. This may be the reason why so many more doctors chose to return to Austria from England than from America after the end of hostilities.

While the migration of the sciences is a matter of great national concern, only the most advanced subject specialists will be capable of appreciating the full significance of the fact that Erwin Schrödinger, one of the greatest thinkers in physics of his generation, was forced to leave Austria. Schrödinger first left Germany for Switzerland, whence he received a call to a chair in Berlin as the successor to Max Planck. After 1933 emigration was the only course open to him. Although offered a chair in Edinburgh, he chose Graz, but was again forced to leave. An offer from De Valera brought him to Dublin, where he was to stay until his return to Austria in 1956. What such a disturbed life meant for advanced thinking in physics is hard to tell. The effect of emigration on the Institute for Radium Research of the Austrian Academy of Sciences is equally hard to quantify. What is certainly clear is that no area was immune. Not only all the social and physical sciences, but also such professions as engineering and architecture, were affected by the pressures which the Nazi regimes placed upon their members.

Perhaps as a result of the division of Germany and the emergence of Marxist criticism, it was recognized early on in Germany that a subject like 'Germanistik', by its very nature and its very name, had always run the risk of national bias and was in need of revision, in just the same way as history in Germany had tended to be nationalistic history. While the sciences could claim to be objective and not to be so conditioned by social factors, subjects like 'Germanistik' and history were inevitably seen as more subjective and more clearly products of a certain society at a certain time. Throughout these volumes there is a note of regret that more has not been done as regards the revision of Austrian history by Austrian historians. In the same way, although a certain readiness is expressed to review the history of 'Germanistik' under National Socialism, not many pages are devoted to such semi-taboo subjects as the continuing tradition of the Nadler School, or the Kindermann School of theatre history. Such matters are not, however, passed over in complete silence:

> Die Nadler-Schule dagegen blühte auch im "Ständestaat" weiter, mit dem sich Nadler als deklarierter großdeutscher Katholik durchaus zu arrangieren verstand. Der "Anschluß" bedeutete für ihn die Erfüllung seiner politischen Wünsche ... Von einer starken Mehrheit der deutschen Literaturwissenschaftler in Österreich kann mit Sebastian Meissl gesagt werden, daß sie nicht dem Anpassungsdruck nachgaben, sondern im "Anschluß" auch an ein nationalsozialistisches Deutschland ein nationales und kulturelles Ziel verwirklicht sahen, dem man durch privates und öffentliches Bekenntnis im Denken und Verhalten vorgearbeitet hatte.[2]
> [The Nadler School, on the other hand, continued to flourish under the corporate state, with which Nadler, as a declared Catholic proponent of Greater Germany, was well able to reach an understanding. For him the Anschluss meant the fulfilment of his political desires ... Of a large majority of German literary scholars in Austria it can be said, with Sebastian Meissl, that they did not give way to the pressure to conform, but saw Austria's incorporation even into a National Socialist Germany as the realization of a national and cultural goal for which they had paved the way by public and private declarations in thought and conduct.]

'Germanistik' in North America was to gain greatly from the influx of specialists from Germany. The second section of the Spalek/Strelka survey of German exile literature since 1933 is able to produce an impressive list of Germanists who have settled and been active in colleges all over the United States.[3] The list of Germanists from Austria, however, is not quite so long because, as has been suggested, the thinking of many university professors was actually in line with much of National Socialism, and hence they saw no need either to revise their opinions or leave the country, unless they happened to be Jewish. One or two, nevertheless, did leave and find sanctuary in North America, most noticeably Marianne Thalmann and Franz Heinrich Mautner.[4] What 'Germanistik' in general and the Germanist in particular stood to gain from the experience of exile is neatly summed up in this volume by Egon Schwarz, who taught at Harvard.[5] According to Schwarz, 'Germanistik' became more pragmatic and less nationalistic, orientated more towards the Enlightenment than Romanticism. The literary canon was changed, progressive authors were included, the stress was shifted from the abstruse to the accessible, the works of those writers who had been banished from the Third Reich were found worthy of special attention. Whole movements such as Expressionism, which had been cast out by the Nazis and their forerunners, made a successful comeback. Authors formerly abused, like Heine, could have whole courses devoted to them; symposia were devoted to such individual writers, and new editions of their works were published. In addition, the intellectual left was rediscovered. The Frankfurt School was recognized as important. It was permissible not only to look for possible linguistic interpretations of works but also to place them in their historical and social context. Schwarz stresses not the uniqueness of the Anglo-Saxon empirical tradition, but the advantages of combining the traditions of the Viennese school with English and American approaches.

Apart from valuable excursions such as these, the sections in these volumes on 'Germanistik' have little to offer the informed reader, who will learn more about Musil in exile or Broch in the United States from other sources, not least from the Spalek/Strelka volumes already mentioned. Berthold Viertel, whose essays on the theatre are briefly analysed, is perhaps more interesting for the fact that he spent almost as much time in England as in the United States even though this meant long separations from his wife, Salka, who was well settled as a script-writer in Hollywood. Viertel was possibly also more significant and successful in film than in his theatre work. Certainly, the poems he wrote in exile in London are better than the plays he wrote in the United States. To some extent, the sections on literature and theatre in exile have been overtaken by more up-to-date research, especially that by Sylvia Patsch on Austrians in exile in Great Britain.[6] Patsch is able to show significant contrasts between the corresponding success or failure of Germans and Austrians in exile in Great Britain. In general, she succeeds in showing firstly that, as one might expect, journalists were more adaptable than creative writers in coming to terms with the new language and the new media and that, again in very general terms, Austrians were more flexible than Germans in their readiness to change from German to English. The United Kingdom received far more Austrians than Germans, and the Austrian Centre (briefly discussed) was really more important than the Free German League of Culture. Some indication of the ratio is given by the fact that over the years some sixty to seventy thousand German-speaking exiles were admitted to the United Kingdom. The Free German League of Culture had around 1,500 members at its peak, whereas the Free Austrian Centre could count on between 6-7,000 paid-up members. Altogether the Austrian presence in England was extremely significant, ranging from Oskar Kokoschka, who was the President of the Free German League of Culture, to Robert Neumann, who became so successful in writing in English that he seems to have been completely lost to histories of Austrian literature as a result. Much remains to be said about the Austrian women writers who found refuge and continued to write in Britain, like Hilde Spiel, Martina Wied and Hermynia zur Mühlen.

The final section of the second volume explores various other countries of exile, in essays covering France, Switzerland, Belgium, the Netherlands, Sweden, the Soviet Union, Mexico, Brazil, Turkey, Palestine, Shanghai and Australia. In his study of Germans in exile in the Soviet Union, David Pike has depicted the great suffering among those who chose Russia as a place of exile, and shown how few survived.[7] Austrians in Russia seemed to have shared the same fate to a greater or lesser extent, though perhaps is it only now possible for the full story of terror and reprisals to be told. Austrians in Great Britain never had to face such suffering, however great the hardships of internment; and, as has been seen, they were extremely well organized as regards cultural, theatrical, artistic and even scientific matters.

The final problem to which this survey returns again and again is whether those in exile should go back to Austria. For some exiles this was a matter of race and religion. If Jewish, they may have had less desire or inclination to return to a land which had brought about the destruction and death of their families and their own banishment. For others it may have been a matter of age and circumstance. If they had left Austria at an early enough age, married and had family abroad, they might have been less likely to uproot themselves. Yet the pull was strong, many did return, and for many the disappointment was great; anti-Semitism was still prevalent, and later the Waldheim affair confirmed their worst suspicions. Remigration was to prove harder than emigration in many respects.

These are volumes which have to be read more than once. What they present is not easy material. The bulging footnotes on the packed pages of these bulky volumes show not only that not everything has yet been digested, but also that much remains to be done. If this is the beginning, then it is a worthy beginning which deserves to be encouraged. It is unlikely that one person will be found who can produce a more manageable survey for the general public, but this is a task which needs to be tackled.

Notes

1. So, for example, the Deutsche Forschungsgemeinschaft for ten years from 1974 to 1983 had a 'Schwerpunktprogramm' devoted to research into German-language exile. One outcome of this was the volume *Die Erfahrung der Fremde*, edited by Manfred Briegel and Wolfgang Frühwald (Weinheim/Basel, 1988), which includes in its impressive bibliography of all the many publications resulting from this research programme the massive four-volume *International Biographical Dictionary of Central European Emigrés 1933-1949*.

Since then the Society for Exile Studies has also published in *Exilforschung* 1988 a volume devoted to the 'Vertreibung der Wissenschaften und andere Themen'. It too covers research into the exodus of the sciences from Germany and Austria.

2. Erika Weinzierl, 'Wissenschaft und Nationalsozialismus', *Vertriebene Vernunft* II, p. 55.

3. *Deutschsprachige Exilliteratur seit 1933*
   1. *Kalifornien* Teil 1, ed. John M. Spalek and Joseph Strelka (Berne, 1976).
   2 *Kalifornien* Teil 2, as above.
   Deutschsprachige Exilliteratur seit 1933
   1. *New York* Teil 1, ed. by John M. Spalek and Joseph Strelka (Berne, 1989).
   2. *New York* Teil 2, ed. by John M. Spalek and Joseph Strelka (Berne, 1989).

4. Sebastian Meissl, 'Nestroy im Exil. Der Literaturwissenschaftler Franz Heinrich Mautner,' *Vertriebene Vernunft* II, 575-83.

5. Egon Schwarz, 'Die Vertreibung aus Wien, perspektivisch gesehen', *Vertriebene Vernunft* II, 529-37.

6. Sylvia M. Patsch, *Österreichische Schriftsteller im Exil in Großbritannien: ein Kapitel vergessene österreichische Literatur: Romane, Autobiographien, Tatsachenberichte auf englisch und deutsch* (Vienna, 1985).

7. David Pike, *German Writers in Soviet Exile, 1933-1945* (Chapel Hill, 1982).

The Poet as Anthropologist

On the Aphorisms of Franz Baermann Steiner

Jeremy Adler

Franz Baermann Steiner, *Fluchtvergnüglichkeit. Feststellungen und Versuche*, Eine Auswahl von Marion Hermann-Röttgen (Stuttgart, Flugasche-Verlag, 1988). 146 pp., DM 29,80.

Although Max Brod symbolically concluded his study of German literature written in Prague, *Der Prager Kreis* (1966),with Hermann Grab, who died in the United States in 1949 but is only now gaining wider recognition as a major prose writer,[1] other commentators have shown that what, for want of a better term, may be called the Prague School of German literature lived on in exile long after the society that produced it was destroyed.[2] The decimation of the Prague Jews and subsequently of the Prague German community effectively blocked or at least hampered the recognition of the surviving writers, even if they were spiritually adopted by Austria and some, like Johannes Urzidil, did manage to reach a wider public. Franz Baermann Steiner is one of the more important of these figures. He was born in Prague in 1909, and died in Oxford in 1952. Though he was better known in England than in Germany as a poet, Steiner's work was recognized by fellow poets like Johannes Bobrowski, Ilse Aichinger and Erich Fried, and Paul Celan (according to Fried) rated him as one of the century's finest writers. But Steiner was not only a poet. Like two of his closest friends, Elias Canetti and H. G. Adler, he was a 'Doppelbegabung' who combined scholarship (notably social science) with literature. It is as an anthropologist rather than as a poet that he enjoys widest recognition.[3]

Anthropology, too, rather than poetry, determined the course of Steiner's career.[4] As a child, before he turned to writing, his main interests lay in natural science, especially entomology, biology and botany; however, poor eyesight prevented him from using a microscope, and so (developing an interest prompted by his flirtation with Marxism in 1926-8), Steiner took up ethnology. Somewhat unexpectedly, he enrolled for the study of linguistics at the German University of Prague in 1930, specializing in Semitic languages. That summer, he went to the Hebrew University at Jerusalem to learn Arabic, and stayed with the Jewish philosopher Hugo Bergmann, Kafka's schoolfriend. According to the dissertation on Steiner by Alfons Fleischli, the visit had a double effect: it helped Steiner redefine his personality as a Jew, leading him to regard himself as 'an

Oriental born in the West'; and it also prompted him to find a new theoretical basis for his scholarship. Focusing increasingly on social science, he used his knowledge of the East to relativize Western science.[5] Steiner completed his studies with a thesis on Arabic in 1935 and then went on to Vienna to concentrate on ethnology, specializing in Arctic ethnology, a life-long interest. In 1936 he went to London to study under Malinowski. Then, in 1938, after a field trip to the Russian Carpathians, his attention turned to the Institute for Social Anthropology at Oxford, and through the mediation of the classicist Christopher Cookson, who had been the host of the Expressionist poet Ernst Stadler during the latter's tenure of a Rhodes Scholarship, Steiner became a Fellow of Magdalen College. At the Institute, Radcliffe-Brown recommended him to write a second dissertation, and Steiner devoted the next fourteen years to a thesis on slavery, a study he regarded as a 'duty' and a 'sacrifice'.[6] It took so long not just because of Steiner's perfectionism but because, tragically, the draft and all his material were lost in 1942, at a time when, according to Radcliffe-Brown, the work was almost publishable. It took seven years to reconstruct. In 1949 'A Comparative Study of the Forms of Slavery' was accepted under Radcliffe-Brown's successor, Evans-Pritchard. That autumn, Steiner was given a temporary post at Oxford, and the following year he was finally awarded a Lectureship there.

Steiner's anthropological method is more wide-ranging than his small output might lead one to expect. Evans-Pritchard has written of his 'monumental learning',[7] and it is indeed Steiner's extraordinary width of reference which is one of the first things to strike the non-specialist reader of Steiner's anthropological essays. This forms the basis for his comparative method. For example, his *Taboo* contains 'everything of any significance which has been written about taboo';[8] and his 'Chagga Truth' is similarly impressive. The essay opens with a general analysis of the concept of 'truth' in which, with considerable methodological self-awareness, Steiner distinguishes the logician's from the philosopher's 'truth', and takes in Greek, Roman, Hebraic, Teutonic, Celtic and African ideas.[9] The comparative method is evident again in 'Towards a Classification of Labour'[10] which is now regarded as 'one of the more definitive studies of its topic',[11] and it is central to his 'Notes on Comparative Economics'.[12] These papers discuss first principles, and the latter was intended to form the basis for a book on the economics of primitive peoples. One of the specific forms that the comparative method takes in Steiner's hands – possibly stimulated by the sociologist Marcel Mauss,[13] and no doubt by Evans-Pritchard's methods in *The Nuer*[14] - is an early variety of structuralism. But Steiner also maintained a linguistic orientation, yet extended the scope of etymological and semantic method to include social *practice:* in 'Chagga Truth', this entailed examining precisely what Wittgenstein, at about the same time, was calling a 'language game'.[15] Clearly, Franz Baermann Steiner was at the forefront of his field as an anthropologist. Yet those who knew him also recognized that his science was informed by his beliefs. Mary Douglas has drawn attention to his attempt, in his own daily life, 'to handle the problem of ritual cleanliness' (Douglas, p. vii). Iris Murdoch, who has evoked both Steiner and Canetti in *The Message to the*

Planet,[16] summed up Steiner thus: 'In spite of his melancholy, he was always a cheerful, happy person, very tender, very full of feeling. He was a good man, a religious man in a deep sense.'[17] If these qualities inform Steiner's anthropology, they take on a yet more determining role in his literary work.

Anthropology has had a decisive impact on poetry at least since the appearance of Frazer's *The Golden Bough*,[18] and it is symptomatic of this influence that the twentieth century's key poem, Eliot's *The Waste Land*, should cite Frazer in the notes and embed Eastern knowledge in an analysis of Western ills.[19] Franz Baermann Steiner was rare, if not unique, among modern poets in being himself an anthropologist, and this has important consequences for his writing. The discipline affected his work in various ways. Most simply, 'ethnic' materials sometimes provided him with sources which he reworked, as in his 'Lied von den Gleichnissen' ('Song of Comparisons'), which is subtitled 'Variationen auf drei Ostjakische Rätsel' ('Variations on three Ostyak riddles').[20] A more complex situation obtains in his poem 'Elefantenfang' of 1942, which is all that came of his earlier plan to write a sociological study of the cultural use of elephants:[21]

ELEFANTENFANG

Die zahmen tiere drohten schweigend,
Köpfe gesenkt vor schwarzem meer,
Das rastlos mahlte in der friedung,
Gellte, schnob.

Doch als die wildlinge, bemeistert
Von hungertagen und verschnürter welt,
Nicht kraft mehr fanden, alte angst verstanden,
Liess man die zahmen zu.

Die schlugen ein mit rüsseln und mit zähnen.
Erbarmungslos der wohlgenährten hass
Dem waldruch galt, dem fernherkommen:
Strafte mit lust.

The poem has been translated by Christopher Middleton:[22]

CAPTURING ELEPHANTS

The tame beasts menaced silently,
Their heads they bowed to the black sea
That churned and churned in the pen,
Trumpeting, shrill.

But when these wild ones, mastered now
By days of hunger in a world strung up
Had no more strength, knew ancient fear,
The tame ones went to them.

With trunk and tusk these stove the wild ones in.
Fat bodies' hatred, without pity aimed
Against the jungle smell and foreign kind,
Wreaked glad revenge.

The diction and attitude here still recall Rilke's poetry of captivity in his *Neue Gedichte* (New Poems), especially 'Der Panther', which pioneered the evocation of a caged beast in modern German verse.[23] Like Rilke's poem, Steiner's represents both the pathos and the wider symbolism of the animal's dilemma. Yet whereas Rilke shows an exotic creature in a Western prison, Steiner uses verse to transport the reader to the foreign context, and reconstructs the animal's alterity through precise anthropological knowledge. However, the most important way in which anthropology relates to Steiner's verse lies not in his choice of subject, but in his handling of attitude and moral viewpoint.

Sir Maurice Bowra has praised Steiner's 'uncomforting dissections of the modern soul', which recall T. S. Eliot, and produce a 'sharpened insight and trained sensibility' in the reader.[24] This quality can be found in some of Steiner's best poetry. If the results are strong when the poems embrace the tangible world, they are most remarkable when they focus on the inner self, as in 'Gebet im Garten' (Prayer in the Garden)[25] or the great cycle *Eroberungen* (Conquests).[26] Yet Steiner by no means adopts a quasi-scientific objectivity. Rather, his verse draws on his own, very personal, methodological subtlety. For example, in his splendid set-piece, 'Kafka in England', written in 1946 and revised in 1952, Steiner exploits his technique of cultural comparison to relativize two very different communities. By juxtaposing England with the fate of Central Europe, he establishes a viewpoint tinged with tragedy, yet satirical and affectionately humane.[27]

KAFKA IN ENGLAND

Weder via Belsen, noch als dienstmädchen
Kam der fremde, keineswegs ein flüchtling.
Dennoch wars ein trauriger fall:
Die nationalität war strittig,
Die religion umlispelte peinlichkeit.

„Haben sie Kafka gelesen?" fragt Mrs Brittle beim frühstück,
„er ist recht unausweichlich und ziemlich fundamental!"
„haben sie Kafka gelesen?" fragt Mr Tooslick beim tee.
„man versteht dann die welt viel besser –
Doch freilich ist nichts real."
Miss Diggs sagt: „aber wirklich?
Ist das nicht reaktionär?"
Nur der kleine Geoffrey Piltzman
Träumt: „wer?

Ich meine, wer daran verdient,
Sie müssen doch tot sein,

Ich mein die leute in Prag – nun, wer auch immer ...”
Doch aus dem tor bricht trotzdem der schimmer...

The poem has been translated by Michael Hamburger:[28]

KAFKA IN ENGLAND

Neither via Belsen, nor as a maid of all work
The stranger came, by no means a refugee.
And yet the case was a sad one:
His nationality was in doubt,
His religion occasioned lisping embarrassment.

“Have you read Kafka?” asks Mrs Brittle at breakfast.
“He’s rather inescapable and quite fundamental, I feel”.
“Have you read Kafka?” asks Mr Tooslick at tea,
“Then you’ll understand the world much better –
Though nothing in him is real”.
Miss Diggs says: “Is that so?
I thought that was reactionary. Don’t you?”
Only little Geoffrey Piltzman
Dreams: “Who?

“I mean, who does well out of this,
They must be dead, after all,
I mean those people in Prague - well, no matter what name....”
Yet the glory of him shines through the gateway all the same.

As a set-piece, the poem recalls the social satire of Heine and T. S. Eliot, yet differs in its handling of multiple viewpoints. The poem has several strands: it telescopes the fate of Kafka’s work on its arrival in Great Britain with that of Jewish refugees; juxtaposes these with the annihilation of their brethren in the death-camps; satirizes Kafka’s cultural appropriation by the English; ironizes the Jewish assimilation of local values; and concludes by re-establishing a value-system derived from Kafka’s work.

For the English, the word ‘Kafka’ has become a formula, to be invoked at their rituals (breakfast, tea), a mere token for exchange in the discreet power-struggles of small-talk. The trite views ironize the speakers – and do so all the more effectively because of their truth-content – yet the comic names imbue the irony with a genuine (if slightly condescending) warmth. By contrast, the Jewish boy, Geoffrey Piltzman, seems to deserve our sympathy, and he, at least, thinks of the fate of the Prague Jews; yet irony enters this sympathy, too, as he concentrates on the fate of the royalties, not the human victims. For the English, Kafka has become a commodity for conversational exchange; for the boy, a genuine commodity. He has assimilated to English society (as his hybrid name tells), and conforms to the stereotype of a Jew. His sadness is that he has lost the religious horizon which would enable him to formulate an adequate response to the fate of his own people. Neither the English nor the Jews prove capable of absorbing contemporary reality. Finally, the speaker recalls the conclusion to

Kafka's parable 'Vor dem Gesetz' (Before the Law) in *Der Prozess* (The Trial). Notwithstanding the human tragedy of the Jews in Prague, and the sordidness of life in exile, the metaphysical order remains intact. Thus, the poem's ironies and cultural relativization (the heirs of Steiner's anthropological method) serve to reveal the inadequacies of human life against the horizon of a divinity; this unnamed power appears in the very inability of humankind to glimpse the transcendental world.

Steiner's aphorisms more overtly combine his twin talents of poet and anthropologist. Their first appearance in a volume almost forty years after his death fills a major gap in our knowledge.

Elias Canetti is quoted by Alfons Fleischli as having first suggested to Steiner that he put down his thoughts in aphorisms.[29] Steiner seems to have started writing them in 1942 (not long after Canetti began his 'Aufzeichnungen'). He produced several thousand over the next ten years, and ultimately they replaced his poetry as his main creative outlet. His method was to jot down thoughts in little notebooks, on bus-tickets, napkins and the like, later revising them, copying or sticking them onto larger pages, which he stored chronologically in small ring-binders. About twenty of these have survived in the 'Nachlass'. Later, a friend typed up about half of them, some 6,000 items from the years 1942 to 1947. These are contained in three quarto binders. According to an unbound sheet in Steiner's hand, about seventy are dedicated to Iris Murdoch. The collection is in no sense definitive, and in any case does not include important later pieces.

Steiner called his aphorisms 'Feststellungen und Versuche' (roughly trans-latable as 'Essays and Discoveries'). The name suggests something of their character and variety. They include short essays, parables, pithy observations, lyrical apophthegms, prose poems, and mysterious poetic dialogues between unnamed speakers. Steiner described the subjects in a letter written in 1948, when he envisaged an edition:

> Ich bin dabei, das Beste auszuwählen. [...] Das Zusammenstellen hängt davon ab, ob die Dinge in 3-4 kleinen Bändchen erscheinen sollen, oder ob ich mit einem umfangreicheren Prosaband beginnen kann. Käme es zu der Gruppierung in kleine Bände [...] würde ich die Gebiete, so weit dies überhaupt möglich ist, sondern, etwa so: 1. Bd. Moralia-Religiöses, Gedichte in Prosa; 2. Bd. Soziologisches, Religionssoziologisches, Glossen zur Geschichte, Völkerpsychologie, etc.; 3. Bd. Literatur und Kunstkritik; 4. Bd. Sprachphilosophisches, damit zusammenhängende ästhetische Themen, Besprechung einzelner Wörter etc. Wenn man aber an umfangreichere Bände denken könnte, würde ich ein abwechslungsreiches Kunterbunt vorziehen. So sind die Dinge ja auch niedergeschrieben worden. (Fleischli, p. 59)
>
> [I am in the process of selecting the best. [...] The arrangement depends on whether the things are to appear in 3-4 little volumes, or whether I can begin with a larger book of prose. If they were to be grouped in little volumes [...] I would divide up the subjects as far as this is possible, approximately as follows: 1st vol. moralia-religious themes, poems in

prose; 2nd sociology, sociology of religion, notes on history, psychology of nations, etc.; 3rd vol. literary criticism, art criticism; 4th vol. philosophy of language, related aesthetic subjects, discussions of individual words, etc. But if larger volumes were possible, I would prefer a more varied mixture. After all, that's how the things were written down.]

Hitherto, only a small selection of Steiner's aphorisms has been available.' [30] The present volume is a shortened version of a dissertation supervised by Heinz Schlaffer.[31] Given the editorial problems and the difficulty of finding a publisher in the West German 'Literaturbetrieb', Marion Hermann-Röttgen has made a personal selection of some of the most interesting pieces. Selecting means imposing some kind of order. She has picked 563 items and arranged them in 11 sections, based on possible chapter headings at one time considered by Steiner himself: 1. Ohne Vers and Titel; 2. Der Übernächste; 3. Sprachliches and Wörtliches; 4. Vom Dichten; 5. Zur europäischen Literatur; 6. Zur deutschen Literatur; 7. Von Völkern – Um den Menschen; 8. Welt und Gott; 9. Der Andre; 10. Dunkel und Licht; 11. Zeitlichkeit. [1. Without Rhyme or Title; 2. The Next but One; 3. Language and Words; 4. On Poetry; 5. European Literature; 6. German Literature; 7. Peoples - Concerning Mankind; 8. World and God; 9. Others; 10. Light and Shade; 11. Temporality.]

Generally, the divisions are helpful, although a handful of pieces counted as notes on German literature (Nos. 163-5) might better belong with European literature. The edition concludes with a short biography, an editorial note, and an interesting discussion of genre, which attempts to define Steiner's shorter prose as 'Bemerkungen', 'Aphorismen', and 'Denkbilder' respectively ('Observations', 'Aphorisms', 'Lyrical Thoughts'). The 'observations' are the largest group, and have no specific formal characteristic; the 'aphorisms' are more closely structured; and the 'lyrical thoughts' or 'ideas' are more poetic and refractory in character. These latter are essentially 'open-ended', and can be characterized as 'symbolisch gestaltete Denkmodelle' ('symbolic models'; p. 145), requiring meditation rather than rational analysis. Hermann-Röttgen divides them into two main types: the 'lyrical' and the 'dialogue'. However, the genre of the aphorism depends on the interaction of three interconnected elements, since besides 'form' and 'content', the 'tone' or 'manner' occupies a critical role, equally affecting the shape of the piece and the very meaning of its statement. Hermann-Röttgen's classifications work well enough with respect to form and content; but one also needs to consider the prose pieces with respect to their mode or tone. Although, according to form and content, Steiner's shorter prose largely comprises 'observations' and 'aphorisms', as Hermann-Röttgen rightly points out, their dominant mode or tone is, I think, that of the 'Denkbild', 'lyrical thought', or 'idea'. The consistent use of this mode can turn a relatively straightforward empirical observation into a more mysterious utterance. This (as we shall see) can occur when Steiner comments on modern psychology, on a translation, or on a Kafka text.

Varying Hegel's definition of tragedy, and following Neumann's masterly survey of the aphorism,[32] Hermann-Röttgen pertinently argues that Steiner's aphorisms emerge from the 'Konflikt einer individuellen Erfahrung mit einem gedachten Ganzen' ('the conflict between individual experience and an intellectually conceived whole'; p. 142). Often, the observations seem to reflect on the tragic consequences of this clash, attempting to uncover an inner self by means of an endeavour which utilizes the knowledge, but scorns the method, of the human sciences. The way in which Steiner dispatches psychology implicitly defines his own concerns:

> Der Psychologe zwingt uns zur Selbstbetrachtung und Einkehr, aber er schickt uns bloss auf den Boden unsres Meeres wie einen Taucher. Da gehen wir in der gewichtigen, modernen Taucherrüstung umher, beäugen, was wir sehen wollten, abermals durch das Fenster und bleiben fremd. (No. 496)
> [Psychology forces us to contemplate ourselves and to look within, but it simply sends us to the bottom of our inner sea like a diver. There we walk about in a heavy, modern diving suit, stare at what we wanted to see through a window, as before, and remain cut off.]

As here, Steiner's aphorisms generally shun the technology of intellectual constructs (except when defining philosophy in No. 295!), and attempt to unlock a silent inner world. Typically, they exploit imagery to reach through to an inchoate realm, disregarding the 'unconscious' to seek out a more basic stratum of the self.

The inwardness of Steiner's aphorisms is an obvious obstacle to their reception, and distinguishes his handling of the form from many earlier varieties. Traditionally, the aphorism gains appeal by combining inquiry with performance. And the performance, of course, is double-edged, being both the writer's literary act, and its correlative effect on the reader. The peculiar dialectic of the aphoristic style is that the formulation turns a reflection into an act, and an act into a reaction. Accordingly, satire, wit, and wisdom are the genre's familiar barbs and currency. They all occur in Steiner, too. But just as he rejects Rousseau's 'freie Bravour des Bekennens' ('open bravura of confession'; No. 161) he often – and this in itself is a way of disarming the reader – eschews wit and accessible wisdom. Instead (as the editor points out, p. 145), he instils meditation. This is where we find Steiner's authentic voice: a brooding heart, illuminated by a vivid intellect. His art does not seek to dazzle. It remains muted. It is not an art of energy, but one which heightens the reader's sense of vulnerability, and increases our capacity to suffer. Thus Steiner reverses the gaze from externals to the self:

> - Sind es die Trommeln des Aufbruchs oder das Hämmern eines Besuchers an der Tür?
> - Keins von beiden. Es ist deine pochende Wunde. (No. 19)
> [- Is it the drums of departure or the hammering of a visitor on the door?
> - Neither. It is your beating wound.]

The challenge which many such pieces pose is to discover exactly what, in every sense, they are 'about'. But therein also lies their heuristic power, their spiritual persuasiveness. Clearly, two extremes of Steiner's performance are constituted by the objective discipline of social anthropology and a variety of personal theology schooled in Judaism, Buddhism, and the Tao. Sometimes, the poles obviously meet, as in the following comment: '"Bedeutung und Struktur" scheint mir noch die beste Übersetzung von Tao te King' ('"Meaning and Structure" in the end seems to me the best translation of Tao te King'; No. 86). Elsewhere, the links are less clear. Between the extremes, there lies a special fascination with language and literature, and here one perhaps finds some of the most accessible pieces. Steiner's interests reflect back on his own paradoxical manner: his taste can absorb such literary opposites as Lichtenberg and Hölderlin, Hebbel and Stifter, Sterne and Wordsworth. Among the moderns, Trakl, Eliot and Canetti are obvious points of reference.

Kafka is a special case. Steiner's attitude to Kafka[33] contributed very considerably to his self-understanding, and helps determine his intellectual position in relation to other contemporaries like Adorno, Benjamin, and Scholem. Adorno had high praise for Steiner's view of Kafka, finding in him confirmation for his own interpretation: 'Meine Vorstellung von Kafkas antinomistischer Theologie trifft bis ins innerste zusammen mit Steiners These' ('My concept of Kafka's antinomistic theology coincides with Steiner's thesis, down to the very central core').[34] Thus Adorno's judgement on Steiner's unpublished essay 'Der Magus von Prag'. Interestingly, Steiner also entertains the view of Kafka as a Kabbalist which has been most persuasively put forward by Scholem.[35] But Steiner rejects this kind of reading for one more commensurate with his own perspective. Importantly, Steiner stresses the textual rifts in Kafka which militate against a mystical interpretation:

> [Kafka] wechselte immer wieder die mystische mit der historischen Ebene, da er schliesslich, trotz allen mystischen Elementen und trotz allem, das über ihn gesagt wird, kein Mystiker war (also auch kein 'verkappter Kabbalist'), sondern ein jüdischer mythischer Denker. (No. 214)
>
> [(Kafka) constantly shifted from a mystical to a historical level, because in the end, notwithstanding all the mystical elements and notwithstanding everything that is said about him, he was not a mystic (and hence not even a 'disguised Kabbalist'), but a Jewish mythical thinker.]

The fractures and dual perspective that Steiner discerns in Kafka also typify his own prose, which may either switch from one frame of reference to another, or smelt contrary ones into a single statement. Perhaps 'mythical' would be an appropriate term for many of his aphorisms, too.

How precisely Steiner uses the term 'myth', and in his usage combines specialized knowledge and individual experience, emerges in some comments on Kafka's *Ein Landarzt* (*A Country Doctor*), discussed by Fleischli, but not included here. Steiner focuses on what he calls the 'Wunde-Axt-Problem' ('Wound-Axe Problem'):

> Die Wunde, die 'man nicht ansehen kann, ohne zu pfeifen' führt in den Brustraum. Lose assoziiert ist die Axt, die solche Wunden schlägt [...]

Unwillkürlich denkt man an die Streitaxt und die Literatur, in der ihre furchtbaren Wunden beschrieben werden. Es ist die altnordische. Wenn die Luft in die Leibeshöhle eindringt – die alt-isländische Fóst-bratra-saga [...] beschreibt dies aufs schrecklichste – entsteht ein pfeifend-gurgelnder Ton. (Fleischli, p. 61)

[The wound, 'which one cannot look at without whistling', opens into the chest. There is a loose association with the axe which cuts wounds of this kind [...] Involuntarily, one thinks of battle-axes and the literature which describes their terrible wounds. It is Old Norse literature. When the air penetrates the cavity of the breast – the Old Norse Fóst-bratra Saga describes this most gruesomely – a whistling-gurgling sound emerges.]

Steiner comments on Kafka:

Er hat die Axt verwandelt – sie pfeift nicht selbst – und die Axt – eine Holzfälleraxt. Das letztere ist nicht sinnstörend, im Gegenteil, es stärkt das tödliche Element: die Axt legt ja ganze Bäume um, geht an die Wurzel, an das Leben. (Fleischli, p. 61).

[He transformed the axe – it does not itself whistle – and the axe [becomes] a woodman's axe. This latter does not disturb the sense, on the contrary, it heightens the deadly element: for the axe fells whole trees, attacks the root, attacks life itself.]

Steiner's reading of *Ein Landarzt* exploits closely controlled associations. It combines three main ingredients: knowledge of the text; knowledge of its supposed myth; private experience. The motor that joins these three in a new whole is an act of mythical 'transformation' ('Verwandlung'), as alluded to in the aphorism itself. But each of these three layers is itself complex. The textual knowledge is saturated with further knowledge of Kafka. For Steiner conflates the *Landarzt* imagery with related images from two other texts: the image of the tree recalls Kafka's early prose aphorism, *Die Bäume* ('The Trees');[36] whilst that of the axe alludes to Kafka's celebrated letter to Oskar Pollak of 27 January 1904, in which Kafka asserts: 'ein Buch muss die Axt sein für das gefrorene Meer in uns' ('A book must be the axe for the frozen sea within us').[37] Thus Steiner recombined three relevant images (wound, axe, tree) to create a new pattern in his own reading, which centres on an old mythical image, with its own unique marker (the whistling wound). Two transformations occur: Kafka's (knowing or unknowing) changing of the saga; and Steiner's transformation of Kafka. Consequently, Kafka's text appears in a mythical light; and Steiner's controlled associative exegesis contributes to, or at least reflects upon, the creation of a variant to the old myth. Such exegesis itself partakes of myth.

A likely model for this intellectual transformation of myth may be found in Pindar and Hölderlin.[38] In an important aphorism which Hermann-Röttgen printed in her thesis but excluded from her edition, Steiner observes:

bei Pindar erscheinen Aktualität und Mythos in einem Raum, und die Aktualität, soweit von der Dichtung erfassbar, gewinnt ihren Sinn durch die Beziehung zum Mythos.

[in Pindar actuality and myth appear in a single space, and actuality, insofar as poetry can grasp it, gains its meaning through the relation to myth.] (p. 23f.)

Juxtaposing myth with actuality overtly provides the method of the *Landarzt* aphorism; but the technique also operates in the more hermetic pieces, where Steiner introduces what might be called truncated or latent myths, that is, motifs or images which seem to invoke some archaic but ultimately undefined process. This can be seen in the series of interrelated aphorisms written in June 1946 which Steiner entitled 'Höhlensprüche und -Gedanken' (Cave-Texts and Thoughts). Hermann-Röttgen prints the sequence as the first piece in her selection (albeit missing out the title). It opens by introducing a quasi-mythical realm where the landscape takes on human attributes: 'Um der Höhlen willen falten die Berge sich und wissen es nicht' (The mountains fold for the sake of the caves and do not know it). This hermetic natural imagery recalls Hölderlin's similar use of the *image* of a stream for an avowedly *rational* purpose in his ninth Pindar Fragment.[39] A sense of mystery prevails, since the mountains remain in ignorance of their function: knowledge belongs to some unknown entity, perhaps to man, but not to the mountain itself. Later, it becomes apparent that the caves are a metaphor for humankind: 'da sind jetzt wir die Höhlen' (now we are caves). But the metaphorical resolution only introduces a further question, namely the question of what the mountains are or represent. Man and meaning seem here to be embedded in a mute and chthonic sphere. Just as the aphorism yokes a metaphor (caves) to an absolute metaphor (mountains), so man and reason seem grounded in, and leading back to, the mutely inexplicable world of Nature.

Steiner's mythical transformations have a personal and existential basis, too. Just as the wound in *Ein Landarzt* can be understood to extrapolate from a personal dilemma (tuberculosis), transforming it into a universal metaphor; so Steiner's actual (heart-)disease may provide a biographical starting-point for his own concern with the pain within, with the cave, and with the wound in the chest. This does not explain Steiner's views. But it perhaps helps one see more clearly how in some pieces he managed to create so peculiarly intimate a sense of myth.

Notes

1. See Hermann Grab, *Der Stadtpark und andere Erzählungen* (Frankfurt, 1985); translated by Quentin Hoare, *The Town Park and Other Stories* (London and New York, 1988).
2. See H. G. Adler, 'Die Dichtung der Prager Schule', in Manfred Wagner (ed.), *Im Brennpunkt ein Österreich* (Vienna, 1977), pp. 67–98 ; Jürgen Serke, *Böhmische Dörfer. Wanderungen durch eine verlassene literarische Landschaft* (Vienna and Hamburg, 1987).
3. For a bibliography of Steiner's anthropological publications, see Alfons Fleischli, *Franz Baermann Steiner. Leben und Werk*, Dissertation (University of Fribourg, 1970), pp. 122-3. For an appreciation, see E. E. Evans-Pritchard, 'Preface', Franz [Baermann] Steiner, *Taboo* (London, 1956; Harmondsworth, 1967).
4. For the biographical data given here, see Fleischli, pp. 11-26.

5. H. G. Adler, 'Franz Baermann Steiner', *Deutsche Universitätszeitung* 10, no. 3, 7 February 1955, p. 13.
6. Letter to Paul Bruell, 13 April 1947; see Fleischli, p. 24.
7. E. E. Evans-Pritchard, 'Obituary. Franz Baermann Steiner', *Man*, 3 (1952), p. 121.
8 E. E. Evans-Pritchard, 'Preface', *Taboo* (Harmondsworth, 1967), p. 13.
9. 'Chagga Truth', *Africa*, 24 (1954), 64-9.
10. 'Towards a Classification of Labour', *Sociologus*, 7 (1957), 112-30.
11. Clifton D. Bryant (ed.), *The Social Dimensions of Work* (Englewood Cliffs, NJ, 1972); see 'Introduction', p. 3. Steiner's article is reprinted here, pp. 18-34.
12. 'Notes on Comparative Economics', *The British Journal of Sociology*, 5 (1954), 118-29.
13. The claim is made by Marion Hermann-Röttgen, *Fluchtvergnüglichkeit*, p. 134.
14. Mary Douglas points out that structural anthropology was disseminated from the early years of this century and took an important turn in E. E. Evans-Pritchard's *The Nuer* (Oxford, 1940). A copy of this book was in Steiner's library. See Mary Douglas, *Purity and Danger. An Analysis of the Concepts of Pollution and Taboo* (1966; London and New York, 1984), p. vii.
15. Contrary to a popular misconception, 'language game' denotes *both* linguistic practice *and* the human activity to which language pertains. See Ludwig Wittgenstein, *Philosophische Untersuchungen/Philosophical Investigations* (1946), tr. G. E. M. Anscombe (Oxford, 1958), pp. 5-5e.
16. Iris Murdoch, *The Message to the Planet* (London, 1984). The unkind reviewer in *The Times Literary Supplement* treats the book as a kind of a *roman à clef*, and sees Marcus Vallar as Wittgenstein and Canetti, and Alfred Ludens as Kafka. The extent to which this leads to a fair reading is arguable. However, insofar as the text does recall real people, one should note that Ludens also evokes Franz Baermann Steiner, who was really a friend of Canetti, as he was of Iris Murdoch herself. See Clive Sinclair, 'Is there anybody out there?', *The Times Literary Supplement*, 20 October 1989, p. 149.
17. Sue Summers, 'The Lost Loves of Iris Murdoch', *You. Mail on Sunday*, 5 June 1988, pp. 17-20 (p. 20).
18. See Robert Frazer (ed.), *Sir James Frazer and the Literary Imagination* (London, 1991).
19. T. S. Eliot, *The Complete Poems and Plays* (London, 1969), p. 76.
20. Hans Eichner, 'The Poetry of Franz Baermann Steiner', *German Life and Letters*, 7 (1954), 180-6; see p. 185f.
21. Franz Baermann Steiner, *Unruhe ohne Uhr. Ausgewählte Gedicht aus dem Nachlass*, ed. H. G. Adler (Heidelberg, 1954), p. 39.
22. Michael Hamburger and Christopher Middleton, *Modern German Poetry 1910-1960. An Anthology with Verse Translations* (London and New York, 1962), p 275.
23. For a translation of 'The Panther' see R. M. Rilke, *Requiem and other Poems*, translated by J. B. Leishman (London, 1935; 1949 2nd edn, ff.), p. 91; a much better version is in [R. M.] Rilke, *Selected Poems*, tr. J. B. Leishman (Harmondsworth, 1964), p. 33.
24. Sir Maurice Bowra provides a most illuminating discussion of Steiner's poem on the armistice, '8 Mai 1945'. However, one might disagree with Bowra's conclusion. Bowra sees a weakness in the poem in Steiner's alleged lack of an overview, caused by his refusal to adopt a political standpoint. Against this one might argue that Steiner does adopt a wider perspective, but that it is the viewpoint of an anthropologist, who uncovers the meaning of barbaric ritual, which survives intact in modern society. See C. M. Bowra, *Poetry and Politics* (Cambridge, 1966), pp. 1-3.
25. Steiner, *Unruhe ohne Uhr*, pp. 88-95.
26. Franz Baermann Steiner, *Eroberungen. Ein lyrischer Zyklus*, ed. H. G. Adler

(Heidelberg and Darmstadt, 1964).

27. Steiner, *Unruhe ohne Uhr*, p. 51.

28. Hamburger and Middleton, *Modern German Poetry*, p. 277.

29. Conversation between Elias Canetti and Alfons Fleischli, summer, 1967. See Fleischli, p. 58.

30. For earlier publications of Steiner's aphorisms, not all of which are printed in *Fluchtvergnüglichkeit*, see 'Aphorismen', *Literarische Revue*, 4, Heft 1 (1949), 44; 'Aphorismen', *Eckart* 23 (1953), 70; *Eckart* 23 (1953), 75 and 303; 'Aus dem Nachlass', *Merkur*, 8 (1954), 32-41, 'Sprachliche Feststellungen und Versuche', *Merkur*, 10 (1956), 966-73; 'Sätze und Fragen', *Neue Deutsche Hefte* 29 (1956), 336-8.

31. Franz Baermann Steiner, 'Kurzprosa. "Feststellungen und Versuche". Eine Auswahl', ed. Marion Hermann, unpublished dissertation (Stuttgart, 1983).

32. Gerhard Neumann, *Ideenparadiese* (Munich, 1976), p. 829.

33. A selection of Steiner's aphorisms on Kafka appeared as 'Aus den Notizen über Kafka', *Merkur*, 8 (1954), 39-41.

34. Letter from Theodor W. Adorno to H. G. Adler, cited by Hermann-Röttgen, *Fluchtvergnüglichkeit*, p. 132 .

35. See Gershom Scholem, 'Zehn unhistorische Sätze über Kabbala', in Scholem, *Judaica* 3 (Frankfurt 1973), pp. 264-71 (p. 271): and Walter Benjamin, Gershom Scholem, *Briefwechsel* (Frankfurt, 1985), passim.

36. Franz Kafka, 'Die Bäume', in Kafka, *Erzählungen und kleine Prosa*, 2nd edn (New York, 1946), p. 44.

37. Franz Kafka, *Briefe 1902-1924* (Frankfurt, 1958), p. 8.

38. For evidence of Steiner's preoccupation with Hölderlin, see his poem 'An Hölderlin', his 'Notizen über Hölderlin' and the essay by H. G. Adler, 'Das Hölderlinbild Franz Baermann Steiners', *Hölderlin Jahrbuch*, 9 (1955/56), pp. 232-40.

39. See Jeremy Adler, 'Philosophical Archeology: Hölderlin's "Pindar Fragments". A translation with an interpretation', *Comparative Criticism*, 6 (1984), 23-46 (p. 45f).

Part Three
Reviews

Brian Keith-Smith (ed.), *Bristol Austrian Studies* (Bristol: University of Bristol Press, 1990), xvi + 274 pp., 21 ills., £18.

A reader picking up *Bristol Austrian Studies* expects to find that the place-name in the title simply means that the volume was published by Bristol University. It is however far more closely associated with Bristol than that, being entirely written by present and former members of the Bristol German Department, edited by a member of that Department and containing a tribute to its late distinguished head, Professor August Closs. Brian Keith-Smith in his editorial introduction draws a parallel between this volume and 'the joint papers and symposia produced by scientists working together in research groups'. It is a sign of the times that scholars in the humanities should feel the need to legitimize what they do in this way. The volume, full of interest as it is, does not show any signs that this reviewer could see of team-work in any meaningful sense, though it does bear witness to the work of a distinguished German Department which has suffered more cuts than many in recent years.

The chronological scope of the volume ranges from the Middle Ages to the present day but focuses exclusively, and to an extent which is unusual today, on Austrian *literature* rather than on a more widely-based conception of Austrian studies. By and large too, the literary figures and texts examined are the expected ones: Nestroy, Stifter, Schnitzler, Hofmannsthal all have essays devoted solely to them (Hofmannsthal has two), while Raimund and Grillparzer make an appearance in Ken Mills's contribution. Though Kafka is a surprise in this context, he is scarcely an unknown name, so it is only in the contributions by Peter Skrine on the late eighteenth-/early nineteenth-century dramatist Heinrich Joseph von Collin and by Marie-Louise Chalcraft on contemporary Austrian women's writing that we make the acquaintance of lesser-known authors and works. Anthony Harper's piece on Laurentius von Schnüffis may also come into this category for non-Baroque specialists.

As with any such volume, there are differences in quality, both in the writing and in the originality and depth of the scholarship. Frank Shaw on the Babenberg Dukes, Peter Skrine on Collin and Colin Walker on Nestroy and the Redemptorists are for this reviewer the outstanding essays. Some of the other pieces on major authors, which show no cognizance of any secondary literature published in the last twenty years, may be symptomatic of the state of Bristol University Library. Cuts or no, however, the Bristol German Department demonstrates here that it is very much alive and kicking.

HELEN WATANABE-O'KELLY

John Komlos, *Nutrition and Economic Development in the Eighteenth-Century Habsburg Monarchy* (Princeton: Princeton University Press, 1990), xvii + 325 pp., $39.95.

This innovative and ambitious book is written with two objectives in mind. Although it focuses on the Habsburg monarchy as a case-study, it attempts to construct a model for understanding the dynamics behind industrialization in the modern world. At the same time it profiles and evaluates the relative success of the Habsburg political economy during the era of so-called enlightened monarchs such as Maria Theresa and Joseph II. What is most revolutionary, however, is the author's methodology, which traces the effects of both industrialization and domestic reform through changes in nutrition and human stature. It is a measure of his success that his study has, at this writing, recently won the Austrian Cultural Institute's book prize for 1989–90.

The author begins his work by challenging the notion of economic take-off posited by leading theorists such as Walt Rostow and Alexander Gerschenkron, in favour of more recent explanations suggesting gradual and intermittent, but fairly persistent economic development over a period of centuries. Crucial to the author's thesis is his stress on the interdependence of economic and population growth throughout early modern Europe. He argues that cycles of economic expansion in the thirteenth, sixteenth and eighteenth centuries were cut short by nutritional crises which literally stunted the growth of populations that invariably encountered decreased fertility and resistance to disease, higher infant mortality, and even outright starvation. It was this 'Malthusian trap' that stood squarely in the way of what has come to be known as the industrial revolution until some European societies – including Austria and England – were able to meet their growing societies' nutritional needs at the end of the eighteenth century.

Although he follows population trends closely, the author traces changes in living standards by measuring his subjects' height, rather than their income. He points out that, whereas 'human stature is a proxy for nutritional status' (p. 42), wealth and income did not necessarily guarantee access to adequate sources of food. As examples he contrasts the superior stature of the relatively poor agrarian populations of Habsburg Galicia and Hungary to those of the 'Erblande' as well as Ireland to England, and even the southern American colonies (including their slaves') to New England. His evidence for the Habsburg monarchy rests primarily on 'Kriegsarchiv' records of tens of thousands of army recruits from Galicia, Hungary, Bohemia, Moravia and Lower Austria, as well as from cadets, enrolled in the monarchy's military schools. He does, however, frequently supplement and corroborate his findings with published data relating to America and other parts of Europe.

The author finds that the stature of Habsburg soldiers rose steadily during the first half of the eighteenth century, presumably due to the well-documented incidence of good weather, low food prices, and higher real wages. It then declined over the next three decades as explosive population growth throughout the monarchy (as high as 50 per cent in the Bohemian crownlands) sharply cut into nutritional levels, partly by inducing lower real wages and higher staple prices. Significantly the decline was greatest in more economically developed areas such as Lower Austria and more heavily industrialized parts of Bohemia, rather than in agrarian areas like Galicia and Hungary. The Malthusian trap was beginning to spring on the monarchy, as well as on other parts of the Continent and England, where average stature declined by a full inch.

Yet by the century's penultimate decade there began a dramatic recovery in levels of nutrition and hence in the stature of the Austrian soldiery, that lasted well into the next century. The author attributes this to the determined intervention of the Habsburg regime, which he documents chiefly from the extensive body of published German and Hungarian language scholarship. He concedes that the monarchy's rivalry with Prussia may have played some role in these reforms, especially in its attempts to maintain a sufficient peasant tax base for its military build-up. He stresses, however, that it was motivated principally by the unfolding subsistence crisis, both out of a genuine concern for popular suffering and a fear of domestic instability following the outbreak of several domestic risings in the Bohemian lands.

Whatever the regime's motivation, he credits it with four achievements: a limited, but persistent reduction in the economic power and privileges of various élites, most notably noble landlords and guilds; the promotion of manufacturing by numerous means, often at expense of the guilds, existing monopolies, contemplative religious orders, and foreign competition; the protection of the peasantry's welfare *vis-à-vis* landlords; and more efficient integration of Galician and Hungarian food supplies with the nutritional needs of the growing industrial class of the 'Erblande'. The extent of its intervention persuades the author that the monarchy had become an 'incipient welfare state' (p. 128) by the end of the century.

CHARLES INGRAO

Helmut Bachmaier (ed.), *Franz Grillparzer*, suhrkamp taschenbuch materialien (Frankfurt: Suhrkamp, 1991), 462 pp., DM 22.

To commemorate the 1991 Grillparzer bicentenary Suhrkamp have produced a collection of essays designed to illustrate the various phases of Grillparzer criticism. For the Grillparzer scholar this affords a nostalgic revisitation of such venerable names as Johannes Volkelt and Friedrich Gundolf. But the non-specialist is equally well served with what turns out to be an interesting illustrated review of the changing faces of twentieth-century literary criticism.

The collection is introduced by an essay by Robert Pichl which provides a concise review of the history of Grillparzer criticism, and then concentrates on the post-war period, in which Pichl identifies two broad streams in *werkimmanente* interpretations, respectively inspired by two of the major figures of post-war criticism: Emil Staiger and Herbert Seidler. Pichl's account of Grillparzer studies, however, does not altogether correspond to Bachmaier's actual choice of essays in this volume. As the most important early critic, for example, Pichl selects not Volkelt but August Sauer, who produced the first scholarly edition of Grillparzer's works. Admittedly, given the substantial body of Grillparzer criticism, the editor had an impossible task in attempting to make a truly representative choice. Indeed, of the earlier critics either Strich or Scherer might have been preferred to Volkelt, and Joachim Müller or Ilse Münch to Gundolf (Pichl himself also mentions Bietak's seminal monograph associating Grillparzer with the Biedermeier period). But it is the post-war period that provides the real surprises. True, the editor reprints Staiger's important essay on *König Ottokar*, and includes an extract from Heinz Politzer's stimulating monograph of 1972, but instead of Brinkmann's chapter on *Der arme Spielmann*, we have a rather laboured essay on this story by Roland Heine. The inclusion of Max Kommerell and Ingrid Strohschneider-Kohrs at the expense of major post-war scholars such as Walter Naumann, Gerhard Baumann or Friedrich Sengle is bound to cause some surprise, and the British Germanist may regret the exclusion of W. E. Yates, J. P. Stern or Martin Swales.

The four original contributions representing the very latest in Grillparzer research are frankly disappointing. A long article by Hilde Haider-Pregler on the reception of *Das goldene Vließ* scarcely offers a new view of Grillparzer, and two articles by Thomas Horst and Dieter Borchmeyer, on the somewhat peripheral issue of Grillparzer's antagonism to the music of Wagner and Weber, rather duplicate each other. The best of the new essays is a sensitive study of *Ein Bruderzwist in Habsburg* by Hans Höller, though this concludes with an enigmatic and unexplained comment on Klesel: 'Nur eine Gestalt hätte den Weg eines politisch machbaren Friedens gewußt: Klesel, der in der Sekundärliteratur fast nur als Schurke und Verräter gehandelt [sic] wird' ('Only one figure could have found the way to a politically feasible peace: Klesel, who has been treated almost exclusively as a villain and traitor in the secondary literature'). As Klesel has not been mentioned previously in the article, the former point is in need of development; the latter point is no longer true.

The collection concludes with essays or comments on Grillparzer by other major writers. These provide an interesting alternative view to that of scholars and critics, though whilst Kafka's enthusiasm for *Der arme Spielmann* is of acknowledged significance, one may question the wisdom of devoting a whole page of text to the following brief item from the diary of Musil: 'Las Grillparzers *Selbstbiographie* ... Meisterhafte Schilderung einer alten Wohnung ... Das ist vornehmer Chronistenstil; so sollte mein Roman geschrieben sein!' ('Read Grillparzer's autobiography ... Masterly description of an old apartment ... That is a noble chronicle style; that is how my novel should be written!')

BRUCE THOMPSON

Jürgen Hein, *Johann Nestroy*, Sammlung Metzler vol. 258 (Stuttgart: Metzler, 1990), viii + 144 pp., DM 19,80.

Gerald Stieg and Jean-Marie Valentin (eds), *Johann Nestroy, 1801–1862, Vision du monde et écriture dramatique*, Publications de l'Institut d'Allemand d'Asnières No. 12 (Asnières: l'Institut d'Allemand, 1991), 301 pp., 120 F.

For an author or a topic to become '*Metzlerfähig*' means it is generally accepted as part of the canon, and one might think that meant the groundwork had been done on it and the basic schools of thought marked out. Jürgen Hein's monograph on Nestroy paints a quite different picture. It is full of pleas and recommendations for further research, a shopping list of requirements for the future: filmography, discography, proper statistics and information on Nestroy's tours (with reviews), on contemporary performances of his plays outside Vienna, especially in North Germany, plus comparison with the local dialect farce traditions in those areas, individual interpretations of all the plays, in-depth analysis of the language Nestroy uses ('Hochdeutsch'/real dialect/'Bühnendialekt') and the way he uses it, theatre practice (a real can of worms: why are there fewer musical interludes, why does he write fewer plays as time goes by, what happens to the versions of his own plays when, for example, a three-acter is cut to one act to meet the craze for three plays in an evening?), and so on and so forth.

However, the work is by no means wholly queries and demands. It tries to describe quite clearly areas and directions of possible research which are demarcated by means of precise statements such as 'es führt kein Weg vom Handeln der Possenfigur zur Deutung der "Weltanschauung" ihres Schöpfers' ('no path leads from the actions of the character in the farce to an interpretation of the world-view of that character's creator', p. 36) or 'Nicht im Zeigen der sozialen Widersprüche liegt die Leistung Nestroys, sondern im künstlerischen Aufdecken der Sprachlichkeit und Spielhaftigkeit des gesellschaftlichen Rollenspiels' ('Nestroy's achievement does not lie in showing social contradictions, but in the artistic uncovering of the linguistic and play-acting elements of the system of social roles', p. 56) or 'Die Theaterwelt [...] wird zur szenischen Metapher, die Biographie, Realität und Fiktion, gesellschaftliches und künstlerisches Rollenspiel übergangslos verbindet' ('The world of the theatre turns into a theatrical metaphor which joins seamlessly biography, reality and fiction, the artistic and social playing of roles') (p. 32). Thus Hein attempts to rule out the sloppy thinking which bedevils so many well-meaning attempts to deal with Nestroy, and is not entirely absent from the best efforts. (He is even guilty himself of an overly direct life-work equation on p. 26, where he states that Nestroy's disillusionment over his romantic youthful love shaped his relationship to the opposite sex and emerges in the world of his plays.)

Since Hein is prepared to be so explicit about what is essentially unfruitful or unscholarly speculation, it is a pity that he does not provide a more critical bibliography, and spare future scholars those dissertations which are no more than uncommented and unanalysed catalogues. The bibliography is in fact very good, though in some ways confusing, because it is effectively a series of bibliographies, relating to the series of research areas that Hein sets out, and confusion can arise when he refers in one section to an article or book which is only mentioned in the bibliography of a later section; however, the index of *all* the personal names mentioned can help here.

The list of Nestroy's plays with details of first performance, number of performances in his lifetime, name of the character he played, source of the plot, secondary literature, and so on, is fairly helpful, but it does not emerge clearly from the details about the textual tradition whether the text is actually based on an autograph MS, or whether the reference to the catalogue of Nestroy autographs is only to a fragment. Unambiguous statements of this kind might have been more useful than page references to works which may not be readily accessible to all.

The proceedings of the international Nestroy colloquium held in Paris at the end of January 1991, and appearing before the wine is dry in the bottom of the glasses, provide ample evidence of the centrifugal nature of Nestroy scholarship, just as Hein depicts it. The writers may have mingled physically, but there is little evidence that they did so mentally. The contributions are in French or

German (with some Latin needed to understand Wolfgang Neuber's *terminos technicos artis universalis rhetoricae explicandae*), and many of the expected names are there. Walter Obermaier performs his usual indispensable task of providing basic raw material and sensible observations on it - the sort of thing which must eventually build up to a Nestroy biography - in this case, insights into the background and careers of the the the theatre-reviewers as a step towards evaluating their writings. W. E. Yates corrects the image of the 'scribbling genius' who 'scarce blotted a line' by showing the care with which Nestroy constantly re-worked his text. Gerald Stieg, Sigurd Paul Scheichl and Wendelin Schmidt-Dengler all deal with essentially related subjects: Stieg with the complex question of dialect in Nestroy, Scheichl with the 'Stilbruch', particularly the one produced by the juxtaposition of 'Hochdeutsch' and dialect, and Schmidt-Dengler with Nestroy's treatment of allegory, which is effectively brought down from its pedestal and installed in the 'Vorstadt' on a permanent basis, as a kind of doorstop-cum-footscraper. If these three had got together with Roger Bauer, whose topic was actually the question of parody/travesty/satire, beginning in the late eighteenth-century Austrian Enlightenment, then a very profitable piece of collective research might have resulted. And Volker Klotz's interesting account of *Heimliches Geld, Heimliche Liebe* (expanded from an *Akademietheater* programme) also has some telling passages on the use of allegory with a Viennese face. Hugo Aust, with his customary stylistic elegance, compares Nestroy's and Walt Disney's techiques of creative adaptation; but since there are two other essays on Nestroy's use of French originals (Jeannine Charue-Ferrucci on *Dreißig Jahre aus dem Leben eines Lumpen* and Gérard Schneilin on *Der Zerrissene*) as well as a paper by Jean-Marie Valentin on a French adaptation of Nestory's *Zu ebener Erde und erster Stock*, with a complete text of the French version taking up the final hundred pages of the book, it would have been very useful to have these scholars working *together*, in order to establish some set of general conclusions about Nestroy's methods. As it is, the essays highlight the diverse approaches and vocabulary of the individual scholars, and the distinct problems and features of the individual plays, rather than the common elements which might have been expected to emerge. In English universities, at any rate, we are being encouraged to think more of the scientific model of joint research. In view of this book, and Hein's account of the state of the art, Nestroy research could only benefit.

MIKE ROGERS

Stefan H. Kaszynski (ed.), *Galizien – eine literarische Heimat.* Seria Filologia Germanska 27 (Poznan: Uniwersytet Im. Adama Mickiewicza, 1987), 255 pp., 400 zloty.

'Heimat' is a loaded word: it recalls 'Heimatliteratur', a regional literature with an anti-urban, anti-modern and anti-democratic animus. This volume records the proceedings of an international symposium held at Poznan in 1984, before Edgar Reitz's film gave dubious respectability to the concept of 'Heimat', and the contributors are more disposed to analyse than to celebrate the notion. All agree that celebrations of the home region gain literary value when the writer has the honesty to admit that his home is irrecoverably lost. Hence the hero of this book is Joseph Roth, for whom the concept of 'home' becomes explicitly problematic. In 'Die Büste des Kaisers' (1935) Graf Morstin, having outlived the Habsburg Empire, is forced to ask himself what 'home' means: 'Was ist überhaupt Heimat?' Klaus Bohnen gives an acute analysis of the various answers Roth provides for this question, ranging from his biographical origins in Galicia to the fictional home constructed in his novels. Gerald Stieg, in a characteristically scintillating and incisive paper, examines the self-deceptions lying in wait for a writer like Manès Sperber, who transferred the nostalgia of 'home' from his Galician birthplace to Vienna, and therefore found himself colluding with the literary establishment to deny the anti-Semitism that, as Stieg shows, still persists in Viennese culture.

Roth and Karl Emil Franzos, the best-known German-language novelists to come from Galicia, are the subjects of several of the best papers in this collection. Margarita Pazi provides an important forty-page study of Franzos, drawing on unpublished materials in the Vienna Stadtbibliothek and elsewhere, while Hartmut Steinecke makes a modest and persuasive plea for his rediscovery and Maria Klanska places him in the context of the Haskala (the Jewish Enlightenment). Norbert Oellers discusses the miraculous and, to most readers, embarrassing conclusion of Roth's *Hiob,* while Gotthart Wunberg returns to the concept of 'home' by analysing Roth's last essay, 'Die Eiche Goethes in Buchenwald'. Here Roth comments, with a quiet but devastating irony reminiscent of Karl Kraus, on the reverence for German culture shown by the concentration-camp officials who have preserved at Buchenwald, near Weimar, the oak-tree under which Goethe wrote 'Wanderers Nachtlied'. Here, as Wunberg points out, Roth implicitly acknowledges that the German tradition of 'Humanität' has been consigned to the irrecoverable past, like the Jewish traditions Roth mourns elsewhere: both survive only as travesties.

Of the more general essays, the most rewarding is that by Zoran Konstantinovic, who combines a valuable survey of Lemberg's German-language literary history with a short account of a recent visit to what is now Lviv. Other contributors deal with such Polish writers as Józef Wittlin, Stanislaw Vincenz, and Julian Stryjkowski. It is regrettable that certain authors who are better known to Western readers, notably the fantasy-writer Bruno Schulz from Drohobycz and the Hebrew novelist S. Y. Agnon from Buczacz, are mentioned only in passing. Several contributors address the question of how the physical landscape of Galicia became transformed into a recognizable literary landscape with standard components such as market-places swamped in mud; but they do not deal with it convincingly. The generally high standard of this collection, however, makes it valuable for anyone curious about the literature produced in Galicia, once a multi-cultural province and now scarcely recognizable as the western Ukraine; though the non-specialist should first read Martin Pollack's *Nach Galizien: Von Chassiden, Huzulen, Polen und Ruthenen* (Vienna, 1984).

RITCHIE ROBERTSON

Jürgen Serke, *Böhmische Dörfer: Wanderungen durch eine verlassene literarische Landschaft*
(Vienna: Zsolnay, 1987), 480 pp., DM 49,80.

A handsome quarto volume, with an eye-catching dust-cover depicting a
collapsing hybrid baroque building – collage or trompe l'oeil? – profusely
illustrated with authentic historical photographs, and clearly structured: a
superior coffee-table book perhaps, but topical in its subject matter as few such
are? Certainly any member of the educated public would be grateful to the host
who provided him or her in this volume with the opportunity to relive half a
century of European history (1938–89) from the perspective of Czecho-Slovakia
and its German-speaking literary élite, the more so since its author is careful to
document where appropriate the relationship between these writers and the
Czecho-Slovak state and culture. Indeed, otherwise well-informed readers may
be surprised to learn of the extent to which individual *deutschböhmisch* writers
functioned as mediators of Czech literature or were themselves translated into
Czech.

But a coffee-table book is one in which the text is by definition subordinate
to the picture. Not so here – despite the extraordinary quality and information
value of those photographs of long-forgotten first editions, extracts from works
published in short-lived exile newspapers, intimate and always poignant
portraits of the family life of a systematically eradicated culture. The global
dimension of the sources of these illustrations (p. 480), as well as the number
derived from personal archives, including Serke's own, give an indication of
what we are actually being offered here. For *Böhmische Dörfer* is, despite the
historical authenticity of its documentary material and the mass of well-digested
information, a very personal book. It is at one level yet another persuasive
example of post-war Germans' melancholy and high-minded tributes to the
memory of Jewish culture in German-speaking lands. It functions also as oral
history, in the sense that it clearly owes a great deal to its author's interviews
with the survivors and their families, who then became friends and collaborators
(H. G. Adler and his family perhaps, as a case in point, or the children of Leo
Perutz, whom he photographs in their home in Israel).

Böhmische Dörfer: the incidental provocation in the ironic title of the sister
crown-land of Moravia, birthplace of so many great names, and at present
preoccupied with notions of separate 'nationhood', is surely unwitting, as is the
traditional *pars pro toto* use of 'Sudetenland' for the whole of *Deutschböhmen*. But
for the rest the consciously selective approach is anything but idiosyncratic;
indeed it constitutes the book's special achievement. Kafka and Rilke appear,
as do Werfel, Freud, Ebner-Eschenbach, not in the 'literary' section, but in the
company of Hitler, Stalin, Dubcek, Husák etc. in the emotively captioned and
powerfully written historical introduction: 'Europa starb in Prag' (pp. 7–85), as
part of the context. The body of the book is devoted to portraits of some forty-
seven German poets of 'Bohemia-by-the-sea', life history, oeuvre and reception.
Of these, fifteen receive in-depth treatment (pp. 86–376); eighty pages are
devoted to the remainder. The first group includes Johannes Urzidil, Camill
Hoffmann, Leo Perutz, and H. G. Adler, with more than thirty pages being

devoted to some, such as Hans Natonek and Hugo Sonnenschein. By contrast, and despite Serke's concern to offer a balanced assessment of Brod's own literary work, Max Brod finds his place in the second section.

The central aim of the book is 'Ehrenrettung', of the status, extent and enduring worth of German literature in Czecho-Slovakia and its protagonists, both as individuals and collectively, and particularly writers of forgotten or, in Serke's view, unjustly neglected works. Of equal concern to him is the rehabilitation of the good name of others, such as that of Hugo Sonnenschein (=Sonka), victim of Auschwitz, but who died branded as a German collaborator in a Stalinist Czech jail, with, as Serke implies, the *nihil obstat* of prominent members of the international PEN. He is not afraid to name names – of famous publishers, distinguished academics, established international authors, who allegedly failed, some through ignorance, some crassly or even cynically, in their duty to these their colleagues. For all but a handful of the writers discussed here were Jews, and others, such as Paul Leppin, were categorized as such by the Nazis. Serke, combining in his extremely polished and fluent style high-level investigative journalism with detective work, integrates in his textual and photographic record ample quotations from the poetic (and scientific) oeuvre of his authors, which document the terrible fate of all but a few, while at the same time underpinning their significance in the history of modern literature.

Without doubt this is a work to be read reflectively, if not uncritically, by teachers and authors of German literary history, and one whose intimate knowledge of subject and acute sense of the historical context will make an unfamiliar period and phenomenon accessible to the student reader.

EDA SAGARRA

Ákos Moravánszky, *Die Architektur der Donaumonarchie* (Berlin: Ernst & Sohn, 1988), 228 pp., DM 76.

In setting as the subject of his book 'the main architectural trends in the Austro-Hungarian Monarchy from 1867 to 1918', Ákos Moravánszky is confronted by a vast body of material and considerable problems of organization. Dismissing both chronological and regional approaches, he chooses to arrange his material thematically, taking as chapter headings such topics as 'Die Geburt der modernen Großstadt', 'Die Architektur des Historismus', 'Der Jugendstil und seine Varianten', 'Nationale and folkloristische Bestrebungen', and 'Die Rückkehr zur klassischen Formensprache'. This abandonment of a chronological sequence has the great merit of denying the teleological reading of late nineteenth- and early twentieth-century architecture as an inexorable progression towards the brave new world of functionalism and the white architecture of 'Neues Bauen'. Although Moravánszky apologizes to the reader for jumping back and forward in time, the chronological shifts are unobtrusive and generally handled with considerable narrative skill. The lack of a regional focus, however, is more disturbing, as the particular characteristics and contributions of the fascinating ethnic mix that made up the Austro-Hungarian Empire disappear beneath the search for shared stylistic motifs. While Moravánszky alludes, for example, to the preference of the Prague architects for Parisian rather than Viennese models, the reasons for this preference and its political implications are not developed further.

In a satisfying way the structure of the individual chapters reflects the overall structure of the book. Vienna is the recurring starting-point and the introductory chapter, entitled 'Gesellschaft und Kultur der Monarchie', is focused primarily on the Viennese context. Following this pattern, successive chapters take as exemplars the Viennese experience of urbanization, Jugendstil, engineering architecture, or pre-modern rationalism, and then set off into the Empire for comparable buildings. Although the Viennese model is clearly essential to any account of Austro-Hungarian architecture, the format is unfortunate in that it forces the author to tell once again the oft-told tale of 'Vienna 1900'. Indeed, the general introduction reads like a précis of Schorske's account and rehearses the same uninformative generalizations that are invariably offered in attempts to link the various artistic currents that fomented in the Austrian capital at the turn of the century. We are told by Moravánszky, for example, that Kraus, Loos, Schönberg and Wittgenstein were all concerned with 'die Ausdrucksformen der Probleme der Gesellschaft'. The Viennese starting-point means that the accounts of the contributions of such luminaries as Otto Wagner, Joseph Maria Olbrich, Josef Hoffmann and Adolf Loos also cover well-trodden ground. It should be noted, however, that Moravánszky is particularly skilful in pointing out the theoretical premises behind the works of the Viennese masters. In a few sentences he delineates very well the influence of Semper on Wagner, or of Schopenhauer and Lipps on the evolution of Jugendstil.

The reader already acquainted with the Viennese context may wish that Moravánszky had shifted the weight of his narrative away from the centre, and more towards Bohemia and Moravia, Hungary and Slovenia. The diversity is remarkable, and Budapest alone can offer the wonderfully folkloric and Byzantine creations of Ödön Lechner, the Nordic churches of Károly Kós and Béla Jánszky, and the dazzling, protomodernist facades of Béla Lajta. The reader is offered tantalizing glimpses of these marvellously inventive buildings, but is left speculating on the finer detail. Exactly what did Lajta learn, for example, during his time as an assistant to Alfred Messel in Berlin and Richard Norman Shaw in London?

Such detailed information, however, is hardly to be expected from a book that sets out to survey a complex of unique yet interrelated architectural cultures. With his enviable command of the principal languages of Central Europe, Moravánszky is especially well able to delineate this wider context. Now that the doors of Eastern Europe are more open to the West, we can look forward to closer studies of the individual stones in the mosaic that Moravánszky has laid out. Access to Western printing should also improve the graphical quality. Although published in West Berlin, *Die Architektur der Donaumonarchie* is printed in Hungary. Even allowing for Moravánszky's understandable preference for contemporary photographs, the quality of the reproductions is very poor.

IAIN BOYD WHYTE

Steven Béla Várdy and Ágnes Huszár Várdy, *The Austro-Hungarian Mind: At Home and Abroad*, East European Monographs (New York: Columbia University Press, 1990), x + 374 pp., $40.

What is a mind, in the sense used here? And, given that this question can be answered, did Austria-Hungary as a whole actually possess such a composite? Our authors tackle their subject subtly, first defining 'mind' as the comprehensive outlook of the educated classes, and then (to meet the twentieth century) extending their range to embrace whole ethnicities. The Dual Monarchy defined itself as two polities linked for certain vital purposes in a species of juridico-political limited liability company. Each unit – at least at the higher levels – was culturally dominated by its largest ethnic group: 'Austria' by German speakers, 'Hungary' by speakers of Magyar; and the results of their interaction can fairly be termed Austro-Hungarian. In discussing who owed what to whom, however, it is necessary also to consider contributions from other, less powerful ethnic groups, like the Czechs in 'Austria' and the Croats in the Hungarian unit.

While Part One of this work is a 'dual' affair entitled 'Austro-German and Hungarian Romanticism', Parts Two, Three and Four are apparently devoted to largely Hungarian themes. If 'Baron Joseph Eötvös on Liberalism and Nationalism in the Austrian Empire' still straddles the 'dual' monarchy, 'Trianon and the Hungarian Minority Question' certainly does not, and 'The Hungarian-American Experience' deals with exile from the Magyar base. The nature of Hungarian history from 1526 guaranteed a profound Austrian influence on Magyar culture, which continues even today, though by the end of the eighteenth century it had been joined by influences from Britain and France. Nikolaus Lenau and Karl Beck, discussed here, originated from Hungary but were key figures in Austrian circles. But even here, with an essay on 'The Image of the Turks in Jókai's Historical Novels', a strongly Hungarian topic obtrudes. The dominant subject of Part Two and the beginning of Part Three is Baron Joseph Eötvös. Born into the deeply Germanized upper aristocracy of the Magyars and brought up by a benignly influential and pious mother, he represented a type of liberalism which, while known in Britain and France, has been most characteristic of *Mitteleuropa*. He was wedded more to what was theoretically desirable than to what was certain or even probable. Not so Count Stephen Széchenyi, his Anglophile and overshadowing senior, a reformer who, though committed more to Hungary than to Austria, was often blessed with Imperial co-operation. With individuals so prominent and influential in a pre-democratic age, it was sufficient in most fields for a mere handful of leaders to think in terms of the Dual Monarchy to ensure the potent and clear-cut existence of an 'Austro-Hungarian mind'.

The truncated Hungary of 1920 and since, virtually uni-ethnic and politically sovereign, has never wholly discarded its Austrian affinities. It had the misfortune to be on the wrong side in both World Wars, and war and Communism caused many Magyars to emigrate to the United States. Writing of the period before the Treaty of Trianon, our authors show a sense of the Habsburg Empire that is rich, accurate, and perceptive. They grasp the cosmopolitan role of Vienna and the distinctive character of its culture, which ensured that Budapest in turn became impregnated with 'Danubian' qualities beyond what the Austro-Germans or the Magyars could have produced alone. The Várdys highlight the metropolitan qualities of both cities, with Budapest displaying an almost Paris-like zest for self-admiration and contempt for the corners of its fatherland. Although Professors Body and Stourzh have already done much to celebrate the distinction of Baron Eötvös, the materials here help to ensure that his merits are recognized. Those in Part Three, on Transylvania before its allocation to Romania at Trianon, are also important. For the Horthy period and the years of exile, the authors' mood shifts somewhat. They are acutely conscious of Hungary's political separateness and its economic and social disruption. Their analysis remains excellent, but a note of apprehensive pessimism creeps in, though relieved by a strong sense of the Magyars' achievement in adversity. Until World War II, Magyars were 'insiders' *par excellence*, but American exile produced the psychology of the outsider, since it compelled émigré Magyars to undergo experiences akin to those of the 'outsiders' of the Lands of St Stephen – Slovaks, Romanians, Ruthenes, Croats, Serbs, and even the despised gipsies. Nevertheless, the Magyar spirit was indomitable, and the Várdys themselves are living proof that Austrian influences did not weaken the integrity of the Magyar mind.

MICHAEL HURST

Robert Pynsent (ed.), *Decadence and Innovation: Austro-Hungarian Life and Art at the Turn of the Century* (London: Weidenfeld and Nicolson, 1989), xiv + 258pp., £25.

Decadence and Innovation consists of a selection of papers on various aspects of Austro-Hungarian art and life at the turn of the century which were delivered at the School of Slavonic and Eastern European Studies in London in December 1986. It follows an earlier volume of essays on central European *fin-de-siècle* culture, *Intellectuals and the Future in the Habsburg Monarchy* (1988), edited by László Péter and Robert Pynsent. Like its predecessor, *Decadence and Innovation* sheds new light on the role of the arts in the regional centres of Budapest, Cracow and Prague as well as in the capital Vienna.

The editor, Robert Pynsent, has selected twelve essays from a total of forty-nine conference papers, apart from his own conclusory essay which comprises about half of the book. Pynsent's choice aims to provide a balance between the traditional importance attached to Vienna as the centre of artistic innovation and the neglected significance of cities like Budapest and Prague in the formation of a *fin-de-siècle* aesthetics. Essays which display a cosmopolitan or comparative range include Edward Timms's study of the imagery of the city in Vienna and Prague and Pynsent's conclusory piece which draws parallels between trends in England, France, Germany, Austria and Bohemia. Certain essays focus on the role of minorities in the capital, for example, Steven Beller's examination of the Viennese Jews' contribution to art and education or Monika Glettler's account of the plight of the Czechs in Vienna at the same period. Beller emphasizes the complexity of the demographic data concerning Jewish involvement in art and education; he rejects both George Steiner's thesis of a Jewish cultural hegemony and Carl Schorske's tendency to underestimate the extent of Jewish involvement in these areas. Glettler assesses the problems of assimilation facing the Viennese Czechs following Karl Lueger's nationalistic *Gemeindestatut* (introduced in March 1900). Other contributions to the volume provide detailed studies of Hungarian and Czech art and culture: Jiri Kudrnác on Czech *fin-de-siècle* criticism; André Karátson's examination of paradox in Hungarian Symbolism; F. T. Zsuppán's survey of the Hungarian Feminist Movement (1904–14) and Peter Wittlich's analysis of synthesis in the Czech visual arts. In these chapters a complex, antithetical process of decay and innovation emerges in which monolithic nationalism, so powerful an ideology earlier in the century, began to be questioned and undermined by a generation of cosmopolitan intellectuals suspicious of simplistic notions of ethnic uniqueness and essence. In his essay on the Self in Czech art, Wittlich highlights this trend:

> Writers like F. X. Salda, Antonín Sova, Otokar Brezina or J. S Machar demanded there that art be true to life [...] Humanity takes precedence over nationality. They replaced a demagogic idea of the unity of the nation with the demand for self-determination, for the free individuality they considered to be the only rational basis for a prosperous national collective (p. 82).

Pynsent concludes the volume with a wide-ranging discussion of all aspects of European *fin-de-siècle* culture in the West and in Central Europe. In the last few pages of his essay Pynsent compares the decadence of the 1890s with that of the 1960s. The analogies drawn between these two periods of social transition, both of which witnessed changing attitudes to society, religion and sexuality, are original and persuasive.

Decadence and Innovation is an important monograph on central European life and culture at the turn of the century. At a time when the concept of *Mitteleuropa* is beginning to re-emerge as a geo-political entity, this book is a valuable addition to our knowledge of its intellectual ancestry.

ALFRED THOMAS

Jacques Le Rider, *Modernité viennoise et crises de l'identité*, Perspectives Critiques (Paris: Presses Universitaires de France, 1990), 432 pp., 195 F.

In this volume Jacques Le Rider has produced an erudite and far-reaching sequel to and development of his *Der Fall Otto Weininger*. The aetiology of cultural anxieties, hatreds, and discontents which Le Rider constructs here is very much derived from that most symptomatic 'case' of the Viennese *fin-de-siècle*. Le Rider's thesis is that the twin pathological crises of identity which motivate Weininger's *Geschlecht und Charakter* – the sexual and the racial – are more or less endemic in the culture of Viennese modernism. The dual crisis is seen to inform the operations of the cultural criticism which burgeoned in Austria around the turn of the century, so that the diagnosis of degeneracy is typically organized around essentialist models of gender and racial identity. Such constructions and their crisis are equally shown to underpin the more subtle aesthetic practice of the age.

Le Rider's reading investigates both types of ideological crisis and shows how they conspire in and spawn the crisis ideology of modernity in its peculiar Austrian constitution. This he traces in what he sees as the three prime movers in the withdrawal into the idea of subjectivity: the genius, the mystic, and Narcissus. Viennese modernism embraces these solipsistic figures only to cast transcendent models of selfhood into the crisis of self-division. The various attempts to recuperate subjectivity are seen to end in the straits of 'das unrettbare Ich'.

The work operates very much in the spirit of this journal, adopting a multidisciplinary approach to a period of cultural history that was particularly intense in the interaction of its cultural forms. The author acknowledges his debt to Carl Schorske's pioneering work, and takes recourse to the latter's strategy of as it were arranging the boldest of Kaffeehaus symposia between artists, philosophers, scientists, and politicians. By and large the study bears out Le Rider's contention that a broad comparatist cast will yield mutually enriching encounters between the protagonists in the cultural crisis. Only occasionally does Le Rider strain the potential of this method. Devotees of individual protagonists will feel that while, given the scope of the study, the readings of the works at issue are bound to be economical, reference by association to writers outside the period should be more stringently so, if the focus of the argument is not to dilate into syncretism. As Le Rider succinctly puts it himself: 'Comparaison n'est pas raison'.

However, the study performs a valuable service to scholarship on this period by researching the interface between the two familiar, but by no means exhausted, *fin-de-siècle* issues of race and gender. By investigating the angles of what he styles the 'epochal triangle' of Male/Female/Jew, Le Rider shows admirably that what is at stake here is the other – desired, feared, and hated. More especially, he highlights the many cases where the ambivalent fascination is turned into crisis by the recognition, however subliminal, of inner otherness. 'Self-hatred' is the watchword here, and working on the basis of the Weininger paradigm, the author lays bare the strategies of projection which this condition elicits. At the same time he traces the, often morbid, desire to incorporate the 'other side' in order to salvage an altered state of selfhood.

In terms of the failed enlightenment project of racial emancipation, Le Rider furnishes a range of examples of the problematic double-bind of assimilation. There is the self-hating Jew seeking to assimilate by default to the other of Germanic culture (Weininger, Kraus); or Jews who assimilate as other with the idea of a collective Jewish identity (Herzl, Beer-Hofmann). And there is a similar division in terms of sexual identity. The 'twilight' of the patriarchal order sees the sons of 1900 divided between the posture of masculine protest (in the Adlerian sense of asserting a virile identity), proceeding both by means of and against the fathers, and the attempt to espouse the other of a new matriarchy (Otto Gross) or a new androgyny (Musil).

The most critical intellects are those which are doubly bound. And it is here

– particularly in the cases of Freud and Musil – that Le Rider at once reveals the most suggestive implications of his study and its inherent methodological limitations. His glosses of such complex matters as Musil's ironic mysticism and the sexual ambivalence which underlies it are less satisfactory than the sections on Hofmannsthal or Beer-Hofmann which are sustained by close textual reading. At the same time he furnishes a framework and a stimulus for more specialized enquiry, not least in his exposition of the philosophical base of the crisis of subjectivity as a compound of the theories of Nietzsche, Mach, and Freud.

Le Rider has prepared the ground for himself and others to excavate in depth what he calls 'a major site of the archaeology of the postmodern'. It remains to be seen whether theories of postmodernism will yield a trenchant perspective on those elements of the hybrid edifice of the 'Wiener Moderne' which are constructed, as it were, after the event of modernism. It is clear, at any rate, that the conventional categories of modernist aesthetics fail to accommodate the dialectical structures of that culture, its amalgam of what might indeed be called post-modern with resolute vestiges of the pre-modern. In this sense Austrian modernism furnishes an extraordinary paradigm case for the cultural ambivalence of European modernism as a whole. A paradigm, that is, in the sense that it is exemplary by virtue of its difference: its impossible melding of revolution and reaction, liberation and constraint. This volume represents an important development in our understanding of that paradigmatic difference. Its author will doubtless loom large in further developments.

ANDREW WEBBER

Célia Bertin, *La femme à Vienne au temps de Freud* (Paris: Stock, 1989), 351 pp., 148 F.

A young woman walking along the Maria Theresienstrasse as fast as her long skirt will permit, the couture of the Secession, lilacs in the Prater, chocolate and *strudel* – these all are part of the backdrop against which the impressionistic scenes of this first survey of women in Vienna from the *belle époque* to the Anschluss are set. And the figure intended to link these various scenes is Freud. Sketches of his women patients, pupils, colleagues, friends and family – Emma Eckstein, Anna Freud, Lou Andreas-Salomé, Marie Bonaparte, Martha Freud amongst many others – are interspersed with vignettes of women as various as Marie von Ebner-Eschenbach, Pauline Metternich and Bertha von Suttner. Brief outlines of women's education, fashion, and daily life give added highlight, as does the information on those women connected with psychoanalysis who are relatively little known. Hermine Hug-Hellmuth, Eugenie Sokolnicka and Sabina Spielrein, for example, are not forgotten. And of course neither are the women of whom the stuff of the Vienna 1900 legend is made. Sissy, *das süße Mädel*, Katharina Schratt – they are all there. When such women are gathered together as is done here for the first time, the significance of women in Vienna in the first decades of this century can no longer be overlooked.

Yet could it be that this gallery of prominent women deceives? Does what is in essence a collage of brief biographical sketches of privileged women tell us anything about that ghostly abstract 'woman', as the title of the book would

175

claim? This is a question Bertin does not address or even acknowledge. And obviously for her 'woman' does not include the majority of the female population of Vienna, for working-class women are relatively absent from this portrait gallery. Their atrocious working and living conditions are indeed mentioned, but no attempt is made to give them their due significance or to integrate them into the whole. In addition, the text is tinted with a touch of 'women's lib' jargon which does nothing more than curtsey to an unthinking creed of women's oppression. It is a pseudo-liberationist display which is made all the more unfortunate in that only the briefest mention is made of those Viennese women who really did do something for women's emancipation, more than any number of frustrated Alma Mahlers or neurotic Doras – women like Rosa Mayreder, the feminist theorist, and Marianne Hainisch, a leading organizer of the middle-class women's movement. Even when they are mentioned, their significance is completely distorted, for they are made the conservative handmaidens of the Christian Socials. And not only feminist clichés abound. Bertin allows herself a large number regarding Viennese women, their looks and character, fears and desires. However, she never questions these clichés, nor does she offer any original interpretations of the biographical material she has used. The book is also fragmented, for Freud's presence is not strong enough to draw the diverse material together. An adequate scholarly apparatus is lacking, and there are many factual and printing errors. Although Bertin has taken a step in the right direction, Vienna's women still deserve something better.

HARRIET ANDERSON

Hannah S. Decker, *Freud, Dora, and Vienna 1900* (New York: The Free Press/ Macmillan, 1991), xii + 299 pp.

The purpose of Hannah Decker's meticulously documented study is, as stated in the preface, to 'mine Freud's text as one would a rich lode, following its many glimmering veins so that his young patient emerges as an historical figure in her own right' (p. xi). Despite the romantic metaphor, Decker de-emphasizes the evaluation of this famous case-history, initiated by Steven Marcus, as a masterpiece of modernist literature. This is not to say that she ignores the insights into the text secured by subsequent feminist interpretations. In fact, one of her main goals is to demonstrate that Freud's flawed understanding of female sexuality and the female psyche contributed to his major miscalculation in the analysis, the failure to recognize the nature and the extent of the countertransference involved in the therapist-patient relationship. As befits her expertise, Decker argues most effectively when she writes as a determined, but sympathetic critic of psychoanalysis. Yet what clearly interests her most is restoring the identity of Ida Bauer in all its historical complexity to the young woman whom Freud reduced to a recalcitrant hysteric and whom he deliberately re-named Dora when he first published his findings in 1905.

The most convincing chapter is the first, in which, proceeding from Freud's remark that the usual methods of hydro- and electrotherapy remained ineffective, Decker describes the painful and often violent consequences of 'faradization', 'galvanization', and the 'percussion' involved in certain hydropathic methods to which Ida Bauer would have been subjected in conventional treatments. Chapter Seven contains a revealing reading of the unconscious motivations behind Freud's preoccupation with this case based on his choice of the fictional name Dora. Here Decker questions Freud's own explanation of this selection; weighs the importance of various literary models including several annoyingly powerful female characters with related names in plays by V. Sardou, the French dramatist to whose work Freud had been exposed during his student days in Paris; and, finally, quite brilliantly links Freud's Dora to Josef Breuer's youngest daughter of the same name who was born in the same year as Ida Bauer. The latter connection suggests, as Decker deftly shows, that the name 'Dora' signalled Freud's anxiety about this case having involved him in the same kinds of troubling issues of transference and countertransference that had marked Breuer's treatment of Anna. Although the many 'boxes' that pile up in the text lead Decker to discuss the mythological figure of Pandora, she curiously does not mention the most prominent contemporary treatment of the myth: Frank Wedekind's controversial play *Pandora's Box*, the earliest version of which appeared in 1895. Whether Freud had read Wedekind before he wrote *Dora* is unknown; we do know, however, that the Psychoanalytic Society discussed *Spring's Awakening*, Wedekind's quite relevant examination of adolescent sexuality, in 1907 and that Freud was invited to and probably attended a private performance of *Pandora's Box* arranged by Karl Kraus in 1905.

Throughout the book Decker emphasizes a crucial factor in the case that, in her view, Freud egregiously ignores: his patient's Jewishness. To what extent Freud can be faulted for failing to take up the issue of Ida Bauer being a Jew surrounded by anti-Semitism (p. 126) remains a complex question. Indeed, whether he actually avoided talking about the topic with her and other patients is equally difficult to ascertain. That there are no traces of such matters in the published case-histories should not be surprising. Freud was at pains especially during the early years of the movement to prevent psychoanalysis from being labelled a 'Jewish science' and would certainly have suppressed any public record of such discussions.

Exactly what effect Ida Bauer's Jewish background had on her and her highly assimilated family is perhaps more difficult to determine than Decker is willing to admit. In the apparent absence of biographical documents that would illuminate these attitudes directly, Decker makes excellent use of the records of the Jewish Community of Vienna (Israelitische Kultusgemeinde) and especially of the well-researched parallel life of her famous brother Otto, the prominent Socialist theoretician. Unlike many other Jewish Socialists, Otto Bauer officially remained within the Jewish community and, despite the anti-Semitic implications of his Marxist views, seems to have made a kind of separate peace with his heritage. This equivocating fraternal behaviour makes the decision of Dora and her Jewish husband to convert to Protestantism shortly after their son was born in 1905 look particularly radical. Decker believes that Dora was motivated not only by concern for her son's future but also by Jewish self-hatred. Yet the evidence of Herzl's and other prominent Jews' attitudes toward baptism does not necessarily allow us to 'know the kind of feeling and thinking that went into Dora and her husband's decision to convert with their infant son' (p. 155).

Just how complex the motives for baptism could be may be demonstrated by the example of Karl Kraus, of whom Decker incorrectly claims that he 'tried, in turn, Catholic and Lutheran conversion' (p. 219, n. 62) and that 'neither brought him inner contentment' (ibid.). The error that Kraus ever became a Protestant aside, Decker's confident pronouncement on his 'inner contentment' betrays a superficial knowledge of his literary biography at best. She seems to be unaware, for example, that Kraus publicly announced his decision to leave the Catholic Church as part of a polemic published in 1922 against Max Reinhardt's use of the Salzburg Cathedral for theatrical performances. In fact, Decker's references to Karl Kraus, who appears primarily as a 'Jew-hating' (p. 200) satirist and as a sponsor of misogynistic ideas, suggest a rather tenuous grasp on the niceties of Viennese cultural history. Not only does she take unsubstantiated information about Kraus from George Clare's *Last Waltz in Vienna*, which is more a family memoir than a reliable historical account, she also depends almost exclusively on outdated secondary sources for her characterization of Kraus's attitude towards women. This leads to a number of mispresentations including a badly botched quotation from Kraus's essay 'Der Prozeß Riehl' (cf. p. 201 and *Die Fackel*, No. 211, p. 26), on a celebrated case involving the owner of a bordello, that falsifies the satirist's view of prostitution. Decker assumes that Ida Bauer would have found nothing but confirmation of the 'derogation of women' (p. 200) in the *Fackel*, yet the reluctant analysand could have also found support for her suspicions about a therapeutic method that sometimes served the therapist's rather than the patient's needs. Not only does one of Kraus's aphorisms begin with the insight that 'Every conversation about sexuality is a sexual act' (*Die Fackel*, Nos. 275–6, p. 27), a point that Decker herself belabours in her justified criticism of Freud's verbal bluntness in sexual matters during his sessions with Ida Bauer (pp. 113–20); the satirist also once characterizes psychoanalysis as 'the occupation of aroused rationalists who trace everything in the world to sexual causes – with the exception of their occupation' (*Die Fackel*, No. 300, p. 26).

Decker's failure to consult the now considerable literature on Freud's relations with his literary contemporaries also makes her frequent references to Schnitzler look extremely uninformed. While she does recognize that *Fräulein Else* is 'startlingly reminiscent' (p. 109) of Dora's story, she clearly does not realize the extent of the parallels between the two texts. She neglects the daughter's oedipal fixation on the father in both instances as well as Schnitzler's construction of his character's dreams as implicit interpretations of her predicament, which relates to Freud's focus on dream materials in the case-history. In fact, considering the dearth of biographical information that Decker had at her disposal, she would have been well advised to exploit the sociological analogue offered by Schnitzler's perceptive portrayal of a young Viennese woman, whose Jewishness, moreover, figures in the text in subtle ways. An even more useful source in this regard would have been Schnitzler's novel *Der Weg ins Freie*, which shows how a broad range of middle-class Viennese Jews including two young women comparable to Ida Bauer react to the growing threat of anti-Semitism. In the case of 'Miss Else,' as Decker refers to Schnitzler's story, perhaps she exploits the rich text so diffidently because the bowdlerized American translation she quotes omits several of the more explicit physiological and sexual passages and therefore seemed to her less compatible with the frank rhetoric of Freud's case-history.

Relying on translations causes at least one interpretive slip with regard to the *Fragment of an Analysis of a Case of Hysteria* itself. In the process of advancing an important argument about Freud's position *vis-à-vis* Ida Bauer's father, Decker equates Philipp Bauer's 'handing over' his daughter to Freud for treatment with Dora's feeling that she had been 'handed over' to Herr K. (cf. p. 95 and p. 237, n. 38). In the first case, the German equivalent is 'übergab'; in the second, it is 'ausgeliefert'. Since the two words, though close in meaning, differ widely in their emotional tone, working with the original text would have dictated a more cautious approach to such an equation.

Occasionally, Decker tends to overinterpret the impressive evidence she has gathered. At several junctures, she stresses the fact that Freud made Ida Bauer a year older than she was when she began treatment, eighteen instead of seventeen. Yet it would have undoubtedly been more important to Freud that she was fourteen rather than thirteen when Herr K. first forced a kiss on her. Fourteen, not eighteen, was both the minimum age for the registration of prostitutes and the age of consent in *fin-de-siècle* Vienna. If as Decker contends, Freud unconsciously sympathized with Herr K., then making Dora fourteen at the time of the first sexual overture would have protected the bourgeois doctor's unconscious attachment to social and legal propriety.

The objections raised at some length here do not obviate the value of Hannah Decker's book as a careful adjudication of the case-history involving Freud and 'Dora'. As cultural history, however, her study falls short of making the substantial contribution to our knowledge of 'Vienna 1900' implicit in the title.

LEO A. LENSING

Gail Finney, *Women in Modern Drama: Freud, Feminism, and European Theater at the Turn of the Century* (Ithaca and London: Cornell University Press, 1989), x + 234 pp., $27.50.

Gail Finney's study examines the representation of women in Schnitzler's *Reigen*, Wilde's *Salomé*, Wedekind's Lulu plays, Synge's *The Playboy of the Western World*, Hauptmann's *Rose Bernd*, Ibsen's *Hedda Gabler*, Hofmannsthal's *Die Frau ohne Schatten*, Shaw's *Candida* and Strindberg's *The Father*. All quotations are in English to accommodate students of drama. In a short introductory chapter Professor Finney suggests that rapid social change in the nineteenth century and a new consciousness of oppression induced a double response in women of feminism or hysteria and that men in turn reacted to these responses either by feminism or the hysterization of women, that is, the reduction of women to their biological functions and the pathologization of the female body. This double spectrum acts as a grid through which to read the plays. Thus Synge's Pegeen Mike and Hauptmann's Rose Bernd exemplify the two responses in women, and *Rose Bernd* is a study, by an author who himself later glorified motherhood as woman's essence, of the hysterization of a woman by the male characters. The figures of the daughter and the mother/wife within the Freudian family provide further organizing principles for grouping the plays under five headings. In the first section Schnitzler is compared with Freud on a range of issues; the second, on Wilde and Wedekind, explores the *femme fatale* or sterile daughter; the third, on Synge and Hauptmann, centres on daughters subject to the law of the father; the fourth, on Ibsen and Hofmannsthal, and the fifth, on Shaw and Strindberg, examine reluctant mothers and powerful mothers respectively.

Freud is not cited as an authority but as the author of metaphoric representations which can be compared with the plays, and in general he comes off rather badly, notably in the comparison with Schnitzler: the role-reversals in *Reigen*, where the sexually active actress contrasts with the effete Count, subvert Freud's conventional definition of feminity as passivity. The liberating potential which Schnitzler discovers hidden within the 'dark continent' stands in tension, however, with a sense of entrapment within a dying culture, and sexual vitality masks the death wish. Schnitzler can be accounted, then, an ambivalent fellow-traveller of feminism in a range stretching from Shaw and Wilde at one extreme through to the conservative Hofmannsthal and the misogynist Strindberg. Professor Finney is less concerned with the author's feminist credentials, however, than with reading the texts as a woman to resist oppressive positions and uncover competing subtexts which express the tensions of the age. A reading of *Salomé* for its repressed homoeroticism finds masculine attributes in the heroine, which Aubrey Beardsley also saw. The Lulu plays are taken as a radical attack, marred only by the attribution of masochism to women, on the reduction of women to spectacle in *Erdgeist* and commodity in *Die Büchse der Pandora*. A comparison between the dysphoric plot of *Hedda Gabler* and the euphoric *Die Frau ohne Schatten* centres on the question 'to be or not to be a mother'. Professor Finney resists the euphoria in a comparison of Hofmannsthal's play with *Faust*: Faust is allowed his excursion into freedom whereas the Dyer's Wife is dragged back into her identity as a proper female. Finally Professor Finney discovers similarities between the powerful mother created by the feminist Shaw and the misogynist Strindberg.

The term hysterization presents problems. Is it a discursive figure or a psychosomatic event in women's lives: were women held to be prone to hysteria, while being actually no more hysterical than men, whose psychic problems attracted more elevated labels; or were women made prone to hysteria by being so held? One cannot judge that from looking at characters in male-authored plays. The term bears too many disparate meanings: femininity as sickness, the reduction of woman to womb, *and* the sexualization of women. It thus obscures the widespread antithesis between the Mother and the Whore or Hetaira and also the effects of class difference on the gender stereotypes: hysteria as sickness has a middle-class aura – it requires leisure, but Hauptmann's monomaniacal, instinct-driven working-class women have great physical stamina. The Freudian family also tends to mask the cross-cutting of class and gender in the construction of the non-bourgeois sexual woman and the antithetical hysterical or repressed bourgeois wife/mother. Nor does the Freudian triangle quite accommodate Salomé, daughter of a powerful mother rather than an Oedipal father. The schematic interpretative grid has compensating advantages, however, in strong readings and pointed cross-cultural comparisons in a study which wears theory lightly. This is a highly readable, stimulating contribution to feminist drama criticism.

ELIZABETH BOA

Bruce Thompson, *Schnitzler's Vienna: Image of a Society* (London: Routledge, 1990), ix + 213 pp., £30.00.

Adrian Clive Roberts, *Arthur Schnitzler and Politics*, Studies in Austrian Literature, Culture, and Thought (Riverside, CA: Ariadne Press, 1989), viii + 214 pp., $29.00 (paper $18.00).

Marc A. Weiner, *Arthur Schnitzler and the Crisis of Musical Culture*, Reihe Siegen 69 (Heidelberg: Carl Winter, 1986), 173 pp., DM 75.

'I would suggest that in its interaction with art Schnitzler's generation unconsciously expressed its social concerns.' This remark (it would make a good examination question) occurs on p. 64 of Marc Weiner's study of Schnitzler and what is here called the crisis of musical culture. It pinpoints the crux underlying the three very different books here under review. Leaving aside Schnitzler's contemporaries, who receive only scant attention, one comes away wondering what exactly Weiner is getting at and whether his statement actually makes sense, for all its neat formulation. Of course the clarity of Schnitzler's texts conceals a complex artistic sensibility responding to a world which they persuade us is even more complex than they are themselves. Yet they also make us feel that he had no great difficulty in writing about that world; the problem is how to write about Schnitzler.

Bruce Thompson's book seeks to put us in the picture. It is much the broadest of the three, and will be welcomed by readers of English in eager search for clarification. But its catchy title is something of a misnomer. The book is in fact a skilful attempt to analyse the various ways in which Schnitzler used Vienna as the subject-matter for his plays and stories; by 'Vienna' it soon becomes evident that Thompson really means certain sections of Viennese society or, rather, an array of fictitious characters peopling an imaginary world which convinces us that it *is* an authentic portrayal embodying the tensions and concerns of Viennese society at the turn of the century. Since they were drawn from Schnitzler's own experience of life in and beyond the city, Thompson's primary objective might seem to be to establish the degree of accuracy of the portrayal. Yet, rightly and not surprisingly, its emphasis (and the book improves very noticeably in quality as it progresses) gradually shifts as he makes it more and more clear that what Schnitzler did for Vienna was not quite the same as what Dickens did for London, Balzac for Paris or Fontane for Berlin: curiously enough, of Joyce there is no mention. 'His realism is a very limited form of

181

referential realism,' he remarks on p. 170. He might just as well have said so on the opening page to the advantage of his argument and his readers, and by no means to the detriment of a book which many of them will value and find very useful as a compendium of sensitive analyses and synopses of a great many works they have probably read in isolation, but which Thompson helpfully sets in a coherent overall context. The map and gazetteer he provides is a particularly appealing feature which readers will want to take with them when next they visit Vienna.

The human being was Schnitzler's abiding interest; it was perhaps an essentially solipsistic one, but he was enough of a late nineteenth-century realist to be able to project it on to self-contained, convincing characters from Anatol to his writer, Stephan von Sala, and his composer figure, Georg von Wergenthin, and from Fräulein Else and Genia Hofreiter to poor Therese. None of them exists in a vacuum; but Schnitzler, great story-teller that he was, was precisely what Balzac, Dickens and Fontane were not: he was a great dramatist, for whom Hauptmann's dictum held true: 'Ursprung des Dramas ist das [...] mehrgespaltene Ich' ('The origin of drama is the fractured self'). Hence his inability and wise refusal to deal with politics as an end in itself; hence, too, his failure, discussed by Weiner, to find a true collaborator in the musical field despite (or was it because of?) his aptitude as an amateur musician. Naturally enough, politics gets some mention in Thompson's book; but music gets virtually none. At first sight this seems extraordinary: Vienna was after all the centre of the musical world. So one turns to Weiner's impeccably produced volume to discover what Thompson has left out. But there is disappointment in store. Despite his well-intentioned, thoughtful and often informative researches, Weiner is unable to come up with anything much to clarify the hazy picture we already have of Schnitzler in his musical setting; indeed, like Fritz in *Liebelei*, he doesn't even grasp the significance of the little bust of Schubert standing unobtrusively in Christine's room, a poignantly telling hint of the unseen struggle this Viennese professional musician's daughter is waging to keep alive some standard of ideal excellence in a cultural context which, even seventy years before, had often been deaf to genius. The crisis in musical culture is there *in nuce* in that little episode, but Weiner's title seems to seduce him to flights of highbrow fancy in an attempt to identify that crisis with the social changes that are so obviously latent in Schnitzler's ostensibly secure world. 'Wait a moment!' the reader cries, suspecting that the occasional mention of Wagner and Schoenberg is not quite enough to prove the point, and wondering whether Dohnányi and Zemlinsky, or indeed Oscar Straus, briefly and tantalizingly mentioned on pp. 42–3, would not have been apter choices, since Schnitzler's artistic involvement with them was more immediate, and the current reappraisal they are undergoing is altering our perception of the volatile Viennese musical scene during his lifetime.

Like Marc Weiner's book, Adrian Clive Roberts's *Arthur Schnitzler and Politics* tends too easily to deploy familiar or pre-conceived ideas with a show of academic earnestness, but without quite the finesse and flair for the nuances of Viennese culture needed to demonstrate a truly convincing grasp of the musical and political dimensions of Schnitzler's evocation of the 'Jahrhundertwende' world. Sometimes it seems a pity that both authors are not always ready to question the accuracy and relevance of their references: *Schnitzler and Politics*, for example, manages to turn *Leutnant Gustl*, that most transparently subtle of Schnitzler's prose works, into some kind of deliberately contentious allegorical manifesto by over-reacting with anachronistic incomprehension to its ironic thematic complex, and gets off to an awkward start by asserting that Hauptmann, unlike Schnitzler, published essays supporting the war in 1914, a statement which a quick look at the *Centenarausgabe* should have qualified, and which does little to help promote Schnitzler as an anti-war campaigner or, less stridently, as almost the only pacifist voice of his generation. Thompson comes nearer the mark when he points out that the characters of *Der Weg ins Freie* express their author's cynical doubts concerning the genuineness of political beliefs and political activity, and when he describes the obnoxious Flint in *Professor Bernhardi* as the typical smooth-talking politician; yet he then almost destroys his argument by stating that Schnitzler's hostile portrayal of the political scene represents a very negative and one-sided viewpoint. That, surely, calls into question the true nature of Schnitzler's artistic aims and achievement. 'But Schnitzler was also a realist', Roberts reminds us as he examines his anguished reaction to the outbreak of war. The point is an essential one, and it surfaces time and again in the reader's mind. For all three books bring home the realization that, closely interlinked though Schnitzler's literary works are with his own private life and personal views and with the current events and attitudes of his place and time, there nevertheless exists an indefinable yet aesthetically crucial demarcation between the diaries, letters and autobiographical writings and that compellingly subtle imaginative world into which we are drawn in his plays and prose fiction and which, over the years, has taken on an extraordinary life of its own by perpetuating a 'Vienna' that has vanished for ever along with its once hotly debated musical and political problems. Schnitzler's genius was surely that of a realist of the most committed if not the the most referential kind, one, that is, for whom the music of time and the politics of human relationships meant more than the topical issues of dodecaphonic atonality, duelling, or anti-Semitism. Perhaps Weiner's observation, quoted at the beginning, would make better sense if it were rephrased to read 'in his interaction with social and cultural issues Schnitzler consciously expressed his own artistic concerns'.

PETER SKRINE

Hans-Albrecht Koch, *Hugo von Hofmannsthal*, Erträge der Forschung, 265 (Darmstadt: Wissenschaftliche Buchgesellschaft, 1989), x + 181 pp., DM 35.

Benjamin Bennett, *Hugo von Hofmannsthal: The Theatres of Consciousness*, Cambridge Studies in German (Cambridge: Cambridge University Press, 1988), xviii + 391 pp., £40.00

Though there is an enormous amount of secondary literature on Hofmannsthal, we still lack a definitive critical study covering all his work. His writing is so varied that interpretations tend to concentrate on single stages of his career, or on single genres, or even on individual works.

Hans-Albrecht Koch's guide to the maze of Hofmannsthal scholarship answers a real need. It provides an account of the primary material (editions of works and letters, discussed in relation to the unpublished manuscripts), of bibliographical aids and biographies, and of criticism (organized by genre). Surveys of scholarship inevitably date, overtaken by events; but this one has lasting value as an authoritative assessment of over sixty years' publications. The lucid survey of editions and of bibliographical and biographical material is excellent. The discussion of interpretative material, being selective, is bound to prompt more disagreement – particularly, perhaps, the relatively thin chapters on the Chandos Letter and the other prose writings. Nevertheless, of what I would have chosen as the most important items, Koch omits entirely only one, Rainer Nägele's article 'Die Sprachkrise und ihr dichterischer Ausdruck bei Hofmannsthal', *German Quarterly*, 43 (1970), 720–32. It is particularly welcome that while over the years Hofmannsthal studies have generated more than their share of pretentious waffle (Dr Koch registers in his preface the effort of 'translation' required in treating it), readers are directed firmly towards research with a strong factual basis: Werner Volke and Martin Stern are (rightly) prominent names. Misprints are mostly minor (even the ascription on p. 79 to the *German Quarterly* of five hundred more years' existence than it has achieved will not fool many users). This is a book which can be recommended without reservation and which should be on the shelves of every library.

So too should Benjamin Bennett's study, though it is much less readably written. It appeared too late to be listed by Koch, but several chapters are based on earlier articles. It does not answer the need for a comprehensive study – the shorter prose fiction is largely left out of account – but is nevertheless an ambitious attempt at a coherent account of Hofmannsthal's development, which Professor Bennett presents as reflecting his successive attempts to reinterpret the function and significance of the theatre.

The premise underlying this approach is that Hofmannsthal had 'a fundamentally theatrical imagination' (p. xi). Even his early playlets are based on a consciousness of the stage situation as 'a reality realer than reality itself' (p. 84). There is little reference to stage productions or to reception of performances – an obvious limitation in view of the keen practical interest Hofmannsthal took in the theatre, especially in his later years. Rather, the theatre in Bennett's argument has a symbolic function as 'a mirror of society's own symbolic function with respect to human existence metaphysically considered' (p. xiii); the 'fundamental principle' of Hofmannsthal's dramatic writing is 'the creation of significant resonances between the artistically closed world of the stage and the mundanely open reality of audience and theatre, with the aim, ultimately, of effecting a complete reconciliation of the individual and the communal, the artistic and the social' (p. 101).

If the argument is not wholly convincing, this is at least partly owing to its presentation. Bennett's discursive style repeatedly runs the risk of producing argumentative short-circuits. About the 'theatricality' of *Der Tor und der Tod*, for example, he argues that 'if the proper conduct of life is not something that comes from the heart, but is comparable to skilful dramatic acting, then it follows that when the play is performed, the very medium by which we perceive it (play-acting) becomes a symbol of the truth it expresses' (p. 72); if the hypothesis in the conditional clause does not hold then the rest of the argument collapses. The reader also needs constantly to check the translations of passages quoted and the context from which they are taken. One small example is the reference to '*Der Rosenkavalier*, "a Viennese masquerade and nothing more"' (p. 239): the line is *not* about the opera but is a comment by one fictional character (the Marschallin) on a strand in its action.

Bennett eschews local colour, explaining in his Preface that he is not claiming to 'treat Hofmannsthal's work *as* a social or cultural phenomenon'; society and culture are 'seen from the perspective of poetic theory'. What this means is that society is defined dialectically as 'the dissonance or imperfection without which an ideal unity would not be able to manifest itself' (p. 201), or else used in over-sharp contrast to the category 'intellectual', as in the contrast between the 'intellectual' Neuhoff and the 'social being' Hans Karl (p. 122). So much has been written about Hofmannsthal's Vienna that the restriction of the argument to a theoretical level is invigorating; but the lack of social and political background proves a weakness, especially in relation to *Der Schwierige*, which occupies a central place in the study. It is described as 'comedy at the brink of the abyss' (pp. 166–7); but it is so closely related to the upheavals of World War I that the abyss needs to be defined in relation to the historical background. Bennett's intellectualizing of Hofmannsthal's work repeatedly leads to false emphases in the perception of his characters, as in the reduction of Elektra to an essentially 'intellectual mode of being' (p. 114) or the description of Helene as 'loving Hans Karl *as a problem*' (p. 182). The treatment of *Der Schwierige*, with questionable conclusions (for example, the claim that Hans Karl decides to marry Helene 'entirely on the spur of the moment' [p. 185]) side by side with acutely formulated perceptions (such as the description of Hans Karl as 'exist[ing] more deeply than he speaks' [p. 122]), is indeed characteristic of the strengths and weaknesses of this challenging study.

W. E. YATES

Andrew Webber, *Sexuality and the Sense of Self in the Works of Georg Trakl and Robert Musil*, MHRA Texts and Dissertations 30; Bithell Series of Dissertations 15 (London: The Institute of Germanic Studies, 1990), viii + 198 pp., £20.00 / $48.00.

In what was originally a Cambridge Ph.D. thesis, Andrew Webber aims to apply psychoanalytic theory originating both from the pioneers, Freud, Rank and Weininger, and from their successor, Lacan, to the interpretation of works by Georg Trakl and Robert Musil which share certain sexual and bisexual preoccupations. The approach also incorporates contemporary critical theory on textuality, the psycho-sexual problems of 'fixing' gender and identity being equated with the elusiveness of the relationship between signifier and signified.

Narcissism and hermaphroditism are seen to be central in the work of Trakl and Musil and to be intermeshed with the struggle of both writers to shape their work to a more complete and authentic aesthetic whole, a goal which, in the nature of things, eludes them because 'completion' or 'plenitude', metaphorically representable as the suspension of sexual differentiation or as a unified sense of self, are attainable only by a momentary illusion or imaginative suspension of disbelief. The language employed in achieving this suspension itself invariably betrays the very illusion it attempts to create; this leads to the infinite 'deferring' of the desired end into an irresolvable series.

The endless complexities of this sexual-textual node are followed through with great skill, a very high degree of critical perceptiveness, and a combinative flair that is most impressive. There may be at times a sense that the ingenuity becomes a shade fanciful; or that there is a danger of a kind of self-defeating infinite regress, as summarized perhaps in the sentence: 'the goal of the present reading is to illustrate that Trakl's text ultimately evades the reader's pursuit, resisting narcissistic capture much as did the beginning image of legend' (p. 20).

Nonetheless, the chapters on the work of Georg Trakl make an important contribution to the comprehension of one of the most arcane and difficult poets in the German language. His heavily encoded private language and cryptic ciphers have led to a plethora of interpretations, many of which Dr Webber outflanks by analysing the texts as strategies evolved to express the inexpressible, the desire for an unattainable transcendental unity of sense and sensuality, whose frustration is mirrored in the frustration of the reader's desire for a complete and/or positive interpretation.

The section on Musil's *Vereinigungen* is perhaps the most repetitive and the one where the method seems to come closest to being mechanical and strained. But in the treatment of the other Musil works, *Törleß* and *Der Mann ohne Eigenschaften*, the method comes fully into its own and results in some very striking correlations between psychoanalytical writings and the fictional mode. The section on *Törleß* in particular is argued with a tautness which, for this reader, has a positively revelatory power to recuperate some of the most enigmatic aspects of the text.

Andrew Webber's concluding chapter is appropriately (for a Lacanian) entitled 'The Problem of Conclusion', and it is to this section that prospective readers might need to turn first as they decide whether to invest either time or money in an encounter with Dr Webber's demanding arguments; for it is here that the good will and the effort required are clearly set out: 'The problem of sexual difference provides a paradigm at once for the invasion of difference into the sense of self (...) and for the denial of a simple signifying integrity in language' (p. 183). What goes for that paradigm also goes for the book as a whole, *mutatis mutandis*: in the statement 'the paradigm of sexual opposition must be revised into one of dialectic interplay' (ibid.), one could substitute 'the paradigm of the quest for meaning' as the subject of the sentence. Readers must approach this book ready to engage in a dialectic interplay with the text, and anyone with no prior experience of the Lacanian sub-plot is going to need to keep a particularly open mind and be prepared for a steep learning-curve. But this is not an exercise in illustrating Lacan's elusive theories; it is a highly perceptive, acutely sensitive interpretation based upon them, illustrated with a wealth of close reading which cannot fail to be stimulating even to the most convinced anti-Lacanian, if only he or she can suspend scepticism long enough to be receptive to the 'problem of conclusion'. To encounter the intelligence at work here is a pleasure, and well worth the investment.

ALAN BANCE

Stefan H. Kaszynski and Sigurd Paul Scheichl (eds), *Karl Kraus – Ästhetik und Kritik: Beiträge des Kraus-Symposiums Poznan*, Sonderband der Kraus-Hefte (Munich: edition text + kritik, 1989), 204 pp., DM 42.

Gilbert Krebs, Gerald Stieg (eds), *Karl Kraus et son temps. Karl Kraus und seine Zeit*, (Asnières: Publications de l'Institut d'Allemand, Université de la Sorbonne Nouvelle, 1989), 243 pp., 95 F.

Joseph P. Strelka (ed.), *Karl Kraus: Diener der Sprache, Meister des Ethos* (Tübingen: Francke, 1990), 356 pp., DM 78.

A sign that Karl Kraus's posterity has matured beyond its earlier dismissals of a Vienna-bound polemicist is the generally high standard of three international symposia, at the New York State University, Albany and at the Sorbonne Nouvelle (both in 1986) and at the University of Poznan (in 1987), whose proceedings constitute these volumes, which complement one another in various ways. While the dominant theme of the French volume is Kraus and political ideology, the other two volumes address questions of aesthetics and poetics hitherto relatively neglected.

All three volumes contain some outstanding work. Kurt Krolop, in *Karl Kraus – Ästhetik und Kritik*, goes some way towards explaining why Kraus, whose aesthetics is often labelled conservative or epigonal, had such an impact on an innovator like Schoenberg, and even aligns Kraus's conception of 'Wortkunst' with Bakhtin's 'material aesthetics'. While also drawing on the aesthetics of neglected *Fackel* contributors like Leo Popper, the young Georg Lukács' friend, Krolop does not fully exhaust the unlikely relationship here between modernist and neo-Classicist aesthetics. E. F. Timms, who is represented in the other two volumes by studies (familiar to his British readers) on Kraus and World War I, here discovers, in the love of animals, an unusual affinity between Rosa Luxemburg's revolutionary scheme and the misanthropic universe of that 'avenger of nature', Kraus. Whereas Kraus's vain attempt, in a polemic of 1928, to elevate an inmate of Czernowitz mental asylum to the lyrical canon is dismissed by Amy Colin in a footnote to her 'Karl Kraus and die Bukowina' in the Albany volume, in the Poznan volume S. P. Scheichl reassesses Kraus's plea for this 'Irrenhauslyrik' as an important statement of his poetics. Another Poznan study which tests assumptions – in this case about the relation between satire and polemic – is that of B. Brandys on *Die demolirte Literatur*, which, however, falls short of a full appreciation of the satirical mode. Other contributors include C. J. Wagenknecht on Kraus's well-known switch from anti-corruptionist to aesthete, G. Stieg on Goethe as Kraus's touchstone, M. Przybecki on *Die letzten Tage der Menschheit* as an operetta, and H. Lunzer's positivistic documentation of the Akademische

Verband für Literatur and Musik in Wien, the student club which first organized Kraus's readings in 1910–12.

Karl Kraus et son temps presents various new findings: Eckart Früh carefully documents the Communist press's reception of Kraus after 1927 and relates his affinities with them to his increasing hostility to the Social Democrats. Further revision of the image of a reactionary Kraus is attempted by A. Greiter and A. Pelinka, who argue that Kraus was critical of the Austro-Fascist Dollfuss; however, their method (headlines, paraphrasing) falls short of philological standards. A. Betz productively compares *Die dritte Walpurgisnacht* with Joseph Roth's and Heinrich Mann's critiques of the intellectual fellow-travellers of Nazism and discovers the émigré journal *Das Neue Tagebuch* as one surprising source for Kraus. G. Sosnowski's 'Karl Kraus et la France' excludes Offenbach and the Heine essay, but at least clarifies Kraus's idealization of the Entente in 1914–18 and his hostility in 1919–22, and the anti-German rather than conciliatory motives of Kraus's French sponsors for the Nobel Prize. S. P. Scheichl complements E. F. Timms by differentiating Kraus's opposition to the war in 1914 from his full commitment to pacifism in 1917–18. L. A. Lensing successfully demonstrates that Kraus's use of photomontage (from 1911 on) not only anticipated but surpassed Tucholsky's and Heartfield's practice in *Deutschland, Deutschland über alles* (1929).

The affinities found by J. Le Rider between 'Sionisme et antisémitisme' have little directly to do with Kraus; J. Szabo considers the unbalanced coverage of the nationality problem in *Die Fackel*, and articles by J.-M. Paul and J. Bouveresse compare Kraus with Broch and Spengler respectively. Starting from the well-known 'Instanz K. K.', B. Lersch constructs a verbose theoretical framework round Kraus's simplest and most direct text, the anti-Schober poster, but makes interesting comments on the 'diaphorische Struktur' of the satirical voice. More unsatisfactory is A. Pfabigan's '"Frauenverehrung" und "Frauenverachtung"', which has neglected or been superseded by British (and Irish) research, in particular, on Kraus and Wedekind, Freud, Weininger and Wittels. Pfabigan purports to exclude the real Karl Kraus and to deal only with the satirical discourse, but then reduces the male attitudes it critically differentiates to a homogeneous 'orgastic impotence', which he subjects to a crude psychoanalytic treatment, misconstruing Kraus's fully conscious poetics of eroticism as Freudian-type sublimation.

The Albany volume *Karl Kraus: Diener der Sprache*, in which the standard of proof-reading is excruciating, has both the best and worst of current research. Most impressive are S. P. Scheichl's close scrutiny of the stylistics of Kraus's pathos; and especially António Ribeiro's exemplary study of Kraus's Shakespeare reception in the context of a precise evaluation of Kraus's techniques of quotation, which complements earlier East German scholarship on Kraus and the German classics. He sees affinities between quotation and glossing and the 'Theater der Dichtung' of Kraus's public readings of Shakespeare plays; citing the aggressive sense of epigone in the poem 'Bekenntnis', he sees Kraus's revision of the literary canon as a decisive political as well as satirical statement, not merely curatorship. L. A. Lensing's account of the visual arts criticism in

Die Fackel takes us far beyond documenting reception (for example, of Klimt) and on to the satirist's incorporation of visual motifs into textual strategies – though the feuilletonistic model of Daniel Spitzer for the early Kraus's satire on visual art is neglected. This fine essay is, however, marred methodologically; after an initial *caveat* (that Kraus at most only partially composed the art criticism in the early *Fackel*), the subsequent argument assumes – against (negative) archival evidence – that Kraus was, indeed, the author of all such criticisms of Klimt.

K. Weissenberger adds little with his piece on poetic rhythm, but his second study, of Kraus the essayist, contributes to understanding of the genre by distinguishing Kraus's innovative poetological essays, with their intrinsic cognitive momentum, from the conventional essayism of *belles lettres* which constitutes part of his discourse. This is more rewarding than either D. Goldschnigg's study of the essays from *Sittlichkeit und Kriminalität*, indebted as it is to Adorno, Benjamin and Wagenknecht and overplaying the role of the *Fremdwort,* or G. Marahrens's systematic analysis of the structure of the aphorism, a significant contribution to study of the genre, which is flawed by bizarre value judgements (for example, p. 84). R. M. Kully continues the pioneering work of C. J. Wagenknecht with an inventory of Kraus's word-play on proper nouns; J. K. Lyon brings Kraus's and Brecht's literary relations up to date – while neglecting a GDR contribution from 1977 by Günter Hartung – before over-emphasizing their affinities, the most convincing of which is their dialectical thinking.

Insight into Kraus's dialectical practice might be a corrective to some of the clumsier polemical interpretations in this volume, which grind that rusty axe of Kraus's Jewish anti-Semitism to no effect. In 'proving' – without any closer look at a possible rational content of the texts concerned – that Kraus's polemicizing, for example against Werfel, was merely personally motivated, M. Pazi reverts to the pre-scholarly Kraus reception which dogged previous decades. At least D. Daviau, despite failing to distinguish satirical from polemical modes in Kraus's discourse and being unaware of scholarly evidence which vindicates some of Kraus's allegations against Hermann Bahr, attempts a more balanced assessment of the problematic side of Kraus's own criticism. A glaring example of how the critique of stereotypes in literature can degenerate into purveyance of stereotypes in criticism is S. Gilman's 'Karl Kraus, Oscar Wilde and the Hidden Language of the Jews'. Gilman claims that Kraus attacked Jews who 'represented the essence of the Jewish language' and made a distinction between such 'bad' Jews and the 'good' Jews whose language is 'non-Jewish'. The categories are not Kraus's; his alleged 'projection' is itself a projection by the critic, cloaked in post-modernist jargon about an internalized 'code of difference' and uncomplicated by concern for textual corroboration. Gilman does to Kraus's polemic against reviewers of *Salome* (1903) what Kraus accuses a reviewer of – that is, slanting his criticism according to an *idée fixe* about anti-Semitism in the work reviewed. By then admitting that Kraus 'decouples the linkage of homosexuality and the Jews' to talk only of Wilde's 'stage Pharisees', not 'Jews' as such, Gilman subverts his own constructs, without fully conceding that

Kraus's discourse is aestheticist, pitched against both anti-Semitic and Jewish liberal 'philistines'.

Against such approaches, even the 'narrative and paraphrasing Kraus criticism' from which Scheichl dissociates himself would be a blessing – but there is sufficient work of quality in these three volumes to be more optimistic about the future. H. Zohn's anecdotal survey of Kraus in the English-speaking world, that is, the American press reception of his and others' English translations of Kraus, gives no indication of how important the last decade has been for Kraus research.

GILBERT J. CARR

Franz Kafka, *Tagebücher*, ed. Hans-Gerd Koch, Michael Müller and Malcolm Pasley (Frankfurt: Fischer, 1990), 3 vols: Textband, 1065 pp.; Apparatband, 445 pp.; Kommentarband, 341 pp., DM 450.

Franz Kafka, *Der Proceß*, ed. Malcolm Pasley (Frankfurt: Fischer, 1990), 2 vols: Textband, 357 pp.; Apparatband, 351 pp., DM 248.

Malcolm Pasley, *Franz Kafka: 'Der Proceß'. Die Handschrift redet*, with an essay by Ulrich Ott, Marbacher Magazin no. 52 (Marbach am Neckar: Deutsche Schillergesellschaft, 1990), 99 pp.

Few of the volumes in the ongoing critical edition of Kafka's writings have been more eagerly awaited than that of *Der Proceß*, arguably his most important work and the subject of philological speculation ever since 1946, when Max Brod admitted in the afterword to the third edition that his ordering of the chapters might have been incorrect. For those readers awaiting a radically new version of the novel, the present critical edition will come as a disappointment. Basing his decision largely on internal narrative logic, Malcolm Pasley has decided to maintain Brod's original chapter sequence, although he has split the first chapter into two distinct ones ('Verhaftung' and 'Gespräch mit Frau Grubach / Dann Fräulein Bürstner') and relegated the original fourth chapter ('Die Freundin des Fräulein Bürstner') to the status of a fragment; the novel thus retains its original ten-chapter structure. The text itself is largely unchanged. The new edition corrects Brod's occasional misreadings and provides a full account of stylistic variants; it also restores Kafka's Austrianisms, idiosyncratic orthography and sparse punctuation (already familiar from critical editions of *Das Schloß* and *Der Verschollene*), which give the text a more personal and unfinished aspect. But fundamentally we are still confronted with the same novel, the same paucity of motives for Josef K.'s enigmatic arrest and execution.

Although mostly stylistic or orthographic, the variants included in the critical apparatus provide a microscopic glimpse into the 'laboratory' of Kafka's creations as his sentences took shape on the page. In a few cases they reveal a shift in meaning. Thus we learn that Josef K. was 'gefangen' ('caught') in the opening sentence before Kafka shifted this event to a legal register with the term 'verhaftet' ('arrested'). One technical problem is that the substantial passages deleted by Kafka (including for instance K.'s intriguing metamorphosis in 'Das Haus' with Titorelli), which Brod originally placed in the novel's appendix, are now located in the critical apparatus where the general reader will probably not venture.

If it reveals little about Josef K., the new edition of *Der Proceß* does provide a wealth of absorbing material concerning the novel's genesis and what Pasley has elsewhere termed the Kafkan 'Schreibakt' or 'act of writing'. In his editorial introduction to the critical apparatus and, more expansively, in the catalogue essay for the 1990 exhibition of the manuscript at the Literaturarchiv in Marbach (Germany), Pasley explains that Kafka adopted a new strategy of composition to avoid the problem that had plagued his work on *Der Verschollene* two years earlier. Frustrated by his inability to bring that novel to a close, Kafka began *Der Proceß* by writing the first and last chapters before proceeding to the intermediary segments, thus firmly delimiting the novel's beginning and end from the outset. He also worked on the middle chapters simultaneously, switching from one to the other when the narrative bogged down. Thus, whereas he had written his American novel in linear fashion, 'tapping his way' through a dark corridor (to use Kafka's own metaphor) without knowing where his story would lead him, here he wrote 'synchronically', within a fixed narrative frame. What resulted was a novel with a beginning and a conclusion, but only bits and pieces in between.

One of the chief indications Pasley uses to date these various pieces is the physical appearance and size of Kafka's handwriting, which was large and flowing in the early stages but became increasingly cramped as he encountered difficulties in 'driving the novel forward'. Although one may question the positivistic lengths to which Pasley takes the measurement of Kafka's hand, it seems clear that he wrote the bulk of his novel – some two hundred handwritten pages – in an astonishingly brief period between early August and October in 1914. The remaining eighty-odd manuscript pages arose in fits and starts from late October to mid-February 1915, at which point he broke off all work on the novel. Pasley's account makes for an engaging philological drama, and, given the extraordinary import of *Der Proceß*, the two-month period in which Kafka wrote the first and only draft of his novel must count as one of the most miraculous events of modern European literature. The Marbach exhibition catalogue, richly illustrated and equipped with informative essays by Pasley ('Die Handschrift redet') and the archive director Ulrich Ott ('Kafkas Nachlaß'), further testifies to the novel's aura.

Unlike that of *Der Proceß*, the critical edition of the *Tagebücher* can be considered a new text insofar as it offers a (limited) number of previously unpublished passages, an extensive apparatus of historical notes, the inclusion of stories like 'Das Urteil' originally composed in the diaries, and a fundamental reordering of the diary entries according to the notebooks in which they were written rather than a strict chronological sequence. A word of thanks is due to the editors, Hans-Gerd Koch, Michael Müller and Malcolm Pasley, for their wide-ranging research; readers can now find a historical gloss on virtually every person, book or event mentioned in the diaries as well as several maps and handsome illustrations. One may question, however, the wisdom of the new ordering. True, it allows us to discern a formal unity in each notebook, as when

Kafka wrote on 15 January 1914: 'Das Heft fängt mit Felice an, die mir am 2. v [19]13 den Kopf unsicher machte, ich kann mit diesem Anfang das Heft auch schließen, wenn ich statt unsicher ein schlimmeres Wort nehme' ('The notebook begins with Felice, who bewildered me on 2. v. [19]13, this beginning will also serve to end the notebook, if I use a worse word than bewildered.'). Nonetheless, the new ordering unnecessarily preserves the chronological jumble that arose for contingent reasons (such as the lack of space in a particular notebook when Kafka needed to finish a story). Thus we encounter the *second* half of 'Der Heizer' in mid-sentence in the midst of diary entries for 1911 (a full year before it was actually written); only three hundred pages later do we find the first half of the story in its proper place, after the entry for 25 September 1912. In 1914 the jumble gets particularly thick as one must look in three different places for entries written in the same period. The chronological list of entries provided in the commentary volume is cumbersome and unsatisfactory, and so here again the question of a suitable edition for the general public remains open.

The most sensational feature of this new edition is without doubt the inclusion of 'allzu Intimes' ('excessively intimate') material that Brod had excised from the first text of the diaries in 1950 to protect Kafka or persons living at the time. In all there are approximately eighty new passages, most of which amount to only a word or a sentence, a few to more than a page. Many of these deletions concern sexual matters, such as the quite graphic description of a conversation Kafka had with the artist Alfred Kubin about the latter's taste for stout women. The passage reveals Kafka's complicity with the *fin-de-siècle* conception of the animal-woman, without soul: '[Kubins] Kunststück in früheren Zeiten war, Frauen so zu ermüden, daß sie nicht mehr konnten. Dann waren sie ohne Seele, Tiere. Ja diese Ergebenheit kann ich mir vorstellen.' ('Kubin's trick was formerly to tire women out until they were no longer able. Then they were soulless, animals. Yes, I can imagine such submission.') Brod also eliminated most references to the brothels he and Kafka visited on their summer trips together, several homoerotic passages, and occasional anti-Semitic remarks (such as a reference to Walter Hasenclever as 'jüdisch, laut' – 'Jewish, noisy'). Generally, his tendency seems to have been to decorporealize Kafka's existence, making of his suffering a purely metaphysical problem. Thus in May 1913 Kafka wrote: 'Verzweiflung also auch von hier aus. Nirgends Aufnahme,' ('Desperation from this viewpoint as well. No welcome anywhere'), then specifying immediately afterwards: '1. Verdauung 2. Neurasthenie 3. Ausschlag 4. innere Unsicherheit' ('digestion, neurasthenia, skin-rash, inner uncertainty'). Brod let the first entry stand, but excised the second.

In conclusion, one should note that these two critical editions vindicate Brod's often criticized role as editor of his friend's work. Apart from the points noted above, his editions do not vary significantly from the present 'kritische Ausgabe'; it does not seem likely therefore that there will be any fundamental change in the way we view *Der Proceß* or the image of Kafka that emerges from his diaries. The critical edition sets the record straight in small though important details; it provides almost direct access to the manuscripts for the scholar; finally, with its elegant physical appearance (not to mention its astronomical price-tag) it marks the official canonization of Kafka in the pantheon of modern German literature. But the task of interpretation still falls to the reader, who will find new questions, not answers, in the present editions.

MARK ANDERSON

Hartmut Steinecke and Joseph Strelka (eds), *Romanstruktur und Menschenrecht bei Hermann Broch* (Berne: Peter Lang, 1990), 209 pp.

Klaus Amann and Helmut Grote, *Die 'Wiener Bibliothek' Hermann Brochs: Kommentiertes Verzeichnis des rekonstruierten Bestandes* (Vienna and Cologne: Böhlau, 1990), 290 pp., 966 Sch.

Romanstruktur und Menschenrecht contains eleven contributions, nine of which were papers read at the Budapest Broch Symposium held on the centenary of Broch's birth. The articles by Gisela Brude-Firnau and Roderick H. Watt arose independently, according to a laconic editors' note, and were included to provide a fuller picture of Broch research. Although Brude-Firnau's thirty-page contribution, originally written in 1978, adds nothing factually new to our knowledge of Broch's life or works, it serves a useful function as an introduction to the following articles. Watt's 'A Comparative Study of the Original Reception of the English Translations of Hermann Broch's Novels in the United States and United Kingdom' shows in exemplary fashion how the reading tastes and expectations of the educated reading public in each country flavoured Broch's reception in newspaper and magazine reviews. British reviewers more than American were put off by Broch's foreignness, and the term 'Teutonic' is used as a kind of shorthand for obscure and pedantic. Some reviews in Scotland were especially devastating, in effect saying that Broch's novels were abstruse, turgid, wordy in the extreme, pedantic and certainly unfit reading material for a healthy mind. In general, Broch's reviewers – regardless of whether they found him 'Teutonic' or a brilliant and profound artist-thinker – gave the reader the unmistakable impression that his works were impenetrable, or at least very hard going – with the obvious deleterious effect on sales. On one minor point Watt is wrong: the indication in the *Choice* review of *The Guiltless* that the novel is 'recommended for college and university libraries' would probably not hurt sales, but increase them, since *Choice* is a periodical aimed exclusively at librarians. Of special value in this article are corrections to P. M. Lützeler's biography of Broch regarding the reception of *The Death of Vergil* and *The Unknown Quantity*. The former work *was* reviewed in Great Britain and the latter was *not* a complete critical failure in Great Britain and the United States.

In 'Hermann Broch und Mittel-Europa' Endre Kiss attempts to show how Broch's thought is specifically Central European; unfortunately Kiss covers too much ground in limited space, and resorts to repeated references to his other related articles. One cannot help but wonder why an expanded version of the piece was not prepared for this book. Strelka's 'Hermann Brochs Modell einer umfassenden Massenpsychologie' is an interesting summation, but, again, offers little that is new. Zsuzsa Széll's 'Stadt und Land: Ein Motiv und seine Bedeutung' treats Broch's seemingly contradictory attitude toward city and countryside, and shows that the contrast is a significant motif not only in *The Spell* but in his other novels as well. Árpád Bernáth provides, in 'Ein Dichter wider Willen?', a sceptical examination of the heretofore virtually universally accepted judgement of Broch as a 'reluctant' poet or novelist. It is to be hoped that Broch specialists will read this useful, tightly reasoned reassessment. In briefest terms, Bernáth points out that since Hannah Arendt coined the phrase 'Dichter wider Willen' over thirty years ago (as the title of her introductory essay to volumes 6 and 7 of the Zurich Broch edition), most scholars have accepted the implied judgement that Broch's literary achievement is in essence a substitute for theoretical-philosophical works that could directly address the pressing issues of the time, such as the phenomena associated with mass-psychosis. There is no question that Broch's life and work were terribly split between creative and theoretical urges, but is it valid to speak of Broch as the philosopher who, impatient with theorizing, became a novelist? According to this scheme, Broch was first philosopher, then novelist, then political writer, and turned to literature to reach a broader audience. But a reexamination of his publications reveals that from 1909 on his first writings were primarily literary: reviews, literary essays, novellas, and poems. His reviews of philosophical works appeared in *literary* periodicals, and until 1922 they were predominantly about *literature*. And so the question is not why the philosopher turned poet, but why the blossoming writer became a kind of 'secret philosopher', taking courses in philosophy from 1925–30 at the University of Vienna. Bernáth's answer, which unfortunately cannot be elaborated on here, is that Broch aimed, even in his philosophical writings, to transform the function of literature, using new methods appropriate to the modern age.

Steinecke's 'Kunstwerk der Erkenntnis' deals with Broch's theory of the novel at the time he was writing *The Sleepwalkers*. Of primary interest to Steinecke is how Broch integrates 'Wissenschaft' (philosophy, ethics, theories of history, psychology, and mass-psychology) with the action of the novel. *How* this is done is – in the tradition of the encyclopedic or polyhistorical novel – much more relevant in Steinecke's view than the *content* of the theory woven into the novel. Dietmar Goltschnigg provides in 'Robert Musil und Hermann Broch' an interesting and unconventional comparison of the two writers (who are so often mentioned together in passing) based on Elias Canetti's autobiography, and shows that Canetti's praise of Musil, often at the expense of Broch, appears in part to have been based on a faulty remembrance of events or on personal animosity rather than fact. Ernst Schönwiese's 'Erinnerungen an Hermann Broch' provide a few details about Broch not found elsewhere, including quotations from unpublished letters to Schönwiese.

In sum, this volume – unfortunately without index, and unaccountably lacking any information about the symposium or its participants – contains in addition to some rehashing of Broch research a number of useful, informative articles.

Amann and Grote's *Die 'Wiener Bibliothek' Hermann Brochs*, an immensely valuable contribution to Broch scholarship, provides information on how and when Broch's library arose (largely from 1915–30), its complex and tragic history, its composition, and Broch's marginalia in the books now found in the library of the University of Klagenfurt. The philosophical-mathematical portion of the library that Broch built up so carefully in his Teesdorf days, when he was a captain of industry during the day and a secret philosopher-scholar at night, survived the 1930s and the war, and was shipped to the United States, but arrived on 12 June 1951, some twelve days after Broch's death. His son, faced with his father's debts and himself hospitalized, was compelled to sell the library of over 2,000 volumes to a New York bookdealer who was acting as agent for Josef Buttinger, an autodidact bibliophile and a director of the International Relief Association. Buttinger added the Broch library to his massive collection, a 'Library for Political Studies' as it was termed. In 1971 the majority of the books in the collection was given by Buttinger to the University of Klagenfurt. The part of this collection that had been a part of Broch's Vienna library has now been painstakingly identified, sorted, and catalogued, and is available for research on its relationship to Broch's writings. The compilers of this enormously useful bibliography are quite right when they claim that this information will enable future scholars to answer questions which have eluded previous generations of Broch scholars. The book will be a cornerstone of Broch research and should be purchased by all research libraries and Broch specialists.

JAMES HARDIN

David Turner, *Moral Values and the Human Zoo: The Novellen of Stefan Zweig* (Hull: Hull University Press, 1989), 353pp., £24.95.

Volker Henze, *Jüdischer Kulturpessimismus und das Bild des Alten Österreich im Werk Stefan Zweigs und Joseph Roths* (Heidelberg: Carl Winter Universitätsverlag, 1988), 375 pp., DM 75.

Stefan Zweig continues to enjoy a large readership, particularly in German-speaking countries, but scholars have tended to neglect him in favour of such other members of the 'Young Vienna' circle as Hugo von Hofmannsthal and Arthur Schnitzler, whose writings have been deemed more worthy of a close reading. There was, to be sure, a flurry of academic interest in 1981, Zweig's centennial year, when international symposia held in Beersheva, Metz, Fredonia, and elsewhere engendered important publications and Joseph P. Strelka's short but powerful book *Stefan Zweig: Freier Geist der Menschlichkeit* constituted a pioneering analysis of Zweig's major works. The distinction of having published the first in-depth discussion of Zweig's novellas belongs to Dr Turner of the University of Hull, who has adapted and put together several of his essays previously published in various journals and collections and also offers much new material. Displaying a sure command of both primary and secondary sources, Turner writes lucidly and with admirable authority. His analyses are as insightful and incisive as they are cogent and convincing.

Turner properly regards Zweig's work as all of a piece. In his novellas as in his historical biographies (or *vies romancées*), his dramatic works, essays, and letters the emphasis is on personal freedom, intensity of experience and commitment, the full-orbed personality (*Persönlichkeit* in Goethe's sense), and human brotherhood. Zweig was impatient with longer narrative forms and produced only one novel and one fragment. 'The *Novelle* appears to be so much in tune with Zweig's narrative aims,' writes Turner, 'that, if the genre had not already existed, he would have had to invent it.' The author gives pride of place to the psychological and moral aspects of Zweig's stories and attempts to divine their special 'Zweigian' quality. In discussing Zweig's 'explorations of the varied manifestations of the human psyche', Turner displays a becoming awareness of the tensions between the psychological prober and the moralist humanist, but he uses such dubious (because un-Zweigian) phrases as 'inmates of the human zoo' and 'the psychological menagerie'.

In the four parts of his magisterial study, which attempts to define Zweig's place in the history of the *Novelle*, the author deals with the fascinating complexity of Zweig's characters, the function of his settings (time, place, weather, atmosphere), his rhetoric, imagery, and narrative structures as well as the humanistic values he espoused. The psychological content of the novellas is considered under several (admittedly overlapping) rubrics: 1) The Problem of Adolescence, 2) The Eruption of the Unconscious, 3) Single-mindedness, 4) Inner Conflicts, 5) The Battle of the Sexes, 6) Intellectual Feats and Deficiencies, 7) The Psychology of Self-Revelation, 8) The Psychology of Curiosity. Thus Zweig's last work in this genre, *Schachnovelle* (*The Royal Game*), is discussed under rubrics 2), 4), 6), and 7), and *Buchmendel* is analysed under rubrics 6) and 8) as well as under the additional headings Wide Horizons, Beyond Time and Space, and The Brotherhood of Man. As Turner warns against overestimating Sigmund Freud's influence on Zweig and reading his *Novellen* as 'applied psychoanalysis', he makes a charming (and logical) Freudian slip of his own by substituting (on p. 95) *Schlachtfeld* (battlefield) for *Schachfeld* (chessboard).

Turner is aware that Zweig's readability often masks his complexity, and his (far from uncritical) examination of numerous variform trees does not blind him to the unity and majesty of the forest. The publishers have risen to the occasion by producing a very handsome book, but it is regrettable that the visual pun (or inside joke) of one of the two (uncredited) woodcuts on the jacket (a 'white' Zweig playing chess with a 'black' one) will have to remain an outsider, as it were, and that the copious quotations in the original German only will limit the readership of this valuable study.

Dr Henze's book has many of the virtues of a first-rate dissertation: thoroughness, clarity, empathy, and a firm grasp of the historical and cultural background. To some extent it supplements Turner's book, for it discusses some early novellas that Zweig later refused to have reprinted (two from the 1904 collection *Die Liebe der Erika Ewald* and the poignant Jewish story *Im Schnee*) as well as several of Zweig's legends. The author regards these early novellas as *fin-de-siècle* documents of unsuccessful Jewish assimilatory tendencies and a Jew's morbid aesthetic fascination with the decline and destruction of his people, and he reads the legends as superficial appropriation of biblical themes and language.

The close personal relationship between Stefan Zweig and Joseph Roth serves the author as a springboard for his comparative study of the two writers' nostalgic transfiguration of the Habsburg monarchy and the effect of their convoluted Jewishness on their writings. As their utopian constructs dissolved in the acid of reality, both men were faced with the loss of their spiritual and actual homeland and spurned the Zionist solution of a new Jewish life on the Jewish soil of an 'oldnewland'. While Roth, an accomplished 'mythomaniac', was aware of the purely fictive nature of his portrayal of the monarchy, Zweig remained convinced that his ideal of an apolitical cosmopolitanism of Viennese vintage had existed before World War I. He took a flight into the past, as it were; even in Brazil, his 'land of the future', he really sought only a land of the past, and in troubled times he tried to derive strength from great historical and cultural figures. Zweig retained his ideal of Judaism as the ethnically unobtrusive moral leavening of mankind, and in the 1930s he counselled his imperilled fellow Jews to refrain from any political activity. Roth, on the other hand, increasingly evoked the world of the Jewish *shtetl* in the easternmost reaches of the lost empire and masked his essential homelessness with a nostalgic celebration of a transfigured Habsburg realm. Even after the victory of Hitlerism Roth remained obsessed with the idea of a Germanic Catholic monarchy.

Henze reads *Buchmendel* as a caricature of Zweig's own bibliophile pursuits and as a critique of an *Ostjudentum* that the author really neither knew nor cared about. Though the author has a tendency to secondguess his subjects, to 'correct' and supplement their writings and public statements, his informed (and occasionally polemical) discussions of such works as *Jeremias*, *Radetzkymarsch*, *Die Welt von gestern*, *Hiob*, and *Die Kapuzinergruft* from the viewpoint of their authors' Jewish cultural pessimism do shed new light on them. One curious error is Henze's attribution of the illustrations (*Buchschmuck*) of *Die Liebe der Erika Ewald* to the Polish-born Zionist artist Ephraim Moses Lilien rather than to Hugo Steiner-Prag.

HARRY ZOHN

Alan Bance and Ian Huish (eds), *Ödön von Horváth Fifty Years On: Horváth Symposium, London 1988* (London: Institute of Germanic Studies, 1989), vi + 157 pp., £10.95.

For some thirty years after his tragic early death in 1938, Horváth's work remained little known outside a circle of devoted followers led by his friend Franz Theodor Csokor and others who had known him in the turbulent years of pre-war Central Europe. As early as 1961, however, Rowohlt issued nine of his plays, with an introduction by Traugott Krischke, and in the late 1940s and 1950s some plays were beginning to be revived or performed for the first time. It was not until the late 1960s and early 1970s that the 'Horváth renaissance' began in earnest.

Critical work began to appear following Krischke's edition of the *Stücke*: Strelka (1962), Poppe (1965), Kahl (1966), Krammer (1969), Hummel (1970) ... But it was Krischke's massive output as editor, biographer and commentator that did more than anything to bring Horváth to the serious attention of Germanists and, rather more importantly, of the wider theatre-going public. From his *Materialen zu Ödön von Horváth* of 1970 (in which the publisher ranks

197

Horváth alongside Brecht) to a series of biographical studies and critical editions of individual works and the four-volume *Gesammelte Werke* of 1970 (edited with Dieter Hildebrandt and later extended in a softcover edition), Krischke has provided the Horváth scholar with an invaluable service. In Great Britain, the National Theatre's brilliant 1977 staging of *Tales from the Vienna Woods* in a fine translation by Christopher Hampton was the first of a string of professional and amateur productions, many of them the work of Ian Huish, whose edition of *Jugend ohne Gott* (1974) was the first of several texts produced for British schools and universities and who has most recently translated *Figaro läßt sich scheiden*. Hampton has also translated *Don Juan kommt aus dem Krieg* and *Glaube, Liebe, Hoffnung* as well as writing *Tales from Hollywood*, a fanciful play in which Horváth figures prominently.

An uncomfortable question inevitably poses itself: does the *oeuvre* merit such exhaustive attention? The publication of the *Horváth-Blätter* in 1983 showed the warning signs of over-exposure: the first issue contained a sketch of a production of *Glaube, Liebe, Hoffnung,* nine facsimile pages of Horváth's first poetic effort, various photographs with tenuous connections with the author. Horváth's is undoubtedly an impressive talent, and one that is particularly remarkable for its perceptive depiction of the times in which he lived and for its uncanny prescience. Whether it is as great as his followers believe is disputed – the vast critical apparatus now assembled around his work would have amused him greatly, and would not, one suspects, have been anticipated by his contemporaries.

Ödön von Horváth Fifty Years On is a collection of papers, simultaneously published in the Austrian journal *Sprachkunst,* given at a symposium in London to mark the fiftieth anniversary of Horváth's death. A previous symposium, organized in London in 1976, had produced eight short papers, later published by the Austrian Institute. The 1988 symposium has produced eleven, more substantial, contributions.

'Ich bin eine typische altösterreichische-ungarische Mischung: magyarisch, kroatisch, deutsch, tschechisch' ('I am a typical old Austro-Hungarian mixture: Magyar, Croat, German, Czech') was Horváth's own description of his Central European origins. Eva Kun writes about Horváth and Hungary, providing insights not available to commentators without a knowledge of Hungarian, and treating neglected periods of Horvath's residence in the country. The influence of Endre Ady on Horváth's thinking is traced in particular detail in this convincing account of the Hungarian ingredient in Horváth's life.

David Midgley, in a paper on the 'Aetiology of the Banal', looks at *Der ewige Spießer;* Alfred Doppler considers Horváth's late plays in connection with the theme of exile; Johanna Bossinade examines 'Eros Thanatos in Horváths Volksstück' (and argues incidentally for new directions in research on Horváth, focusing on the *Volksstück* as the central part of the *oeuvre*). Ian Huish, in an agile analysis of several works, identifies much familiarity with Freud and traces Horváth's use of Freudian themes in the mouths of his characters and in their actions, and through various symbolic devices.

Horst Jarka investigates interest in Horváth in the United States and finds that, as in Great Britain, there was a flurry of interest in 1939 at the time *The Age of the Fish* (the English title of *Jugend ohne Gott*) appeared, and then more or less complete neglect until *Tales from the Vienna Woods* reached the American stage in Hampton's translation in 1978, when the critics reacted with the same mixture of misunderstanding and caution as their British counterparts. From Jarka's account it appears that Horváth remains neglected in the German departments of American universities – only 30 per cent of those responding to a questionnaire indicated that his works appear in their normal degree programmes. Jarka concludes by asking whether Horváth is yet to be discovered or already forgotten.

Franz Kadrnoska links discussion of *Jugend ohne Gott* with the theme of *Vergangenheitsbewältigung* in its fictional and real manifestations, and in the context of the Waldheim affair, through which uncomfortable realities have again found their fictional expression, this time in Gerald Szyskowitz's *Puntigam oder Die Kunst des Vergessens* of 1988.

Louise Adey makes the essential link between Horváth and his antecedent in the tradition of the *Volksstück*, Johann Nestroy. In a perceptive analysis of the use of language, based on an intimate knowledge of both authors, Dr Adey demonstrates convincingly how Horváth drew on a long tradition of linguistic subtlety in popular comedy, of which Nestroy was the nineteenth-century master. A full-scale study of Horváth in the context of the Viennese *Volkstheater* tradition would be most rewarding; Dr Adey should be encouraged to undertake it.

Jurgen Schröder writes about *Stunde der Liebe* in a welcome essay on a little-known work; Alan Bance returns to *Jugend ohne Gott*, Horváth's masterly short novel which figures prominently in several of the papers of the symposium; finally, Jean-Claude François looks at the relationship between fiction and history in Horváth's works. He concludes with some telling thoughts on reasons for the new-found interest in Horváth:

Er hatte in seinen Stücken und in seiner Prosa jene deutsche Gesellschaft zwischen Kaisertum und Nazismus gleichsam photographiert – aber diese Bilder waren nicht gestellt, nicht offiziell, nicht propagandistisch; sie waren getreu, aufrichtig, zuverlässig. Um eine andere Metapher zu gebrauchen: er hatte die Weimarer Gesellschaft präpariert, und zwar so gut, daß die Medizinstudenten der späteren Generationen seine Präparate noch verwenden können.
[In his plays and prose he had, as it were, photographed German society between Empire and Nazism – but these pictures were not posed, not official, not propagandist; they were faithful, sincere, reliable. To adopt a different metaphor: he had dissected the society of the Weimar Republic, so well that later generations of medical students could still use his specimens.]

Not a bad verdict on an author whose works threatened to slip into obscurity. The papers in this welcome volume, each characterized by an obvious and genuine enthusiasm for their subject – above the level of obsession – demonstrate between them the wealth of possibilities there are for research on Horváth and his works and justify the interest awakened by a dedicated group who have

199

devoted themselves to keeping that interest alive. It must be hoped that they will lead to further exploration of some very promising ideas.

DAVID PHILLIPS

Douglas Jarman (ed.), *The Berg Companion* (London: Macmillan,1989), xii + 301 pp., £29.50.

> The music of Alban Berg has always presented a particularly intriguing paradox, a seeming contradiction between the directness of its expression and the complexity of its surface, a problem compounded by the composer's fondness for number schemes, abstract patterning, and programmatic reference.

The paradox thus formulated by Michael Taylor in his contribution to *The Berg Companion* is explored from a variety of angles in the book as a whole. This produces an overview of Berg's life and music which should interest both the specialist and the layman. Two biographical articles placing the composer in the Viennese cultural context are followed by essays dealing with the songs, the instrumental music, and the operas. Each of these groups consists of an introductory article followed by detailed studies of individual works.

Christopher Hailey's essay offers the most penetrating account of Berg's persona and his cultural milieu in the collection. Hailey proposes that when considered in the context of the contradiction arising from the 'unabashed provincialism' of the Viennese and their aspirations to a cosmopolitan culture, the music of the 'Viennese classics' can be seen as serving an analogous social function to that provided by the international classical vocabulary used in the ostentatious *Ringstrasse*. He writes:

> In Vienna, however, where the letter, if not the spirit, of the Classic Style came to be jealously guarded by the city's academic institutions, this precious patrimony also represented a weighty burden. It was in a sense a legacy imposed from without, a kind of masculine sobriety grafted on to the sensuous spontaneity of Vienna's indigenous musical heritage. It was the difference between Johannes Brahms and Johann Strauss, between the rigours of a sonata and the lyric inspiration of a song.

Hailey's paper explores this dichotomy in relation to the inexpensive seats of the fourth gallery in the Vienna Court Opera, which he characterizes as 'an evocative metaphor for that unique Viennese continuum linking audience and performers, tradition and its cultivation, heritage and its inheritors', and perceptively concludes:

> If Gustav Mahler brought conscious articulation to the instinctual, then it is one of Alban Berg's supreme accomplishments to have embraced and transmitted the warm ambience of Viennese inheritance without compromising the high art of his inherited legacy, to have found *his* resolution of the Viennese dichotomy by making the conscious unconscious.

In the first essay dealing with 'the Man and his Environment', Martin Esslin's tour of the Viennese intelligentsia, I was surprised to read that 'through Loos, Berg found his way into the circle of the avant-garde painters' including Klimt and Schiele, two names hitherto not associated in this way with either Loos or Berg. The other piece in this section is Joan Allen Smith's essay on Berg's character, which abounds in humorous anecdotes about the Berg household, taking as its primary source the unpublished memoirs of Soma Morgenstern. Although the author tells us that she has 'chosen to present the picture of Berg ... with a minimum of psychological conjecture', her analysis portrays Berg as the 'strong-mother-weak-father type' who finds a substitute father in Schoenberg and eventually marries a woman with a neurotic urge to control him.

Since the lifting of restrictions on access to Berg's papers following the death of the composer's widow in 1976, much research has been carried out on the private programmatic elements in Berg's music and his working methods. Two pieces in this collection deal with Berg's passion for cryptography as revealed by the annotations in the score of the *Lyric Suite* and the 'Open Letter' on the *Chamber Concerto*. Douglas Jarman's essay on the *Violin Concerto* places Berg's preoccupation within the general context of the interest in the occult in Germany and Austria, and in particular the writings of Wilhem Fliess, while Barbara Dalen's essay continues the exegesis initiated by Berg himself in the 'Open Letter' and suggests that the *Chamber Concerto* includes symbolic references to the love affair between Richard Gerstl and Schoenberg's wife. Also making use of the recently available autograph material, Patricia Hall's piece on the sketches for *Lulu* is a fascinating account of the composer at work.

The analytical studies in the *Berg Companion* reflect the wide spectrum of present-day music analysis, ranging from its use as a tool for historical enquiry to the study of systems and methods of composition in isolation. The essays on the early songs, the *Altenberg Lieder,* and the instrumental works by Mark DeVoto, Stephen Kett, and Bruce Archibald fall in the first group, in that they follow the categories which Berg himself would have applied to the discussion of his music. The discussion of the opening bars of *Lulu* by George Perle represents the other pole, in its use of a fragment from Berg as a springboard for theoretical speculation which I suspect to be more relevant to explaining Perle, the composer, than Berg.

Derrick Puffett's discussion of *Wozzeck* and *Lulu* in their operatic environment falls apologetically between analysis and historical musicology, for the author believes that the 'highlighting of reminiscences and anticipations', the subject of the essay, though interesting and necessary 'can never replace analysis as a means of "getting into" a work'. Unlike George Steiner (in *The Death of Tragedy)* for whom Berg's music 'distorts Buchner's principal device', by making Woyzeck 'eloquent', Puffett thinks that 'Berg's characters are not lost for words' and consequently considers that 'the interludes have much more the role of continuing dramatic and thematic arguments already carried on at length within the scenes themselves'. Equally striking is his characterization of *Lulu,* 'if not [as] "bourgeois comedy", ... at least [as] a drama of "middle-class family life"'.

Although these articles at times cover the same ground the result is far from tedious, for the various approaches intertwine in the reader's mind, bringing to life the topics under consideration and making this an important and entertaining addition to Berg studies.

SILVINA MILSTEIN

Wendelin Schmidt-Dengler, Martin Huber, Michael Huter (eds), *Wittgenstein* und (Vienna: Verlag der Österreichischen Staatsdruckerei, 1990), 211 pp., 278 Sch.

Wittgenstein felt that philosophy should really be written as a poetic composition. Yet, as Ray Monk points out in his recent biography, his style is curiously at odds with much of his subject-matter, as though a poet had somehow strayed into the analysis of the foundations of mathematics and the theory of meaning. Not surprisingly, many writers have been fascinated by Wittgenstein's constant resorting to simile and metaphor, and none more so than the post-war generation in Austria.

In May 1989 a symposium was held in Vienna to explore the ramifications of this fascination, and to examine the ways in which Wittgenstein himself was a very 'literary' philosopher. *Wittgenstein und* therefore consciously looks both at his impact on Austrian literature, and at the impact of literature upon him. Oswald Wiener remarks: 'der eindruck einiger von Wittgensteins schriften auf die *Wiener Gruppe* (jedenfalls auf mich) war zugleich tief und undeutlich' ('the impression some of Wittgenstein's writings made on the Vienna Group (at any rate on me) was at once deep and indistinct'), but readers of this volume will find that for all the elusiveness of some of the material, the authors have made real attempts to take to heart one of Wittgenstein's most famous maxims: 'whatever can be said, can be said *clearly.*' Perhaps more Germanists should read Wittgenstein.

The volume opens with essays on the literary nature of Wittgenstein's production, central to which are the philosopher's obsession with linguistic clarity as an end in itself, and with an examination of shared motifs in Wittgenstein and Goethe. In a volume otherwise carefully edited and attractively laid out, it is unfortunate that in the Goethe essay mistakes in English were not eliminated (p. 39) and that Bertrand Russell's name is consistently misspelt. One might also have wished for a specific contribution on the impact upon Wittgenstein of the literary culture of the 'Wiener Jahrhundertwende', for Weininger, Kraus, Loos and Hofmannsthal (especially the 'Chandos Letter') were surely of more than passing importance in the development of Wittgenstein's philosophy. In 1931, for instance, he wrote: 'I don't believe I have ever *invented* a line of thinking, I have always taken one over from someone else.' He then cites, *inter alia*, Kraus, Loos and Weininger.

Whereas the contributions on the impact of literature upon Wittgenstein tend to be essayistic and linguistically orientated, the remainder are more traditionally author-based, with contributions on Wittgenstein's significance for modern poetry, the 'Wiener Gruppe', Bachmann, Schutting, Handke and Bernhard.

Common to all the essays is a level of scholarly commitment which makes for consistently stimulating, if not particularly easy, reading, and unlike so many published conference proceedings this is not a mixed bag. Whilst the Foreword rightly makes no claims for the book's completeness, it can be recommended as an important contribution to our understanding of the intellectual fabric of modern Austrian literature. The distinguished contributors are: Chris Bezzel, Rudolf Haller, Martin Huber, Michael Huter, Martin Kubaczek, Burghart Schmidt, Wendelin Schmidt-Dengler, Gisela Steinlechner, Joseph Peter Stern, Friedrich Wallner and Oswald Wiener.

ANDREW BARKER

Elisabeth Young-Bruehl, *Anna Freud* (London: Macmillan, 1989), 528 pp., £18.95.

Anna Freud once quoted a remark of her father's: 'He spoke of how we bring up our children: ... we supply them with a map of the Italian lakes and then send them off to the North Pole' (p. 407). She herself was supplied before birth with a blueprint that she could only comply with: every daughter is a son *manqué*, and her greatest achievements are in some sense a failure. If Sigmund Freud was the originator uniquely empowered, like God, to an analytic parthenogenesis, his daughter was the only child of the theory to be literally reproduced by the listening patriarch. Her story is that of a woman obliged to outlive the father who gave her meaning, in the knowledge both that she was also born too late for him and that nothing she might do must go beyond him. The wish to be a man expresses itself in an admirably stern rationality, a life of chaste daughterhood and passionate friendship, and the fortitude that always exceeds the prescribed feminine. At the same time, Miss Freud precisely followed the model of the good woman: her work never done, active always in a nurturing sphere, reasoning her way through painstaking research on the damage done to children by the War, concentration camp survival, or everyday deprivations, while Melanie Klein as classical ugly sister explores the richer trails of the infant's hidden psychoses. If Klein or Lacan have (as Young-Bruehl implies but does not admit) survived better as oedipal heirs, that is not to deny Anna Freud the primary inheritance of the good child - the continuance of what was most clear-sighted, modest and sane in Freud's work. She was of course defeated in the end by the hideous gamesmanship of the third and fourth generations of IPA-niks, whose names begin to spill in lists into this biography about halfway through its considerable length. Anna Freud hated the politics of administration, and ended worsted by it, but she was extremely good at keeping things temporarily calm by the iron glance from under stooped shoulders. These generations were the unruly gangs of any diaspora inheriting the right to atheism once the Holy of Holies is gone and the Written Law available to the rudest of readers. Freud prepared a genealogical system which ended prey to its over-institutionalization - his own daughter was left outside.

Young-Bruehl is best when she relieves the interminable internecine quarrels with some modest synthesis of her own. She locates Anna's key development in her adolescent struggle against masturbation (a 'vice' Young-Bruehl seems quaintly unwilling to defend, presumably out of homage to this father-daughter plot) by means of creative story-telling and fantasy. Narratives in which Anna is the boy hero inform the later shape of her scientific imagination. She learns from her father how to integrate the personal into the theoretical, going further than his more complete censorship dared: thus the beating fantasy, the excess of altruistic devotion, the origins of male homosexuality (perhaps, via an incest fantasy, Anna's deepest self-image) and, most fascinatingly, the compulsion to lose and be lost, are at the basis of her speculative research. In the most painful and intellectually active period of her life - months spent ill with 'flu while mourning for her father - Anna Freud developed a theory of the identification process in bereavement, and the reversibility of the image of loss, that devoutly extends the insights of *Mourning and Melancholia.*

NAOMI SEGAL

Donald G. Daviau (ed.), *Major Figures of Modern Austrian Literature* (Riverside, CA: Ariadne Press, 1988), 481 pp., $39.95.

The *Major Figures* series is designed to provide English-speaking readers with a six-volume guide to Austrian literature, reaching back in time from the present day to Grillparzer. This, the second volume to be published, presents fifteen authors from a period that stretches roughly from the 1930s to the 1960s. It clearly posed some delicate editorial problems: it had to combine some formidable representatives of literary modernism with later writers of lesser stature; and it had to confront the difficult issues arising from literary responses to a period of political turmoil and cultural uncertainty. The complexity and heterogeneity of this literary landscape is well described in Donald G. Daviau's introduction, which accomplishes the feat of being both thorough and concise. It cannot be said with the same confidence, however, that the chapters on individual authors are uniformly calculated to elicit the critical sympathy of English-speaking readers.

A judicious balance between 'life' and 'works' makes for a vivid portrayal of authors whose international reputation is in any case well established. The creative tensions in the works of Franz Werfel, for example, are very well brought out – tensions between fulsome compassion and fervent anti-materialism, between moral righteousness and self-recrimination. In Joseph Roth we see the inveterate 'Maskenspieler', chronicling the social deracination of his time and providing poignant symbols for lost cultural integration. We are shown Broch's skill in analysing and expounding the psychology and mythology of fascism, and even the august figure of Musil comes alive in the course of a wide-ranging presentation of his intellectual projects. In what is probably the outstanding chapter of the book (by Michael Winkler), the poetic stature of Paul Celan is clearly established with reference to that complex network of 'ciphers, topoi and symbolic images' that informs his work. And the intricacy of poetic imagery aptly dominates the chapter on Ingeborg Bachmann, too, highlighting the tension in her work between the transcendence of the banal and the ironization of idealist absolutism.

But ranged alongside these are a number of authors who, for one reason or another, evidently prompted a degree of critical ambivalence from contributors to the volume. Considerations of breadth of representation may have suggested the inclusion of two poetesses writing in a popular vein: we see Christine Busta evoking the visual detail of the natural world in a spirit of simple religiosity, and Christine Lavant giving child-like expression to the yearning (familiar from Rilke) of a soul adrift between the opposing ideals of simplicity and wisdom. Among an older generation, Alexander Lernet-Holenia appears – with good reason – as the representative figure of 'innere Emigration': an author who had displayed a precocious mastery of German poetic idiom, but whose creative effort during the years of fascism goes to the elaboration of 'symbols of futility'. We are shown the novels of Albert Paris Gütersloh – acknowledged to be abstract and recondite – expounding allegorical pleas for the restoration of the aristocracy, and George Saiko developing equally arcane psychograms of the tortured political identity of Austria. Heimito von Doderer, despite the richer humanity and sensuous detail of his work, is also found to be remarkably self-directed in his treatment of social issues, and that well-documented 'Habsburg myth' that haunts the writings of several of the novelists is apparent in the drama also. We see Csokor moving to the expression of a humanism that lies 'above' politics and that is idealized in the old Empire; and in a later variant of the trend, we see Hochwälder dedicated to the maudlin exploration of mankind's lost capacity for remorse and to the pursuit of 'order and tranquility'. Friedrich Torberg, finally, for whom no great claims are made as a literary writer, becomes an effective media manipulator in post-war Vienna, denying the oxygen of publicity to such critical voices as Brecht and Böll.

It is an ethos of passivity and introspection that predominates in the volume, and it is difficult to avoid the impression that editorial policy could have struck a different balance by including certain authors who are mentioned in the introduction, but nowhere else. We are given Saiko and Gütersloh, but not Ernst Weiss; Torberg and Lernet-Holenia, but not Jura Soyfer; Csokor, but not Horváth. Might space perhaps be found for them in a subsequent volume?

DAVID MIDGLEY

Notes on Contributors

JEREMY ADLER is Professor of German at Queen Mary and Westfield College London. He has published *'Eine fast magische Anziehungskraft'. Goethes 'Wahlverwandtschaften' und die Chemie seiner Zeit* (Beck, 1987) and many studies of twentieth-century Austrian and German poetry.

HARRIET ANDERSON wrote her doctoral dissertation at University College London on the Austrian feminist Rosa Mayreder. Her edition of Mayreder's diaries, *Tagebücher 1873-1937*, was published by Insel Verlag in 1988. She is now giving courses on women's history at Vienna University; her study of the Austrian women's movement is due to be published by Yale University Press.

MARK ANDERSON is Professor of German at Columbia University and author of *Kafka's Clothes* (Oxford University Press, 1992).

ALAN BANCE is Professor of German at Southampton University and author of *Theodor Fontane* (Cambridge University Press, 1982) and numerous studies of twentieth-century Austrian and German fiction.

ANDREW BARKER is Senior Lecturer in German at Edinburgh University. He is working on a book on Peter Altenberg.

ELIZABETH BOA is Senior Lecturer in German at the University of Nottingham. She is the author of *The Sexual Circus: Wedekind's Theatre of Subversion* (Blackwell, 1987) and is now working on a feminist study of Kafka for Oxford University Press.

GILBERT J. CARR is Lecturer in Germanic Studies at Trinity College, Dublin, and the author of numerous articles on Kraus and his contemporaries.

SANDER L. GILMAN is Goldwin Smith Professor of Humane Studies at Cornell University. Besides teaching in the Departments of German and Near Eastern Studies there, he is Professor of the History of Psychiatry at Cornell Medical College in New York. The most recent of his numerous books are *Jewish Self-Hatred: Anti-Semitism and the Hidden Language of the Jews* (Johns Hopkins University Press, 1986) and *Disease and Representation: Images of Illness from Madness to AIDS* (Cornell University Press, 1988).

JAMES HARDIN is Professor of German at the University of South Carolina. Besides articles on Broch, he has prepared several critical editions and analytical bibliographies in the field of baroque literature, and has recently edited an anthology of articles on the Bildungsroman.

HANNAH HICKMAN is Visiting Fellow in German at Salford University. She has published *Robert Musil and the Culture of Vienna* (Croom Helm, 1984; Open Court paperback, 1991) and edited *Robert Musil and the Literary Landscape of his Time* (University of Salford, 1991), and was recently awarded the Klagenfurt Robert Musil Medal.

MICHAEL HURST is a Fellow of St John's College, Oxford. He has published numerous books on nineteenth-century British and Irish politics and now has a particular interest in Central Europe.

CHARLES INGRAO is Professor of History at Purdue University. His books include *In Quest and Crisis: Emperor Joseph I and the Habsburg Monarchy* (Purdue University Press, 1979) and *The Hessian Mercenary State* (Cambridge University Press, 1987).

LEO A. LENSING is Professor of German at Wesleyan University, Middletown, Connecticut, and author of a study of Wilhelm Raabe. He is at work on a biography of Karl Kraus.

DAVID MIDGLEY is Fellow in German at St John's College, Cambridge, and author of *Arnold Zweig: Eine Einführung in Leben und Werk* (Athenäum Verlag, 1987).

SILVINA MILSTEIN is a Lecturer in Music at King's College London and a specialist in twentieth-century music. Her book *Arnold Schoenberg: Notes Sets Forms* (Cambridge University Press, 1992) is based on her doctoral work under Alexander Goehr in Cambridge.

DAVID PHILLIPS is Tutor in German in the Department of Educational Studies, Oxford University, and a Fellow of St Edmund Hall. He has published numerous articles on Horváth.

S. R. F. PRICE is Fellow and Tutor in Ancient History at Lady Margaret Hall, Oxford. His publications include *Rituals and Power: The Roman Imperial Cult in Asia Minor* (Cambridge University Press, 1984) and 'The Future of Dreams: From Freud to Artemidorus', in D. M. Halperin, J. J. Winkler and F. I. Zeitlin (eds), *Before Sexuality: The Construction of Erotic Experience in the Ancient Greek World* (Princeton University Press, 1990).

J. M. RITCHIE has just retired as Professor of German at Aberdeen University. He has published numerous studies and translations, mostly of twentieth-century German literature, including *German Literature under National Socialism* (Croom Helm, 1983).

PAUL ROAZEN is Professor of Political and Social Science at York University, Toronto. His books include *Freud and his Followers* (Penguin, 1979) and *Helene Deutsch: A Psychoanalytic Life* (Meridian, 1985).

RITCHIE ROBERTSON is Fellow and Tutor in German at St John's College, Oxford, and author of *Kafka: Judaism, Politics, and Literature* (Oxford University Press, 1985; German translation published by Metzler, 1988).

MIKE ROGERS is Lecturer in German at Southampton University and the author of numerous studies of Nestroy and Kraus.

EDA SAGARRA is Professor of Germanic Studies at Trinity College, Dublin. Her many books include *A Social History of Germany* (1977) and studies of Fontane and Ebner-Eschenbach.

207

NAOMI SEGAL teaches French at St John's College, Cambridge. Her books include *The Banal Object: Theme and Thematics in Proust, Rilke, Hofmannsthal and Sartre* (published in 1981 as no. 6 in the Bithell Series of Dissertations) and *Narcissus and Echo* (Manchester University Press, 1989).

PETER SKRINE is Professor of German at Bristol University. His most recent book is *Hauptmann, Wedekind and Schnitzler* (Macmillan, 1989).

MARTIN STANTON is Director of the Psychoanalytic Studies Centre at the University of Kent and managing editor of the journal *Free Associations*. His books include *Outside the Dream: Lacan and French Styles of Psychoanalysis* (Routledge, 1983) and *Sandor Ferenczi: Reconsidering Active Intervention* (Aronson/Free Associations, 1991).

KLAUS THEWELEIT is best known as author of *Männerphantasien* (Stroemfeld/ Roter Stern, 1977), an illustrated study of the psychological origins of fascism, published in English under the title *Male Fantasies* (Polity, 1987). His most recent books are *Buch der Könige* and *Objektwahl,* also published by Stroemfeld/ Roter Stern.

ALFRED THOMAS is Assistant Professor of German and Slavic Languages at Rutgers University, Newark. He has published *The Czech Chivalric Romances Vévoda Arnost and Lavryn in their Literary Context* (Kümmerle, 1989), and articles on medieval Czech literature, Czech Romanticism, and modern Slovak literature.

BRUCE THOMPSON is Senior Lecturer in German at Stirling University. His most recent book is *Schnitzler's Vienna: Image of a Society* (Routledge, 1990).

EDWARD TIMMS is Professor of German at the University of Sussex and Fellow of Gonville and Caius College, Cambridge. His publications include *Karl Kraus, Apocalyptic Satirist* (Yale, 1986) and *Freud in Exile: Psychoanalysis and its Vicissitudes,* co-edited with Naomi Segal (Yale, 1988).

HELEN WATANABE-O'KELLY is Fellow and Tutor in German at Exeter College, Oxford. She has published numerous studies of Baroque literature and Adalbert Stifter, and is currently co-editor of *Spectaculum Europaeum: Handbook of Theatre and Spectacle in Europe 1580-1750.*

ANDREW WEBBER is Fellow in German at Churchill College, Cambridge, and is the author of *Sexuality and the Sense of Self in the Works of Georg Trakl and Robert Musil,* no. 15 in the Bithell Series of Dissertations (Modern Humanities Research Association, 1990).

IAIN BOYD WHYTE is Director of the Centre for Architectural History and Theory at Edinburgh University.

W. E. YATES is Professor of German at Exeter University. His books include *Grillparzer* and *Nestroy* (both published by Cambridge University Press in 1972), and he is one of the editors of the new edition of Nestroy.

HARRY ZOHN is Chairman of the Department of Germanic and Slavic Languages at Brandeis University. His most recent book is *'ich bin ein Sohn der deutschen Sprache nur ...': Jüdisches Erbe in der österreichischen Literatur* (Amalthea Verlag, 1986). His many translations include selections from Karl Kraus.

Austrian Studies

Acknowledgements: The Editors gratefully acknowledge the support of the Austrian Institute in London. Thanks are also due to the colleagues listed below for their willingness to serve on the Advisory Board.

Books for review should be sent to Ritchie Robertson, St John's College, Oxford OX1 3JP, England.

Manuscripts for publication should be submitted in duplicate to Edward Timms, Arts Building, University of Sussex, Brighton BN1 9QN, England.

Guidelines: Articles should be written in English and should not exceed 7 500 words. They should be typed double-spaced, using endnotes (not a numbered bibliography) to identify the source of quotations. Quotations should normally be given in the original language, followed by an English translation. A detailed style sheet is available from either of the Editors, on request.

Austrian Studies may be ordered through any bookshop. Since it is designed as an annual publication, it may also be obtained by subscription direct from the publishers, Edinburgh University Press, 22 George Square, Edinburgh EH8 9LF, Scotland.